Corporate Strategic Analysis

Marcus C. Bogue III
Elwood S. Buffa

FP

THE FREE PRESS
A Division of Macmillan, Inc.
NEW YORK

Collier Macmillan Publishers
LONDON

The Free Press
A Division of Macmillan, Inc.
866 Third Avenue, New York, N. Y. 10022

Collier Macmillan Canada, Inc.

Printed in the United States of America

printing number

1 2 3 4 5 6 7 8 9 10

Library of Congress Cataloging-in-Publication Data

Bogue, Marcus C.
  Corporate strategic analysis.

  Includes index.
  1. Strategic planning.   I. Buffa, Elwood Spencer
II. Title.
HD30.28.B64   1986   658.4′012   86–571
ISBN 0–02–903760–3

To Corporate Strategists
"The Movers and Shakers"

Contents

Preface   vii

PART I   PERSPECTIVES

1. Objectives—Why Formulate Strategy?   3

2. Strategic Analysis   13

PART II   INDUSTRY AND MARKET ANALYSIS

3. Industry and Market Structures   39

4. Productivity/Exchange-Rate Effects
    in Global Competition   65

PART III   CORPORATE ANALYSIS

5. Product and Activity Structures   99

6. Diversification and Acquisitions   123

7. Financial Implications of Strategic Positions   147

PART IV   SCENARIO ANALYSIS
AND IMPLEMENTATION

8.   SCENSIM for Strategic Scenario Analysis   175

9.   From Analysis to Plans and Action   214

     Index   241

Preface

Good strategy is fundamental to success. The literature is filled with examples that demonstrate this premise, and we provide some of these case reports. One can be successful without good strategy if luck comes to the rescue. But all we know about luck is that it changes. The better option is to have a good strategy for achieving success, and we bet on strategy as the way to change the odds.

It is our thesis that if a thorough strategic analysis is performed, the viable strategies will be laid bare, and there are likely to be few alternatives. Managers then have a logical basis for formulating strategies, weighing their risks and returns, and finally for choosing a course of action.

While there may be important subgoals in strategic planning, they all finally focus on the ultimate objective—to increase the economic value of the firm. We establish the increase in economic value as the overriding criterion early in Chapter 1, and show how to measure it. We want to acquire or divest on the basis of whether or not business units have clear prospects for adding value, and we want to devise strategies for individual business units that will convert them to value-adding status.

The analysis of the industry and its markets and the study of the product, activity, and financial structures all focus on the competitors who vie for the business—this is what makes strategic analysis productive. It is a common assumption that the competitive world provides a neutral arena, but in fact, the situations are seldom if ever equal for all. Because of the differing configurations and positions of the competitors they have inherently different strengths and weaknesses. Good strategies seek to take advantage of, or create, these structural differences and convert them to long-term strategic advantage.

While analysis is of considerable value in isolating the strengths and weaknesses of the players, it has the additional role of providing a sound basis for strategic scenarios. These scenarios can be analyzed in terms of their risks and returns, both for scenarios for individual business units, and for corporate portfolios, providing a basis for choice.

Finally, while strategic analysis and formulation are crucial, the strategy process cannot end there. Given a specific strategic course, the final result is likely to be only as good as the implementation. Putting any strategy into action requires a careful definition of the strategy that can be communicated effectively and buttressed with the right staff and organization, the design of programs and plans that will lead to the goals, an appropriate allocation of resources to achieve results, and controls to help steer the strategy to its target. The important subject of implementation is our final chapter.

This book is directed to the practicing managers, for they are the ones who can benefit directly. While the materials in the book are academically sound, the emphasis is on practice rather than theory—there are already many books that deal with the theory of strategic choice, strategy formulation, and other important topics. This volume is filled with applications and with market and industry information. All the competitive information in the book is drawn from public sources. In fact, this is one of the most important practical lessons in the book—competitive information is available to everyone if they will simply use it. But it requires careful ''digging'' and analysis to convert it to useful forms. Industrial espionage is unnecessary.

The useful forms of analysis are another lesson of the book. We deal with modes of analysis that have application for industry, markets, and companies. Understanding the use of these existing tools enhances understanding—reinventing the wheel is not an efficient use of time. But in speaking of analytical tools, we are not dealing with the world of management science and mathematical models. We use graphical displays that represent relative competitive position and help managers visualize their situations.

We use some of the graphical displays found in traditional product portfolio analysis, such as the growth/share matrix and share/

momentum charts, but without the strategic implications and prescriptions attached to them. These displays are valuable in providing perspectives to the analyst. But it is important to recognize that our analytical methodology is a departure from traditional product portfolio analysis, beginning with the analysis of the industry and its markets, and focusing on product and activity structures, and their analysis.

Marcus C. Bogue III
Elwood S. Buffa

Part I

Perspectives

Chapter 1

Objectives—Why Formulate Strategy?

In 1980, it appeared that Uniroyal was close to bankruptcy, being leveraged to the hilt, and facing a dramatic downturn in the auto industry as well as a recession. But by 1983, operating income from tires had jumped 60 percent during the first six months compared to the previous year on sales that actually declined 7.6 percent. After-tax income from all operations tripled during the same period to $22.4 million on sales that declined 3 percent to $996 million. Debt was down to 75 percent of equity compared to 154 percent in 1980.

How was this accomplished?[1] Corporate management chose to divest many businesses, including most of their footwear unit and almost all tire operations outside the United States. They closed two U.S. tire plants, and reduced the number of tire lines which had the additional benefit of helping reduce inventories by 40 percent. On the positive action side, they moved strongly into agricultural chemical niches, redressing the balance of their product mix so that the company is projected to be rather different by 1988, as shown in the following table:

	PRODUCT MIX (%), 1982	EST. MIX (%), 1988
Tires	48	40
Chemicals	26	40
Engineered products & services	26	20

Beginning in 1975, A&P decided on a drastic move to close nearly half of its 3468 stores, based on their profitability. Unprofitable stores simply did not justify their existence, and what better measure of their contribution to corporate health than profitability? But the results were a disaster. The shutting of a single store can have drastic effects on a marketing area's exposure, distribution costs, warehousing operations, advertising costs, and its labor situation, as well as on the manufacturing facilities that no longer have an outlet for their products. In other words, there were system effects from taking seemingly logical actions based on local profitability that A&P failed to consider. For example, the reduction in the number of stores in an area can drastically reduce an advantage of scale in functions as diverse as advertising and distribution operations.

An alternative would have been to shut down entire operating divisions, retreating completely from geographic areas where profitability was poor. The store-by-store approach left A&P spread thinly in some areas, sacrificing potential economies that could be gained from geographic concentration.

The initial results were encouraging, reflecting an increase in the size of the average store and sales per store, and the company was profitable in 1975 and 1976. But the system effects had begun to dominate, and profits dropped from $23.8 million in 1976 to $4.8 million in 1977, to heavy losses of $15 million in 1978.[2] The losses became so heavy that by 1979 there was talk of bankruptcy until Tengelmann, a German giant supermarket chain, agreed to buy 42 percent of A&P's stock and became an "investor-partner."[3]

Then there is the fascinating case of Bowmar, first in hand-held calculators, but first to go bankrupt facing Texas Instrument's price competition. TI's advantage lay in its recognition of where the value was added in the process of manufacturing and marketing a calculator. TI manufactured silicon chips that were the heart of many of its products, including calculators. It gained an unbeatable cost advantage that Bowmar could not match, reaping huge profits in chips, which they also sold to Bowmar, but small if any profits in calculators.[4] Bowmar eventually recognized its mistake and acquired chip manufacturing facilities, but it was too late.

TI followed a price-cutting strategy based on its low manufacturing costs. It priced its first pocket calculator at $149, retail. Bowmar then reduced its $179 calculator by $30, but TI retaliated by chopping $30 from its price.[5]

Figure 1-1 shows ten well-known brands of consumer products,

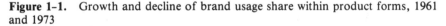

Percentage		0	5	10	15	20	25
Soap for face and hands							
1961	Ivory						
	Lux						
1973	Ivory						
	Lux						
Shampoo							
1961	Prell						
	Lustre Creme						
1973	Prell						
	Lustre Creme						
Hair spray							
1961	Breck						
	Toni						
1973	Breck						
	Toni						
Deodorant							
1961	Secret						
	Five Day						
1973	Secret						
	Five Day						
Perfume and cologne							
1961	Chanel						
	Arpege						
1973	Chanel						
	Arpege						

Figure 1-1. Growth and decline of brand usage share within product forms, 1961 and 1973

SOURCES: For 1961, "Beauty Secrets," *Good Housekeeping;* for 1973, *Target Group Index Reports* for 1974; Reprinted by permission of the *Harvard Business Review.* An Exhibit from, "Forget the Product Life Cycle Concept!" by N. K. Dhalla and S. Yuspeh (January/February 1976). Copyright © 1976 by the President and Fellows of Harvard College; all rights reserved.

paired for their comparative growth from 1961 to 1973. For example, in 1961, Ivory had a 17 percent usage, while Lux had 14 percent. But by 1973, Ivory was up to 25 percent while Lux had declined to only 6 percent. For each pair of brands, there is a winner and a loser. All the brands had been around a long time and might have been considered mature in 1961 in product life cycle terms, yet the winner was able to do something unique that extended the life of the brand compared to the loser—implement a winning strategy.

Strategy Makes a Difference

The several case examples discussed in the foregoing paragraphs all underline the point that strategy makes a difference. While no one strategy can be applied to all cases, that is what makes strategic analysis so fascinating—the situations are different and in a sense unique. On the other hand, there are modes of analysis that make it possible to unravel these complex situations, exposing the strengths and weaknesses of company positions so that winning strategies can be formulated.

The success of the Japanese in penetrating foreign markets has placed competitive strategy in the spotlight. There has been a shift toward global competition that has intensified the interest in strategic planning at all levels, and a recognition that it pervades all functions including finance, marketing, and even production.[6] Indeed George Steiner states, "Strategic planning is inextricably interwoven into the entire fabric of management."[7] But at the heart of the matter are a number of issues: how to analyze industry and market structures, exposing the effects of product and activity* structures; how to take account of competitive interplay of alternatives; how to evaluate the impact of different company financial structures on competitiveness, and international financial flows; and, finally, how to construct viable competitive plans that take account of the risks involved in alternate scenarios. This book is concerned with these issues.

The Level Playing Field

There is an implicit assumption of a "level playing field" as managers address strategic alternatives—that the situation is the same for everyone. In a level-playing-field view of the competitive world, success seems to be based on hard work, dedication, and sometimes even cleverness. There is nothing wrong with these attributes of a management team, but the fact usually is that the situation is not the same for everyone—the playing field is *not* always level but often very hilly. There are structural differences in the geography that can be exploited, and the strategic manager ferrets them out and takes advantage of them. That is the essence of strategy.

In constructing strategic plans, management needs analyses. But ours is not the world of models and mathematics. We need analyses that reveal *structural* differences between alternatives; structural differences within industries, markets, products, and activities. Ap-

*Activities refer to the various steps a company engages in (at an appropriate level of detail) in conceiving, making, marketing, and distributing its products or services. We will enlarge on this point later.

parent advantages, such as short-term price movements, are by their nature fleeting—only structural advantages can be converted to long-term profitable positions.

For example, the structural configuration of the dominant players in industry is often quite different, with one emphasizing marketing or distribution, another emphasizing assembly, and a third being vertically integrated backward into component manufacturing and forward into marketing and distribution. It isn't that any one of these structures is right or wrong, but in constructing competitive plans, one player may be able to position or oppose its strength against the competitive weaknesses of others and thereby win an extraordinary position. Analyzing structural strengths and weaknesses and understanding the geography of the playing field provide the key, but we note that the lay of the playing field is also subject to change. Once-defensible hills can erode, and new hills can grow. We will have much more to say about structural issues in diversification and acquisitions, industry and market structures, product and activity structures, and so on.

Enhancing Economic Value—The Ultimate Strategic Objective

Certainly the focal point of strategy is to enhance economic value for the firm—to take the assets we have and increase their value over and above what we paid for them. Ignoring the accountant's adjustments, book values represent what we have paid for the assets. The economic value of the assets is determined by the stream of future earnings that the assets can generate. This future income stream is largely determined by the strategy pursued by the firm in relation to competitors' strategies. These strategies either enhance or deplete the value of the assets compared to their purchase price. In a broad sense, the equity markets reflect the consensus regarding economic value, so that the market-to-book ratios are indicators of the success or failure in enhancing value. A market-to-book ratio of greater than 1.0 means that the market recognizes an increased value of assets over book values, while a value less than 1.0 means the reverse.

Taking the chemical industry as an example, the 1981 market valuations of the twenty firms shown in Figure 1–2 show a direct relationship between equity returns (return on equity minus the cost of equity capital[8]) and market-to-book ratios. Seven of the eight firms with positive equity returns have market values in excess of book value,

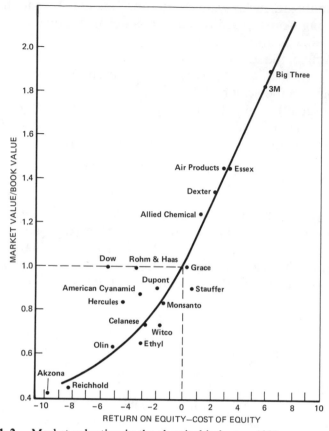

Figure 1-2. Market valuation in the chemical industry, 1981

SOURCES: Company annual reports, and *Value Line*.

while of the firms earning less than the cost of capital, all have market values at or below book values. For positive equity returns the relationship is fairly linear. Firms such as Allied Chemical, with a higher market valuation relative to book, are those that the market expects will improve their future earnings performance as a result of their strategies in relation to those of their competitors. For firms below the line, such as Stauffer, the reverse is true. For firms earning less than their cost of capital, the relationship flattens the more negative the return. At some point, a firm becomes valued not by its earning power, but by its liquidating value—the alternative use value of its assets. Notice Dow Chemical and Rohm & Haas with fairly negative equity returns but market values approximately the same as book values. The market consensus is for vast improvement in the earnings of these firms—to the level of their cost of capital. If this were not so, the market values of these firms would not be approximately equal to book value.

ECONOMIC VALUE

Our purpose here is not to develop a theory of capital asset pricing, but to lay a groundwork for the kinds of managerial actions that can lead to increases in the economic value of a business. Clearly, strategy deals with managerial actions that will have a substantial continuing effect and enhance the long-term economic value of the business. We focus on four factors that contribute to economic values in strategy formulation,

- Scale
- Returns
- Growth
- Sustainability

Scale refers to the size of the strategic opportunity available; the larger the scale, the greater the potential for increase in value. Returns refers to the ability of the strategic opportunity to earn returns *in excess of the cost of capital*. Growth refers to the magnitude of the potential increase in the strategic opportunity—growth businesses with positive returns are adding value. Finally, by sustainability, we separate the short-term from the long-term strategic opportunities. The longer the term, the greater the duration over which the returns and growth can add to the economic value of the firm. We summarize the impact of these four factors on the economic value of the firm in Figure 1–3.

GROWTH/RETURNS

Looking at the components in a firm's portfolio of businesses in terms of growth and returns suggests that business units that are earning in excess of their cost of equity capital and have good growth are the *real* "stars"—they are adding economic value to the portfolio. Those that have good returns and low growth are also adding value, but do not offer as much potential for the future.

Business units with low growth and negative returns are subtracting from the economic value of the firm, and should certainly be can-

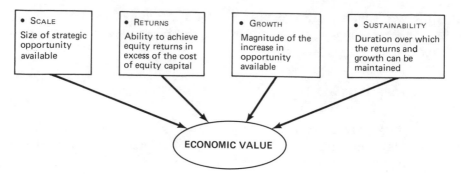

Figure 1-3. Determinants of the economic value of a business

didates for divestiture. These are not necessarily the conventional "dogs." Rather, we are partitioning the low-growth businesses into those that earn in excess of their costs of equity capital and those that do not. The latter group are candidates for divestiture.

Finally, high-growth/negative-return business units are the real question marks. We must either find strategies for converting the high-growth/low-return units to positive return units or get rid of them, for they are subtracting from the economic value of the firm.

An Example. Let us look at the portfolio of NL Industries in 1981 in our terms of growth and returns in excess of the cost of equity capital. NL Industries, Inc. was originally in paint and metals, principally lead products, and also held a 50 percent ownership of Titanium Metals Corporation of America (TIMET). Beginning in 1972 and continuing throughout the mid 1970s they moved strongly into petroleum services, while deemphasizing and actually divesting some of their interests in paints and lead-based products. Figure 1-4 shows a graph of equity returns on an asset basis versus asset growth for their three main lines of business: paint, metals, and petroleum services. These equity returns are defined slightly differently, reflecting returns on assets above the cost of capital in each of the lines of business and risk class.* The areas of the circles represent the sales contribution of each business.

Metals are strongly adding value for the firm and the acquisitions

---

*Equity returns for the three lines of business were calculated by subtracting from the returns on assets, calculated using data in NL's annual report, an estimate of the cost of capital for each line of business. This estimate was derived using the capital asset pricing model obtained by averaging risk estimates for comparable companies. For a more detailed explanation, see Diana Harrington, *Modern Portfolio Theory and the Capital Asset Pricing Model: A User's Guide* (Englewood Cliffs, N.J.: Prentice-Hall, 1983).

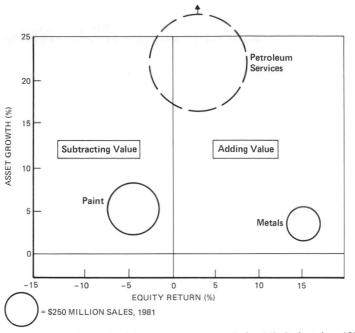

Figure 1-4. Returns (asset basis) versus asset growth for NL Industries, 1981

Sources: Company annual and 10-K reports, and *Value Line*.

in petroleum services are adding value, but paint products are subtracting value. It appears that NL improved its position by divesting of Dutch Boy Paints in 1976 and adding positive return businesses in petroleum services such as Rucker Co. and Ashton Supply in 1977, and Stewart & Stevenson Oil Tools, Basin Surveys, and Petrolog in 1978. Petroleum services not only add value, but the size of their sales contribution is large compared to the other units, so the returns have a large multipier.

Of course, Figure 1–4 represents the situation as of 1981. The issue of sustainability is also of great importance, and we know that petroleum services have since changed drastically. NL's position in TIMET also had some long-term negative aspects in terms of aggressive Japanese competitors and the balance between industry capacity and demand.

Future Values

The objectives of strategy formulation are to direct resources to those business units that will enhance future values. The cases cited at the

beginning of the chapter all indicate that carefully chosen and implemented strategies make a difference in creating growth and returns
above expectations. But strategies do not present themselves, they
must be ferreted out, and that is the function of analysis—to lay bare
the hills and valleys in the competitive terrain in order to see the advantages and disadvantages of all the players, and to anticipate the effects of changes in the terrain. The lay of the playing field is dynamic.

Chapter 2

Strategic Analysis

With increased firm value as the basic objective, the role of analysis is crucial in self-examination and in knowing competitors. The history of strategic analysis is short, and an extremely important element begins with the Boston Consulting Group's (BCG) widely known product portfolio analysis using the four quadrants of the growth/share matrix.[1]

We use some of the graphical displays developed for traditional product portfolio analysis, such as the growth/share matrix and share/momentum charts, but without their attached strategic implications and prescriptions. These displays are valuable in providing perspective to the analyst. But it is important to recognize that our analytical methodology is a departure from traditional methods, beginning with the analysis of the industry and markets, and focusing on product and activity structures and their analysis.

Product Portfolio Analysis

The notion of a "business portfolio" was the key in product portfolio analysis rather than the matrix display, although the growth/share matrix has probably received the greatest attention. An important part of portfolio analysis depends on the concept of the strategic business unit (SBU) developed by McKinsey & Company in conjunction with General Electric. Combining the concepts of the SBU with the business portfolio leads to the fundamental idea that a well managed company contains a mixture of types of SBUs—a recognition that the different needs of the various SBUs can be best accommodated in a portfolio, and that the company is the sum of its SBUs. In the portfolio approach, the weaknesses or needs of an SBU may be shared or supplied by another. For example, a high-growth SBU will likely need cash now, but may be a future high-potential supplier of cash.

The "portfolio grid" of which the growth/share matrix is the most prominent type is usually a two-dimensional display of the SBUs in a company portfolio. The two dimensions usually measure competitive position and market attractiveness—for example, the growth/share matrix measures competitive position as relative market share, and market attractiveness by projected market growth. The experience curve is an integral part of the analytical framework, linking the market growth and competitive position concepts. We will discuss these portfolio concepts more thoroughly below.[2]

Strategic analysis has moved beyond the product portfolio concepts, and even BCG has partially abandoned it for a different approach.[3] Nevertheless, we find the growth/share matrix and the experience curve to be useful devices in analysis, when properly applied. It is the overly simplistic characterizations and prescriptions that follow from product portfolio analysis that should be abandoned, and to a large extent this is happening.

As a starting point, we will review some of the basic elements of product portfolio analysis, and establish the standards for constructing growth/share matrices and the share/momentum chart, an associated display. At a later point in this chapter we will review the basic elements of the experience curve, introducing other analytical tools in future chapters as needed.

THE GROWTH/SHARE MATRIX

A growth/share matrix is constructed by displaying on a four-quadrant grid each business unit in a company as a circle, the area of which is proportional to the sales of the business unit. The horizontal axis is relative market share using a logarithmic scale increasing from right to left, and the vertical axis is the projected market growth rate in percent. Figure 2–1 shows such a growth/share matrix for General Foods Corporation for 1982.

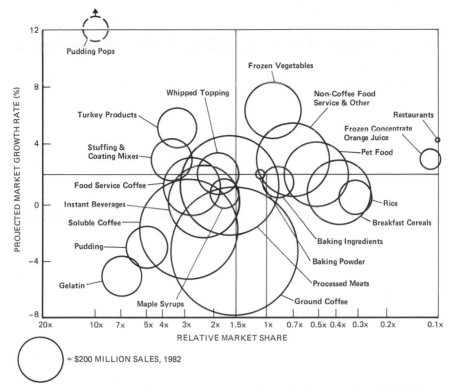

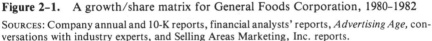

Figure 2-1. A growth/share matrix for General Foods Corporation, 1980–1982

Sources: Company annual and 10-K reports, financial analysts' reports, *Advertising Age,* conversations with industry experts, and Selling Areas Marketing, Inc. reports.

Relative market share is measured as the volume (sales is commonly substituted in practice) of each business unit divided by the volume (sales) of the leading competitor in that business, both stated for a relevant period. The market leader in the business has a relative market share of greater than one, and traditionally a cutoff ratio of 1.5 is set to indicate dominance in a business. Relative market share is used instead of market share because the latter measure does not indicate the strength of a company's position. A 20 percent share could be weak if the leader had a dominant share, but strong in a highly fragmented industry. For example, if there are 80 other competitors each with a 1 percent market share, then 20 percent is a dominant share, but if there is only one other competitor with an 80 percent share, then 20 percent is small. Therefore, relative market share is a more appropriate measure of market position than absolute share.

Projected market growth rate (past growth is commonly substituted) is a measure of the attractiveness of a market,[4] and the dividing line between high and low growth is somewhat arbitrary, about 3 percent in Figure 2–1, since growth in the food business is about the same as the growth of the gross national product. Finally, the third measure of each business unit in the company's portfolio is the contribution of the business to the company represented by the sales for each business, depicted by the areas of the circles plotted on the matrix.

The four quadrants of the matrix have been dubbed stars, cash cows, dogs, and question marks, and have the cash flow implications shown in Figure 2–2. These are traditional descriptors for businesses in each of the four quadrants, and are accompanied by strategy prescriptions. The strategy prescriptions that accompany traditional product portfolio analysis are at best a bit naive, and in some instances downright wrong. Nevertheless, they should be understood, for they provide a starting point.

STARS

The stars are the really attractive businesses in the portfolio, having high market growth and a very strong competitive position by virtue of their large relative market share. While they often generate large amounts of cash because of their strength and position, they also need large amounts of cash to invest in their expanding markets, for promotion, new capacity, and so on. The result is that their net cash flow is usually modest in a well-managed portfolio, and may be either positive or negative. At any rate, their cash needs from the company

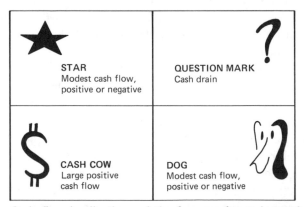

Figure 2–2. Cash flow implications of the four quadrants in product portfolio analysis

are not large. A common strategic mistake is to "milk" a star too early by keeping prices high, resulting in early cash generation. This can result in a "shooting star," since competitors can gain market share through competitive pricing, driving the star to the "dogs," to use portfolio analysis metaphors.

CASH COWS

The cash cow businesses are the main source of cash for the company, because of their excellent relative market share coupled with low growth. In a well-managed portfolio, they generate much more cash than they need for reinvestment to sustain their positions. Again, in the colorful language of portfolio analysis, a mistake is to let a cow drink its own milk.

DOGS

In the third quadrant, the dogs have low relative market share and low growth. These businesses are the least attractive in portfolio analysis, because they seem to have no logical positive direction in which to move. Unless competitors are "overmilking" their cows, they generate little cash because of their poor market and low growth positions, but their saving grace is that they need little cash for reinvestment. Investment in dogs is often a "cash trap" in the sense that it is likely to cost substantially more to improve a dog's position against an entrenched leader in a low-growth market than the improvement can possibly return.

QUESTION MARKS

Finally, the question marks are so-called because they pose a dilemma. They appear to be very attractive because of their high growth, but because of their current poor market share position it would require large amounts of cash to convert them to stars in the face of obvious strong competition. The standard prescription is to "prune and focus," rather than attempt the development of all or the elimination of all. In choosing businesses in which to invest, care must be taken to avoid cash traps—those businesses in which the investment required to gain position exceeds the returns accruing to the improved position.

PRESCRIPTIONS

Given the portfolio of a company represented on the growth/share matrix, product portfolio analysis provides a rationale for the strategic manipulation of the various business units. The company must allocate resources among the business units, and in portfolio analysis cash is the basic resource. For example, it can transfer cash from highly profitable businesses that are mature (cash cows) to business units that have high potential for future profitability (question marks or stars). These kinds of considerations lead to four major strategic moves in portfolio analysis:

- Increase market share
- Hold market share
- Harvest
- Withdraw or divest

Using cash allocation as the mechanism, product portfolio analysis prescribes the best sequence as investing in high-potential question marks to produce stars that will ultimately become cash cows. Question marks that appear to have low potential are candidates for withdrawal or divestment, thus releasing for more promising uses the cash they have been requiring. Stars that are maturing may be allowed to reap their harvest by reducing the investment required to sustain growth, freeing cash for other purposes. Harvesting allows market share to decline by not reinvesting, thereby maximizing short-term earnings and cash flow. Dogs live a dog's life, being constant candidates for harvest, withdrawal, or divestment. Even if retained, their dog status means that they are likely to be resource starved, being thrown a bone only when there is nothing better to do with surplus resources.

THE SHARE/MOMENTUM CHART

The growth/share matrix is a purely static display, and gives no indication of the strategic moves a company is following for its business units. Therefore, it is often accompanied by a second chart, a market share/momentum chart, which shows change in market position for the company's business units. A share/momentum chart is constructed by displaying each business unit as a circle, the area of which is again proportional to sales. The horizontal axis of the plot is past growth for the company, and the vertical axis is past market growth. Figure 2-3 shows a share/momentum chart for General Foods for the 1980–1982 period.

Circles below the diagonal represent business units that grew faster than the market they serve and hence experienced absolute market share gain, though not necessarily relative market share gain. The reverse is true for those above the diagonal. These interpretations are true all along the diagonal line, including the negative-growth quadrants of the chart. Businesses that fall on the diagonal are growing as fast as the market. Those that fall in the lower right of the chart are growing much faster than the market, and those in the upper left are growing much more slowly than the market. Businesses that fall below the diagonal, but in the negative quadrant are gaining market share, but relative to a declining market. Finally, those businesses that

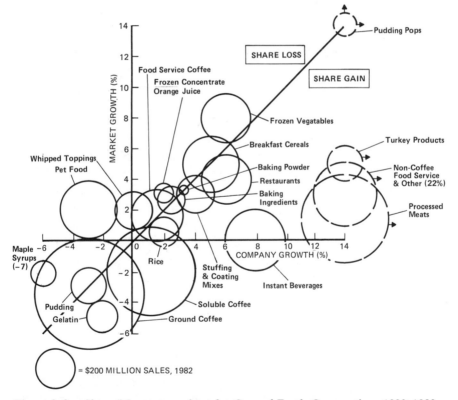

Figure 2-3. Share/Momentum chart for General Foods Corporation, 1980–1982

Sources: Company annual and 10-K reports, financial analysts' reports, *Advertising Age,* conversations with industry experts, and Selling Areas Marketing, Inc. reports.

fall above the diagonal, but in the negative quadrant, are losing share in a declining market.

Examination of the General Foods growth/share matrix and share/momentum chart (Figures 2-1 and 2-3) reveals a very strong portfolio. It is the market leader with 13 of its 21 product lines. Of these, eight are gaining share while four are growing with their markets. The company's performance in the sluggish food industry, which is growing at a real annual rate of only 3 percent, demonstrates its skill and commitment to competing effectively in mature markets. For example, the 1982 introduction of Jell-O Pudding Pops, whose market share is ten times that of the next largest competitor, has proved to be highly successful. General Foods is the only *national* distributor in the frozen novelties market, which is basically regional. Jell-O gelatin and pudding also dominate their markets with relative market shares of seven and five times the share of their nearest competitors, respectively.

Figure 2-3 shows that several of General Foods products are growing somewhat faster than the industry average—turkey products, processed meats, non-coffee food service and other, and instant beverages. Even though restaurants are expected to grow at 4 percent, General Foods is selling this business because of low rates of return (returns not shown). By contrast, coffee, their leading product in terms of sales volume, faces a projected decline in market growth as consumers continue to cut back on coffee consumption.

The characterizations of business units in portfolio analysis have a certain appeal, and everyone can identify businesses that seem to fit. However, we will be interested in fundamental relationships between units and other structural advantages or disadvantages of strategic prescriptions. Are low growth and relative poor market share sufficient reasons to divest a dog? Are all dogs alike? The following summary of a statistical study helps establish the rationale for broadening the analysis of dogs, as well as businesses in the other quadrants in the matrix.

Profitability and Cash Flow Characteristics of Dogs

Hambrick and MacMillan[5] use the PIMS data base to analyze the performance of 1028 industrial product businesses within the framework of portfolio analysis. The PIMS (Profit-Impact-of-Marketing-Strategies) program is managed by the Strategic Planning Institute, and obtains disguised annual data from more than 200 corporations on a total of about 2000 business units.

The 1028 business units were classified into the four quadrants of the growth/share matrix based on their growth rates and relative market share. The line between high and low growth was set at 10 percent. The measure of relative market share was the ratio of a business unit's share divided by the share of its leading competitor, but the dividing line between high and low market share was taken as 1.00. Thus, only the market share leader for a business was classified as having high share. The classification resulted in 114 stars, 315 cash cows, 418 dogs, and 181 question marks.

The performance of the four groups of businesses is fascinating, and belies some of the preconceptions of portfolio analysis. Profitability for the businesses in each of the four quadrants in terms of return on investment (ROI) was

		MEAN (%)	SD
I	Stars	30	23
II	Cash cows	30	23
III	Dogs	18	22
IV	Question marks	20	25

Stars and cash cows had the same ROIs and standard deviations (SD)—growth industries and mature ones being equally profitable. There was approximately a 10 percentage point reward for a high-share compared to a low-share business unit. But dogs and question marks were still rather profitable. Though the relatively large standard deviation indicates that many dogs and question marks were unprofitable, by the same token, many were much more profitable than the mean ROI.

Cash flow in the four quadrants was somewhat more in line with portfolio analysis expectations, with stars having a marginally positive cash flow, cash cows being net cash generators, and question marks having a net cash drain. But dogs had a positive average cash flow. Either portfolio characterizations are too simplistic or there are many cows drinking their own milk—we think the former is true.

The average cash flow from dogs was greater than the cash drain by question marks and the point was made that the absolute size of dogs is likely to be perhaps twice that of the average fledgling question mark, so that the average dog might finance two or more promising ventures.

Given the results of the Hambrick and MacMillan study presented here (there were additional results), it is difficult to see that the average dog deserves its derogatory characterization. The average dog had a good but not brilliant ROI, produced cash, had positive returns in relation to risk, and even tended to exhibit a slight increase in market share. As Hambrick and MacMillan point out, the great majority of U.S. businesses are mature, with estimates in the range of 67 to 90 percent, and more than half of all businesses are dogs in portfolio analysis terms, since there can be only one market-share leader in any business.

Can it be that U.S. corporations should harvest or divest themselves of most of their businesses? Surely the belittling classification is unfortunate, and the prescriptions of resource starvation and withdrawal or divestiture are an oversimplification. Undoubtedly some business units in the dog quadrant may have negative ROIs and cash flow, and indeed may not fit into future plans. But decisions should rest on a careful analysis of industry and market structures, the relation of the unit to the activity base of other business units in the portfolio, the value-added chain, shared costs, competitive and financial considerations, and so on. Naive analysis can be worse than no analysis.

The Experience Curve

It is commonly recognized in manufacturing that as experience is gained through production, unit costs are usually reduced. It was originally thought that the cost improvement was simply a worker learning effect, reflecting the development of skill and dexterity when a task is performed repetitively. Now, however, the effect is recognized as resulting from a wide variety of additional sources, such as improvements in production methods and tools, improved product design, standardization, improved material utilization, reduction of system inventories, improved layout and flow, economies of scale, and improvements in organization. In addition, the concept applies to the organization as a whole, not just manufacturing, though the largest cost effects are usually reflected in direct manufacturing costs. The entire effect might be called "organizational learning." Actually, the worker learning effect is small compared to the total learning, and is one that occurs rather quickly.

When all the experience curve effects are added together we have a measure of the quality of management of a firm. A poorly managed firm would reflect organizational learning that is slower than the industry average, while a company that manages its resources extremely well should expect faster organizational learning than the industry average.

The concepts of the experience curve (also called the learning curve) were first developed in the aircraft industry during World War II. Studies of production costs of military aircraft showed that for each doubling of *cumulative* total output of an aircraft model, the deflated unit costs were reduced by 20 percent of the unit cost before doubling. For example, the second unit produced cost only 80 percent of the first, the fourth unit cost 80 percent of the second, the fiftieth unit cost 80 percent of the twenty-fifth, and so on. Taking a specific example, suppose that the initial unit cost for an item were $10. An 80 percent experience curve would then look like Figure 2–4 when plotted on linear scales.

The initial learning in Figure 2–4 is very rapid, but then tends to level off. However, the process continues into the future with additional cost reductions that can make an important competitive difference. For example, the cost of the one-thousandth unit is $1.08 and it appears from the shape of Figure 2–4 that we have fairly well

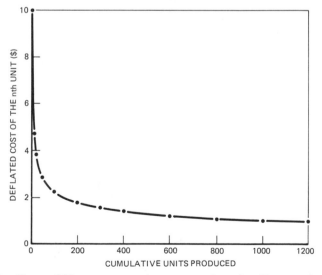

Figure 2–4. Form of 80 percent experience curve plotted on linear scales. First unit cost $10; costs following the first unit are deflated.

squeezed out the cost. But if this item develops a mass market, the 500,000th unit produced would cost only $0.15, 86 percent less than the cost of the one-thousandth unit. Obviously, the experience effect can produce continued important competitive advantages.

In practice, the experience curve is represented on log-log graph paper so that it appears as a straight line. Figure 2–5 shows how Figure 2–4 would look when plotted on log-log scales.

In thinking about the strategic implications of the experience curve that follows, it is important to recognize that experience accumulates at the activity level, rather than the product level. It is within the activities that we find better ways of doing things, better technology, worker learning, and so on. This does not mean that there is no coalescing of experience at the product level, but such a buildup depends on the configuration of activities, and their reenforcement through interrelationships.

STRATEGIC IMPLICATIONS

Several logical strategic observations can be made about the experience curve. First, the market leader in an industry with the largest market share will have produced the largest number of units and should have the lowest cost, even if all firms are on the same percent experience curve. Second, if a competitor develops an advantageous process technology, it may establish itself on a lower percentage experience curve than its competitors, and have lower unit costs even if other firms have the same cumulative output. Third, by allocating

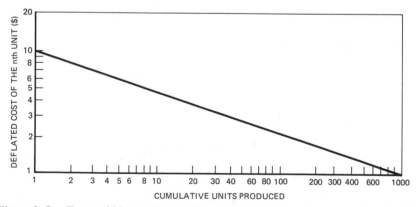

Figure 2–5.   Form of 80 percent experience curve plotted on log-log scales. First unit cost $10; costs following the first unit are deflated.

resources toward mechanization in earlier stages, and automation in the later stages of the product life cycle, a firm can maintain its position on the experience curve, or improve the slope of its experience curve. Such a strategy may be particularly important in the mature phase of the product life cycle where competition is usually focused on price, and therefore on cost, as a means of maintaining profitable margins under price pressure. Finally, a firm with greater experience can use an aggressive price policy as a competitive weapon to gain even greater market share.

Value of Market Share.   The reinforcing effect of large market share leads to low unit cost which in turn leads to high profits and the capability to reinvest, which cycles to reinforce the drive toward lower costs and larger market share. A firm with low volume needs something unique in the marketplace in order to survive, since price cannot be its appeal, given its cost position. Such a firm needs to be able to differentiate itself from the pack, perhaps with the highest quality, or a market niche, in order to charge a price that allows a profitable margin.

Shared Activity Effects.   Another connection between market share and the cost-experience curve is through the activity interdependence of related SBUs. As we will show more clearly in Chapter 5, experience accumulates at the activity level rather than the product level. Therefore, where related SBUs have common activity bases, accumulated experience is compounded, and market share and cost can have a weak relationship.

The effects of interdependence are illustrated by Figure 2-6. When an SBU is independent of others in the portfolio, as in Figure 2-6a, with no shared activities, there is a relationship between product volume and cost position through cumulative experience–cost position is improved through experience, but there is no reenforcement from other product volume.

However, when SBUs are interrelated through shared activity bases, related product experience influences the cost position of other products, and vice versa, as indicated in Figure 2-6b. A portfolio that contains related business units incorporates a natural synergy that provides cost advantages.

Product and Process Technology Improvements.   If products can be designed with economic production methods in mind, costs compared

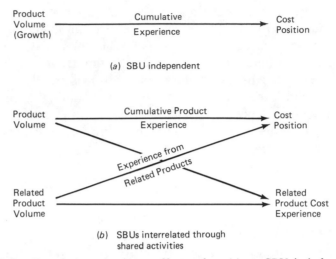

Figure 2-6. Cumulative experience effects when (a) an SBU is independent of others, and (b) SBUs are interrelated with shared activities

to competitors may be advantageous. This concentration on "production design" becomes even more important as volume increases and may involve better utilization of materials, or substitution of more economical materials that may make possible lower cost production methods. Production design may standardize materials and parts so that a wider variety of sizes and types of the product use some of the same parts, allowing higher volume and experience curve effects for those parts and an economy of scale in their manufacture. A company can gain significant operating advantages by integrating manufacturing activities from several business units that use the same or similar processes. Indeed, integration of activities should be one of the good reasons for acquisitions, because the "fit" makes good sense and produces a combined unit with cost advantages.

A newcomer to an industry with a new production technology may come in with a steeper experience curve and be able to establish itself very quickly as a cost-price leader. Note how quickly the initial experience is rewarded in Figure 2-4. On the other hand, if the rivalry in the industry is amongst strong competitors, there will be rapid transfer of new technology—there are few real secrets that are of lasting value.

Cost-Experience Curve for Amateur Photographic Products

One cannot expect a company to hand out product cost data, so the cost experience curve in Figure 2-7 needs explanation. In a separate

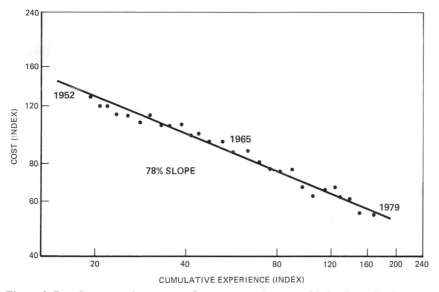

Figure 2-7. Cost-experience curve for amateur photographic business for Eastman Kodak, 1952–1979

SOURCE: Financial Supplement to Company Annual Report, 1979.

Financial Supplement to its 1979 Annual Report, Eastman Kodak published an index of their volume and their prices for amateur photographic products. By cumulating the volume index, deflating their price indexes, and taking their margins into account, we were able to derive their costs for the 1952–1979 period. The result is the 78 percent cost-experience curve shown in Figure 2-7. The curve provides a fascinating record over a 28-year period of the cost-experience curve phenomenon.

The Price-Experience Curve. The experience curve is a cost phenomenon. However, deflated prices following similar curves when plotted against total industry accumulated experience, usually because one company in the industry is the overall price-cost leader. The shape of the price-experience curve will not necessarily be parallel to the cost-experience curve throughout the life of the product. A good example of that fact is the price-experience curve for Eastman Kodak's amateur photographic business shown in Figure 2-8.

The price curve is superimposed on the cost-experience curve in Figure 2-8, showing that in the 1950s and early 1960s Kodak's deflated prices were declining according to an 86 percent experience curve. Obviously, the difference between an 86 percent price curve and a 78 percent cost curve means that margins were increasing during

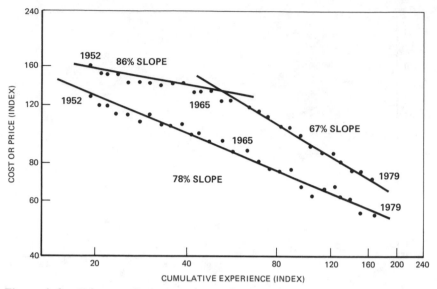

Figure 2–8. Price-experience curve superimposed on cost-experience curve for Eastman Kodak's amateur photographic business, 1952–1979

SOURCE: Financial Supplement to Company Annual Report, 1979.

this period, as shown in Figure 2–8. With such attractive margins in the industry, competitors such as Agfa, Fugi, and even Polaroid were attracted to share in the largesse, just as economic theory predicts.

In order to maintain their position in the amateur photographic business, Kodak reversed the policy of reducing prices at a slower rate than costs were being reduced, and reduced prices faster than cost reductions from the middle 1960s until 1979. The margins in 1979 were back to about where they were in 1952, but the competition in the business is now somewhat more intense. In the long run, cost and price curves must track together, because competition will force this relationship. Therefore, price/margin decisions are of great strategic significance.

Information Sources

Strategic analysis depends heavily on information about competitors. How can we obtain this crucial information without resorting to industrial espionage? Information such as that in Figures 1–4, 2–7, and 2–8 is publicly available, and much more.

First, a great deal of information on publicly owned companies is available in company annual reports or supplements (such as the information on Kodak's amateur photographic business, and on NL Industries cited earlier), but particularly in the more detailed 10-K reports that must be filed with the Securities and Exchange Commission (SEC). In many instances, information inserted in these reports is masked by indexes that are meant to give basic information to stockholders and the SEC, but manipulation of the data can yield the information needed by a strategic analyst.

Then there are data published by industry associations, articles published by newspapers and trade magazines, government reports and documents, and other bits and pieces of data that can be fit into a pattern that is meaningful at the level of strategic thinking. Indeed, careful digging always uncovers more data than can be meaningfully analyzed. All the company and industry data cited in this book were publicly available.

Analyzing Strategic Situations—Plan for the Book

The growth/share matrix, share/momentum chart, and the experience curve covered in this chapter are useful as elements in strategic analysis. In addition, there other devices that we will use, but we will introduce them as needed later in the book.

The statistical study of dogs by Hambrick and MacMillan suggests that there are factors operating that affect profitability other than the classification of a business into one of the four quadrants of the growth/share matrix. Similar comments may be appropriate for the other four quadrants of the growth/share matrix, in the sense that no simple prescriptions are obvious from the position of a business unit on the matrix.

Product life cycle analysis is a useful general concept linking future growth and market attractiveness, and we will use it in characterizing the broad position of a product. But we will use it only indirectly as a part of strategic analysis, partly because studies have shown that it is difficult to judge exactly where a product is in the cycle, and partly because of other problems with it as a basis for strategy analysis.[6] Instead we will use the general structure that follows for analyzing strategic situations, linking value and growth with cost position—the basic objective of strategy is to analyze situations in ways that reveal opportunities that add value to the firm.

INDUSTRY AND MARKET STRUCTURES

An analysis of competitors needs to be broad in context—examining the economies of scope, comparing the activity base of each to see which they are engaged in, and relating this structure to the value-added chain for the industry. Which activities contribute most to value added and which firm's operations emphasize these activities?

For example, in the titanium industry, most major Japanese producers are involved solely in sponge manufacture, an early stage of processing—reduction of the ore to an intermediate stage—that accounts for about 20 percent of the value added. They have not participated in ingot manufacture or, until recently, mill products and fabrications. Some of the U.S. firms are more integrated, being strong in sponge and ingot manufacture as well as mill products, accounting for about 75 percent of the value added. Other U.S. manufacturers have no position in sponge manufacture, but emphasize ingots, mill products, and some fabrications, accounting for about 50 percent of the value added. Finally, there is a group of firms whose activity is solely in fabrication, accounting for perhaps a third of the value added.

None of the firms is involved in the activity of mining the ore, rutile, which has a very small value added. A 10 percent advantage in rutile would not be of strategic value, unlike such an advantage in sponge, ingots, mill products, or fabrication. The rutile seems to be available to all. In addition to their variety of activity bases, the largest, strongest U.S. firms are joint ventures between large materials firms that have many other businesses in their portfolios, while the Japanese firms are specialists in the industry.

Now, the players in the titanium industry have rather different activity structures, providing advantages and disadvantages to each—it is not a level playing field. This is not to say that one of these structures is the right one and the others wrong. But depending on the situation, net advantage may accrue to a firm. For example, the Soviets withdrew substantially from the world titanium market in 1980. The Japanese were able to move quickly to fill the capacity vacuum, but the U.S. joint ventures could not—their sponsors had other businesses that required resources, and they decided that they could not respond.[7] The Japanese now dominate the basic industry and are beginning to exploit this advantage by moving downstream into the other high value-added activities.

Market structures and their degree of consolidation are very important in understanding competitive strength and weakness. Markets tend to go through an evolution from fragmented at early stages, to unconsolidated, and then to consolidated when one producer gains true dominance. In the early stages, competition tends to be on rather friendly terms, since growth usually provides enough business for everyone. But as the market matures with slower growth, competition becomes intense. One competitor may become dominant and consolidate the market, or the market may remain stable in an unconsolidated state for a long period, with several players having similar market shares. But if something happens to destabilize the market, one of the competitors with structural advantages may move to consolidate it.

We use office microcomputer software as an example of a fragmented market, and manifold business forms as an example of one consolidated by Moore Business Forms, Inc. Then we discuss the beer industry in detail through a series of developments following Miller's attempt to dislodge Anheuser Busch from its leadership position. Chapter 3 focuses attention on the analysis of industry and market structures.

INTERNATIONAL STRATEGIC ISSUES

To compete effectively in international markets we must be more productive relative to our own economy than our international competitor is relative to its economy. This differs from our traditional thinking of simply being more productive then the foreign producer. The analysis presented explains the anomaly that has plagued U.S. manufacturers during the last ten years when we lost much of our competitive edge to the Japanese. A relatively small difference in productivity can result in a devastating competitive cost advantage or disadvantage.

The productivity achievements of a company, or even an entire industry, are swamped out by the productivity improvements of the economy as a whole. This fact, developed in Chapter 4, leads to the admonition, "To compete effectively in international markets, be more productive relative to your own economy than your international competitor is relative to his economy."

In Chapter 4 we will discuss these international issues using examples from the steel and auto industries. Auto and steel price experience curves show the impact of oil prices on these energy-sensitive industries, and the effects of differential labor costs in steel and autos.

PRODUCT AND ACTIVITY STRUCTURES

Early in product life cycles, when there is market growth, there is something for everyone and everyone may be growing, but not necessarily gaining market share. At that stage, the market is unconsolidated, but unstable. Someone could move out to challenge for a consolidated position, as IBM has in personal computers. We will discuss other firms with a strong consolidated position, such as Moore in manifold business forms and Steelcase in office furniture.

Experience and comparative activity structures between players can turn out to be terribly important. If a clear leader develops, the experience curve helps to consolidate a cost leadership position that is extremely difficult to dislodge. Thus, the experience curve concept and all its strategic implications will be of great importance in many instances.

The complexity of a firm's activity structure in a business in relation to the value-added stream is a microcosm of the broader industry structure discussed earlier. A firm may have advantages that result from experience in an activity. A low market-share business may contribute to that activity experience, and if the activity accounts for a large fraction of the value added for all products, divestment of the low market share has unintended effects on the enterprise as a whole. A dog may be a thoroughbred golden retriever in such a case. For example, manufacturers of integrated circuits have had important cost advantages in the manufacture of consumer electronics products, such as hand-held calculators and digital watches. Some items in their product line may well have been regarded as dogs, with low growth and low relative market share. However, they contributed to experience in the manufacture of integrated circuits, adding to cost advantages for all products. These are the kinds of topics that we cover in Chapter 5, Product and Activity Structures.

DIVERSIFICATION AND ACQUISITIONS

While the conglomerate thrust of the 1960s and 1970s has waned, there has been no decline in activity to diversify, merge, and acquire. Indeed, one response of smokestack industries facing declining markets has been to diversify into other potentially more promising fields. But another, more common trend during the 1975–1980 period was for firms to acquire within the field of their own expertise, such as the move to acquire Republic Steel by LTV's Jones & Laughlin to form LTV Steel Company, the second largest U.S. steel producer. Firms acquiring outside their own industry have often branched out into services—business services, distribution, finance, and transportation. This has been particularly true for firms in materials conversion and manufacturing.

How should a firm go about focusing on a target? Should it seek out a successful firm with substantial experience in its field—one with a good record of earnings? Should it look for a firm in trouble and buy a tax loss carry forward? Should it look for fundamental demographics to help target firms with a strong future market? Should it scan industry sectors that are consolidated or ones that are not? What are the hallmarks of a good acquisition? These are some of the issues developed in Chapter 6.

FINANCIAL IMPLICATIONS OF STRATEGIC POSITIONS

The competitive environment depends on a number of factors including the threat of new entering competitors, rivalry amongst the players, product substitutions, and the bargaining power of both players and customers.[8] The impact of new competitors can have destabilizing effects on the industry as a whole, producing new capacity and possibly affecting prices. The entry of AT&T as a new competitor in the commercial telecommunications, computer, and other high tech markets has produced apprehension, for it is assumed that they will be a formidable force. While others might face substantial barriers to entry, AT&T has the resources to enter with the scale required for efficient production, and has Bell Laboratories to produce the product innovations.

The cost/price experience curves among competitors can produce an anomalous situation, where an aggressive player's rapid growth results in what we call the margin paradox—the margins of the aggressive competitor improve while the leader with greater experience and lower costs experiences declining margins.

When the cost-experience curve is used as a strategic tool, it may be easy to concentrate only on the variable costs of production that are impacted by labor-saving devices and materializing engineering designs. But prices must cover the capital costs in addition before profit is real. Therefore, the capital structures of different players can be very important. We develop analyses that show that one can be the low variable cost producer and yet, because of differences in financing mix and leverage, require a higher price to survive in the market.

Finally, we examine the phenomenon of the V-curve, the relationship of margins or returns to market shares in an industry. The V-curve relates the profitability of firms to their dominant market strategies, showing that the market leaders and niche players earn higher profits, while those in between these strategies are low earners. These and other financial implications of strategic positions are the subject of Chapter 7.

STRATEGIC SENARIO ANALYSIS

Given analyses of the industry and its markets, international issues if they are pertinent, product and activity structures, the competitive environment, and financial structure impacts, we do not yet have a strategy in place. In Chapter 8, we develop strategic scenarios that anticipate what will happen if strategy alternatives are followed. Assuming different ways of achieving strategic objectives, organizations and their managers have different risk requirements, and they need to be able to assess each alternative in these terms.

We examine scenarios in terms of uncertainty profiles, using a technique called SCENSIM (*SCEN*ario *SIM*ulation). For each alternative, key issues are listed that could impact the bottom line results. These might be competitor responses, events that affect the competitive environment, errors in forecasts of demand, legal issues, and so on. Then the effects of each issue are estimated and an envelope of results is drawn that circumscribes the risks. Two examples are developed: waterflood to increase oil field yield, and alternatives for achieving a capacity expansion.

Risk relationships between business units and the corporation as a whole are identified, given the occurrence of specified events. The risks are classified as controllable or not, so that resources can be allocated toward those elements that are under managerial control. Finally, strategies that meet the risk profiles of management are identified.

FROM ANALYSIS TO PLANS AND ACTION

Though the thrust of this book is directed toward strategic analysis, the result must lead to strategic plans, and finally to implementation of plans, or the entire effort will have been wasted. Chapter 9 puts the entire effort into the perspective of strategy formulation and the process into which analysis fits. We review triggering events and the thrust of strategic plans for both SBUs and corporate levels. The process for developing strategic plans at these two levels is discussed, placing the analytical steps in focus. Finally, when strategic planning is completed, it must be implemented—executives must now manage strategically.

Part II

Industry and Market Analysis

Chapter 3

Industry and Market Structures

"Know your competitors" is the admonition, and to know them is to understand the industry structure in terms of its value-added components and which competitors participate in each, and to understand the structure of the market. It is the structural strengths and weaknesses that are truly significant. What is the lay of the playing field?

There are economies of scale as well as scope. Economies of scale result from the volume of operations, while economies of scope are concerned with the interrelatedness of operations. If a firm attempts small-scale entry, it will have high costs compared to competitors with sufficient scale. While economies of scale are most often associated with the supply, production, and distribution functions, they can be important in marketing, advertising, and other functions as well, particularly when these activities represent a significant portion of the total cost of products. On the other hand, by understanding the scope of activities in an industry and how they may interact for different product lines and business units, it is possible to gain joint economies. Both scale and scope economies may result in a structural competitive advantage for some competitors relative to others.

The nature and structure of the market can have a dominating influence on strategy. If the market is consolidated by one competitor, such as Moore in the manifold business forms field or Steelcase in office furniture, one set of strategic moves may be appropriate, but if it is still anyone's game, quite another strategy may be used effectively.

On the other hand, market dominance does not necessarily imply dominance of the high value-added activities, though the two often go hand in hand. But when the market is dominated by someone who does not control the high value-added activities, such as was the case with Bowmar in pocket calculators, the strategic prescriptions must offer some other strong basis for maintaining position.

Industry and market structure will mean different things to different people, but we refer to the basic activities required, related to the value-added stream—who the competitors are and how they participate in the activities of the value-added stream, the capacity-demand balance in the industry, price trends, growth rates, margins in the industry, and the degree to which markets and requisite activities are consolidated by an industry leader.

Value Added and Activities

A broad comparison of the players in an industry shows how each participates in the value-added steps in the industry from raw materials to finished products. Which companies are integrated and which participate in only a portion of the value-added stream? Are there crucial supply materials, and who controls them? Are some producers at the mercy of others for the supply of critical components?

Figure 3–1 shows the value-added structure for several major competitors in the titanium industry. The chart allocates value, in terms of final selling price, of titanium products over the several stages of processing within the industry. The value added at each stage is the selling price of the product at that stage less the value added of all previous stages.* The height of the bars is proportional to the average value added at each stage of processing. The shading indicates where in the value-added stream various participants are active.

BACKGROUND ON TITANIUM

Titanium is a light, strong, corrosion-resistant metal that maintains its characteristics at high temperatures. It came into prominent use in military aircraft design and has since found a wide variety of applica-

---

*When intermediate goods markets do not exist, value added can only be estimated. It is often more useful in these cases to show proportional cost of the various stages, leaving profit out entirely, or showing it as a final value added item.

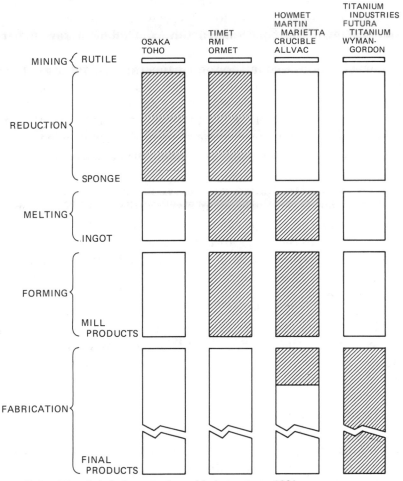

Figure 3-1. Titanium industry value added structure, 1981

SOURCE: *Mineral Facts and Problems* (U.S. Bureau of Mines, 1980), Annual Titanium Supplement to *American Metal Market*, Fairchild Publications (various issues), and conversations with industry sources.

tions—the Soviets have used it for the hulls of their latest submarine designs. In conjunction with the world economic rebound following the 1974–1976 recession, and because of its unique properties, titanium demand and production began to increase dramatically in the 1976–1977 period.

Titanium is a common element found in many minerals. The ore, called rutile, is mined in a number of countries, including the United States, Canada, Norway, South Africa, and the Soviet Union, but

Australia is the principal producer, accounting for more than three-fourths of the world's production. Those who are in titanium-related businesses might be concerned about controlling a raw material source. But the value-added stream depicted in Figure 3-1 shows that the mining of rutile accounts for only a tiny fraction of the total value added, about 1 percent of the average cost of mill products, and political instability does not seem to be a factor—you simply buy it.

The reduction of rutile, typically by some variation of the Kroll process,* produces an intermediate stage of the metal called sponge. Sponge is melted, together with some scrap, in successive vacuum-arc-melting operations to produce ingots, which are formed into mill products. The mill products are produced in standard shapes, such as billets, bars, sheets, and strips, which are fabricated for final applications. As stated, the average value added at each stage of manufacture is in proportion to the height of the bars in Figure 3-1, with fabrication being quite variable depending on the specific application. So far as the basic industry is concerned, reduction and forming account for substantial fractions of the average cost of mill products, about 45 and 35 percent respectively. A 10 to 20 percent cost advantage in the reduction of rutile to sponge could be quite important, whereas the same percentage cost reduction in rutile mining costs would be unimportant.

THE TITANIUM INDUSTRY

None of the structural configurations can be said to be right or wrong—they each have strengths and weaknesses, and that is the value of understanding the structure. The major Japanese producers, Osaka Titanium Company and Toho Titanium Company, are specialists, concentrating on sponge production. As such, they can focus their efforts and learn to do what they do very well, and profit from experience to produce at low cost and high quality. Since they concentrate on sponge reduction, they must rely on other firms—traditionally Sumitomo Metal Industries, Nippon Mining, and Kobe Steel—to further process their sponge into ingot and mill products and, of particular importance, to sell it. Their access to the end-use markets is

---

*The Kroll process of sponge reduction is a batch reactive process in which purified titanium tetrachloride is reduced with sodium or magnesium in an inert atmosphere. Like most batch processes, the scale of the batch has great impact on cost. In sponge production the size of the reactive vessels determines batch size.

very restricted, which greatly reduces their ability to market their product.

The major U.S. sponge producers, the TIMET division of Titanium Metals Corp. of America, RMI, and Oregon Metallurgical Corp. (ORMET), are more integrated, participating in a much broader range of the value-added stream. There may be some economies resulting from integration, such as transportation, or energy savings in a high-energy requirement industry. On the other hand, the broader range of activities requires larger staffs to coordinate and hence results in higher overhead costs. Moreover, corporate effort is distributed over a variety of tasks, with the possible result that no single task is done as well.

The third group does not participate in sponge manufacture, but concentrates further downstream on ingot and mill products, with some fabrication activity. It includes in Japan Sumitomo Metal Industries, Nippon Mining, and Kobe Steel, with Nippon Steel entering in 1983 by converting two excess stainless steel mills to titanium. In the United States the five leading firms are Howmet Turbine Components Corp., Martin Marietta Aluminum, Crucible Specialty, Teledyne Allvac, and Lawrence Aviation Industries. This group is largely at the mercy of the sponge producers for supply and price in times of tight capacity or other reasons for short supply. But when demand falls off it is this group that the sponge-only producers must rely on to market their product. They are integrated within the middle of the value-added chain, servicing sponge producers and fabricators. Finally, the fabricators participate in activities involving the largest average value added in the chain. This group includes such firms as Titanium Industries and Futura Titanium, which supply fabrications to the chemical process industry, and Wyman-Gordon, which forges turbine parts for the aerospace industry.

Recently a fifth group has developed (not shown on Figure 3–1) concentrating on forming mill products from ingot. In this group, for example, ALS is a joint venture of Sumitomo Metal Industries and Allegheny Ludlum Steel Corp. Sumitomo is supplying the ingot and Allegheny Ludlum is forming it into mill products using excess stainless steel rolling capacity, with the products being marketed in the United States and Canada by Allegheny Ludlum. At the same time Wyman-Gordon, the largest U.S. fabricator, has begun a backward integration step into melting and forming.

Clearly, the firms in the titanium industry are positioned quite differently in the range of activities of the value-added stream. In addition, TIMET and RMI, the two major U.S. producers, are joint ventures of other large firms, with NL Industries and Allegheny International owning TIMET, and U.S. Steel and National Distillers and Chemical Corp. owning RMI.

Sponge output is dominated by four producers: two Japanese, Osaka and Toho, and two U.S. producers, TIMET and RMI. Oregon Metallurgical Corp. (ORMET), the next largest sponge producer, is owned about 92 percent by ARMCO.

Capacity/Demand Patterns

Free-world consumption of titanium sponge is divided into three major markets:

United States	55%
Japan	23%
Europe	22%
	100%

The U.S. market is the largest and is also growing very fast, at an annual rate of 19 percent from 1976 to 1981, shown by the consumption line in Figure 3–2. But sponge production capacity in the United States

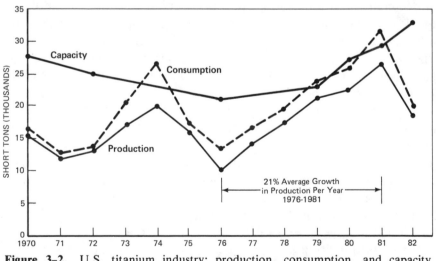

Figure 3–2. U.S. titanium industry: production, consumption, and capacity, 1970–1982

SOURCES: *Metal Statistics: Annual Summary* (American Metal Market), Fairchild Publications, various years; *Mineral Commodity Summaries* (U.S. Bureau of Mines), *Mineral Commodity Profiles* (U.S. Bureau of Mines).

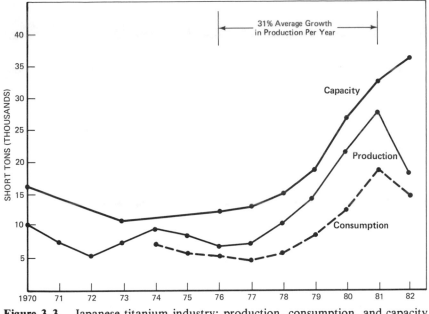

Figure 3-3. Japanese titanium industry: production, consumption, and capacity, 1970–1982

Sources: *Mineral Industry Surveys,* various issues (U.S. Bureau of Mines); Mineral Commodity Summaries (U.S. Bureau of Mines); *Mineral Commodity Profiles* (U.S. Bureau of Mines), Annual Titanium Supplement to *American Metal Market,* Fairchild Publications (various issues).

dipped from 1970 to 1976, partially as a result of government imposed pollution control requirements, and then increased from 1976 to 1982, though not as fast as production and consumption.

The difference between production and consumption of sponge in the United States is made up from imports—in 1981 74 percent came from Japan, a net exporter of titanium sponge. The comparable capacity/production/consumption graph for Japanese sponge is shown in Figure 3-3.

The Japanese have increased sponge capacity much faster than the U.S. producers. From 1976 to 1982, Japan's capacity increased 190 percent, from 12,400 to 36,000 thousand tons. The comparable U.S. figures are 57 percent, from 21,000 to 33,000 thousand tons.

Prices

The price of titanium sponge fell steadily from $13.26 per pound in 1955 to $2.78 by the end of 1973 (both in 1982 dollars). However, shortages resulted in price increases from 1974 to 1980, culminating in

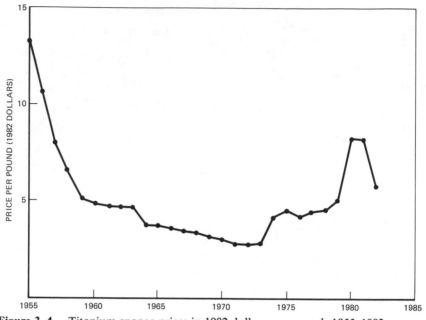

Figure 3-4.   Titanium sponge prices in 1982 dollars per pound, 1955–1982

Source: Metal Statistics (American Metal Market), Mineral Commodity Profiles (U.S. Bureau of Mines), 1983.

a price of $8.11 per pound by the end of 1981. The high 1980–1981 prices reflect the very tight capacity/demand balance at that time. As supplies increased, reflecting capacity additions, prices fell by the end of 1982 to $5.70 per pound. Japanese export prices to the United States generally followed U.S. prices with a $1 to $3 premium. Prices are projected to continue to decline in the long run, since capacities are almost certain to be ample in relation to demand. Figure 3–4 shows a 28-year price graph in constant 1982 dollars.

Competitive Dynamics

Figure 3–5 is a sector chart showing the competitive dynamics of the titanium sponge market from 1977 to 1981 in terms of relative capacity position and growth for the major producers. A sector chart is related to the growth/share matrix and the share/momentum chart discussed in Chapter 2. Recall that the growth/share matrix displays a company's portfolio in terms of scale, market growth rate, and rela-

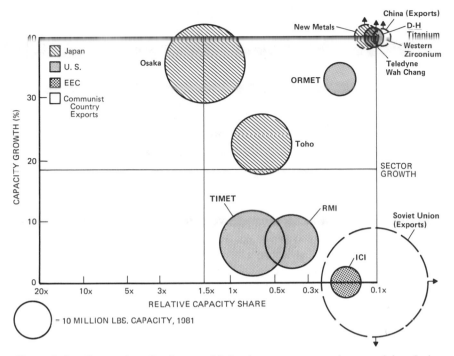

Figure 3-5. Sector chart for free-world titanium sponge capacity growth in relation to relative capacity share, 1977–1981

Sources: Mineral Industry Surveys (U.S. Bureau of Mines); Annual Titanium Supplement to *American Metal Market,* Fairchild Publications (various issues); *Chemical Week,* April 26, 1981, "Titanium No More Boom and Bust Cycles?" pp. 42–46.

tive position for the business units, and the share/momentum chart shows changes in market position for the same business units. The sector chart takes a market- or industrial-sector view instead of a company view—it shows each competitor's position and momentum within a sector. Hence it is better suited to displaying the competitive interactions between companies competing in a particular market or sector, while the growth/share matrix and share/momentum chart are more useful in showing the portfolio of a particular company.

In a sector chart each competitor is represented by a circle that is proportional to its sales (or other suitable measure of scale) in the sector. In Figure 3–5, for the titanium sponge sector, circle areas are proportional to the capacities of competitors for 1981. The circle centers are plotted at the competitor's relative market share and growth rate, and a dashed line is drawn horizontally at the sector growth rate. In Figure 3–5, relative capacity share and capacity growth rate have been substituted for market share and growth rate because of their availability. (As in most heavy industries, sales volume divides among the competitors virtually in proportion to capacity.) For the Soviet Union and China, export growth and exports relative to capacity of the leader were used since only export sales from communist countries affect free-world markets.

Osaka Titanium is the industry leader with 1.5 times the sponge-reduction capacity of its largest competitor, TIMET, but TIMET, Toho, and RMI are all of similar size. Osaka capacity grew at about 36 percent per year during the 1977–1981 period, while all free-world capacity grew less than 18 percent, the sector growth rate.

Not shown on the chart are new entrants, such as International Titanium, whose capacity was not yet on stream by the end of 1981. International Titanium, using a new process developed in conjunction with Ishizuka Research, commenced production in 1982 with 10 million pounds of sponge capacity per year, making it approximately the size of ORMET.

As recently as 1977, TIMET was the free world's largest producer of titanium sponge. But both the major U.S. producers are growing at less than 10 percent, and will become quite small in the industry in a relatively short time. Some of the small U.S. producers have high growth rates, though it is easier for a small firm to show a high growth rate, and ORMET in particular will become a large U.S. producer if it continues to grow at the rates shown.

The speculation is that the Soviets needed their domestic titanium to build their submarine fleet, and withdrew substantial export volume from the world titanium market in 1980, leaving a large capacity gap. The Japanese filled the gap more aggressively than the U.S. producers. Recall that the two larger U.S. producers are both joint ventures of other large companies. One can speculate that perhaps this corporate structure reduced the flexibility of the U.S. titanium companies in moving as quickly as the Japanese to finance the large expenditures for new capacity, or the joint venture companies chose not to invest additional large amounts in the titanium industry, having heavy demands for funds in other business units. In a corporate joint venture, both parties must be willing to invest to add new capacity, making it doubly difficult to expand.

Depending on the age of the facilities and the process used, the U.S. Bureau of Mines estimates the investment in facilities to be in the range of $9000 to $16,000 per ton of sponge capacity. Assuming new capacity at the upper figure, capacity additions between 1980 and 1982 required investments of about $120 million in the United States and $150 million in Japan.

These formidable investment requirements present a substantial barrier to entry, but because they are highly specialized facilities they also present a substantial exit barrier. Overcapacity could become a chronic problem in the industry. Meanwhile, one U.S. producer, D-H Titanium (a joint venture of Dow Chemical and Howmet Turbine Components Corp.), attempted to develop an electrolytic process for sponge production that could reduce manufacturing costs significantly. Such a development would obsolete much existing capacity, but would not necessarily take it out of use, because of the high exit barriers, exacerbating the problem of future overcapacity. Unfortunately the attempt failed and the D-H joint venture was disbanded in 1983.

The slower expansion of the U.S. firms suggests that these firms will continue to lose their once dominant competitive positions to Osaka and Toho. Of course, the Soviets may reenter the titanium market if their appetite for submarine building becomes sated, producing a world overcapacity as severe as it was in the 1960s and early 1970s and a return to price cutting—there is reason to believe in a downward price trend because of overcapacity pressures.

Margins

The gross operating margins (sales minus cost of goods sold), shown in Figure 3-6 for the three U.S. sponge producers reflect their integrated operations in sponge, ingot, and mill products. The low prices of the 1970s, followed by the dramatic price increases in 1980 and 1981 are reflected in margins, indicating that costs were probably not the problem during the low-margin years.

ORMET shows the strongest recovery during the 1979–1981 period, probably tied to its heavy investment in capacity, shown by its 34 percent capacity growth rate in Figure 3-5. TIMET, being more forward integrated into downstream products, did not experience as rapid an increase in margins as did ORMET during 1979–1981. Also, TIMET did not expand capacity as rapidly and may have lost sales, being capacity limited during that period. RMI's margin growth rate parallels ORMET's.[1]

The long-term demand prospects for titanium appear to depend on a variety of contingencies: the question concerning the possible

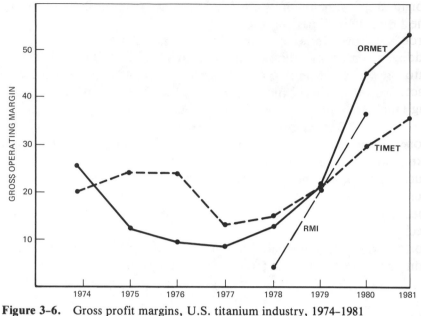

Figure 3-6. Gross profit margins, U.S. titanium industry, 1974–1981

SOURCE: Company or parent annual reports and 10-K reports

TIMET (50 percent NL Industries, 50 percent Allegheny Ludlum Steel Corp.); RMI (50 percent US Steel, 50 percent National Distillers and Chemical Corp.); ORMET (company annual and 10-K reports).

rentry of the Soviet Union into the market, creating overcapacity; the cooling or heating up of the cold war, affecting U.S. demand for defense; the effect of airline deregulation in the United States on the demand for new commercial aircraft; and the possibility of demand expansion for new applications. In the past, industry demand has been dominated by the cyclical defense industry and fast growing commercial aerospace requirements. More recently, the decline in commercial aircraft production has been partially offset by increased defense spending. However, titanium is rapidly penetrating new markets to substitute for such metals as nickel. For example, titanium is being used in the chemical industry because of its corrosion resistance.

As of 1985, both U.S. and Japanese producers have announced substantial expansion plans, which would add substantially to both U.S. and Japanese capacity. But the Japanese have financed a significant portion of the planned U.S. capacity expansion, for example, the 1984 expansion of International Titanium.

Based on the industry analysis, it appears that Osaka is rapidly consolidating titanium sponge on a world-wide basis—they have won the battle, with Toho close behind. While both the large Japanese producers have participated only in the sponge portion of the value-added stream, they are in an excellent position to move downstream into the higher value-added activities of ingot and mill products. In fact, Osaka decided to begin ingot production in 1981 and began adding facilities to do so.

The implications for U.S. firms of the projected Japanese domination of the industry are significant. As the Japanese accumulate experience faster and consolidate their position as the low-cost producers, the U.S. firms will have progressively less influence in the industry, market prices will become progressively more difficult for them to control or even match, and as a result, profits will likely decline. Titanium users in the United States will buy an increasing proportion of the sponge and mill products from the Japanese, and the dominance will move from the United States to Japan.

Market Structure

Our interest in market structure is focused in the degree to which the market is dominated or consolidated by one firm. In looking at markets from this point of view, we are interested in the competitive dynamics of the players in an industry—the relative market shares, growth rates, and how they are changing. We touched on these kinds of relationships in connection with the titanium industry.

Early in product life cycles when growth is high, we commonly have a fragmented market with fluid market structure—regardless of market shares, everyone is growing and each competitor is likely to be quite amiable and courteous about competition. Industry associations flourish. Each firm can grow and prosper without needing to be terribly competitive, though they will grow at different rates and some will be larger than others. Competition is not so much with other firms as it is for new sales, and market-share changes that occur are often related to new product development or extensions into new markets for old products. The situation may remain fluid for quite some time, with no clear winner. The sector chart in Figure 3–7a illustrates this situation, where each circle represents the position of a firm in the industry.

As the market matures and growth slows, competition becomes more keen. Either a clear leader emerges and the market structure

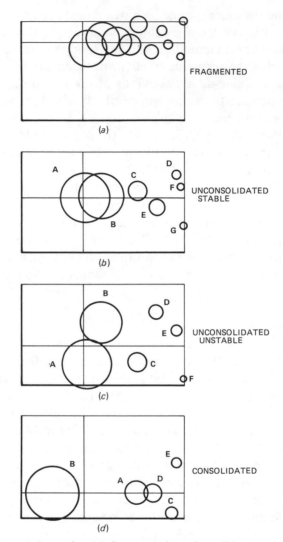

Figure 3-7. Sector charts for (*a*) fragmented market, (*b*) unconsolidated-stable market, (*c*) unconsolidated-unstable market, and (*d*) consolidated market

changes in transition to a consolidated one with a single dominant competitor as shown in Figure 3-7*d,* or it moves to an unconsolidated but stable structure shown in Figure 3-7*b*—markets in which the structure of the competitors is such that a natural segmentation occurs typically in transition to an unconsolidated and stable structure. The most common basis for segmentation is geographic, with various local markets being dominated by certain competitors.

In the unconsolidated stable phase, competition is still not so much between competitors as it is for new products and new markets. Industry associations are still popular and what competition exists between firms is "gentlemanly." This phase, depending on the value-added structure, can last for a long period.

Instability can occur for a variety of reasons. Something may happen in the industry to create new opportunities or uncertainties that will destabilize it, usually an external factor. Deregulation in the airline industry, the Soviet withdrawal from the world titanium market, the development of an innovation in process technology that drastically reduces production cost, a change in the way business is done brought about by a new entrant—these are all examples of events that can cause an industry to become unstable, as shown by the sector graph of Figure 3-7c.

In Figure 3-7c, firm B has challenged the former market leader and is growing rapidly at the expense of both firms A and C. It is unstable because it will not end in the situation shown in Figure 3-7c. There will be resolution, someone will have to win—firm B has taken on the former market-share leader, and one or the other is likely to emerge as the leader.

Of course, this scenario is similar to the situation we described in the titanium industry, where the Soviet withdrawal created an opportunity on which Osaka Titanium capitalized. For reasons alluded to earlier, the former market leaders, TIMET and RMI, did not or could not respond, and by 1980 they lost market dominance to the new leader in the industry, Osaka.

In Figure 3-7d the market has been consolidated by firm B. It now dominates the market with the largest share and is much larger than its competitors, including A, the former leader.

Examples of Fragmented and Consolidated Markets

Figure 3-8 shows a sector chart for the U.S. office microcomputer software market for the 1982–1983 period. Of course, the microcomputer software industry is quite new, and it is no surprise that it is fragmented with extremely high growth—nearly 90 percent growth per year—and a large number of competitors. Notice that Microsoft, the current leader, is only about 1.2 times as large as its nearest competitor, Visicorp. But several others are nearly as large as Visicorp— Digital Research, MicroPro, and Lotus with a runaway growth exceeding 150 percent.

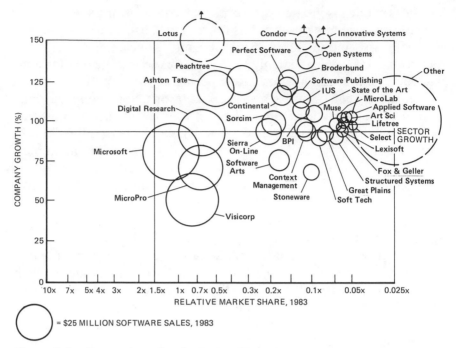

Figure 3-8. Sector chart for the U.S. office microcomputer software industry, 1982–1983 (Hardware manufacturers excluded)

SOURCE: *Future Computing,* estimates for 1983 sales, as of October 1983.

There are several classic characteristics of a fragmented market. The large circle (labeled "other") at the right of the chart signifies the large number of small entrants coming into the market, and as a group, they are growing faster than the market. Though not apparent from Figure 3-8, most of the companies are single product—their fortunes depend on the success or failure of that single product. Only Microsoft is multiproduct. Finally, market share changes are occurring not so much because of competition between companies as by market expansion with new products.

Even though the microcomputer software market is fragmented as of 1983, we are already beginning to see intercompany competition develop. Lotus was the first software company to "win" by destroying an existing competitor—VisiCorp. The Lotus 1-2-3 product is really just a better VisiCalc.

But by 1984, the process of market shakeout had already made substantial progress. As one chief executive of a software startup company put it, "The industry's got one foot on a banana peel and the other in Chapter 11.''[2] The first half of 1984 saw bankruptcies, buyouts, layoffs, and price cutting. For example, Sirius Software, Inc. and its parent Softsmith Corp. filed for protection under Chapter 11. Publisher Readers Digest Associates and ASK Computer Systems withdrew from the business. Management Science America and On-Line Software International reported quarterly losses. Soricum Corp. and Information Unlimited Software were acquired by Computer Associates International Inc. And, VisiCorp and MicroPro International Corp. laid off more than half their staffs. The market was flooded with alternative products—there were 20,000 programs available for the installed base of about 5 million personal computers.[2]

The answers to the strategic market transition questions are not obvious. Will the microcomputer software market quickly consolidate, or will it mature to an unconsolidated stable state? In order to attempt an answer, we must look to the value-added structure within the industry. Is that structure such that differently configured firms will exist and be able to hold different segments of the market?

Figure 3–9 shows a sector chart of the manifold business forms in-

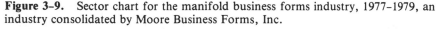

Figure 3–9. Sector chart for the manifold business forms industry, 1977–1979, an industry consolidated by Moore Business Forms, Inc.

SOURCE: Company annual and 10-K reports, *Value Line,* and Standard & Poors' COMPUSTAT.

dustry during the 1977–1979 period as an example of a consolidated market. Moore dominates the market, is growing at a slightly higher rate than the industry, and has five times the market share of its largest competitor, Standard Register. Some of the smaller firms are growing faster, but they are in market segments, rather than being industry-wide producers as is Moore. This does not mean that the smaller firms are unprofitable, for market niches can be extremely lucrative. In the absence of some external destabilizing force, however, it seems very unlikely that a competitor's challenge to Moore could be successful.

A consolidated market can become unstable also, when someone decides to take on the leader, or when some external event destabilizes the market and the leader does not respond to the change appropriately. Usually, however, a strategy of taking on an entrenched leader ends in disaster as, for example, when Lionel Corp. challenged Toys-R-Us in the discount toy store market in the late 1970s, which ended with Lionel filing for bankruptcy.

We will use the beer industry and its development over a 15-year period as an example of market structures and their dynamics, and as a vehicle to illustrate with real examples the other two market structures, unconsolidated stable and unconsolidated unstable.

THE U.S. BEER MARKET, 1968–1972

During the 1968–1972 period, the beer industry in the United States was unconsolidated and fairly stable. Even though Anheuser-Busch was the largest, it was only about 40 percent larger than Schlitz, from whom it had wrested industry leadership in 1957, and Coors and Pabst were not far behind, as shown on the sector chart of Figure 3-10. Miller, the player that turned out to be really aggressive, was only one-fifth the size of Anheuser-Busch with less than 5 percent market share—not really an important competitor at that time.

The main competitive market activities during this period were that the large firms were getting larger, and regional brewers were having difficulty competing with the national brands, and were slowly going away. But there were no real competitive dynamics occurring.

The event that destabilized the industry was the purchase of Miller by Philip Morris. When Philip Morris entered the business through Miller, they chose to compete on a somewhat different basis. They did not lower the price, a common strategy, but increased costs by increas-

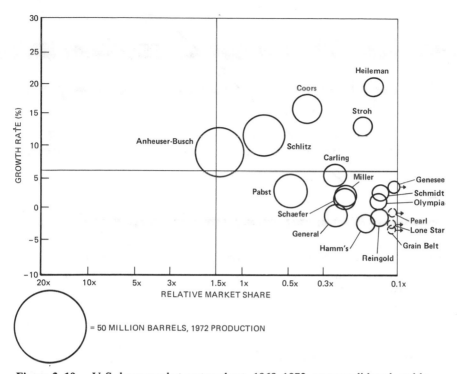

Figure 3-10. U.S. beer market sector chart, 1968–1972, unconsolidated, stable

SOURCES: Company annual and 10-K reports, *Beverage industry* (various issues), and *Modern Brewery Age* (various issues).

ing advertising dramatically, affecting the profitability of the entire industry, including their own. The increased advertising forced all competitors to do so in order to keep up, increasing costs for all. Coming from the cigarette business, perhaps an advertising strategy appealed to Philip Morris as the most logical way to challenge the leaders.

Figure 3–11 shows the general margin/market-share relationship in effect in 1970—the larger the market share, the higher the operating margin, with Miller producing only 5.8 percent, and Anheuser-Busch the leader with almost 18 percent. But the dashed line below the solid line shows the effect on everyone's margins of having to meet the heavy advertising expenses without price increases—a new competitive dynamic had been created in order to stay in the game. Miller had the financial resources to play this game with their new Philip Morris backing.

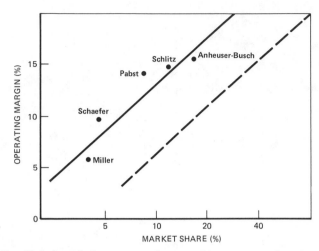

Figure 3–11.   U.S. beer industry operating margins versus market share, 1970

SOURCES: Company and parent annual reports, *Value Line, Modern Brewery Age,* and *Beverage Industry* (various issues).

THE U.S. BEER MARKET, 1972–1976

The effects of the new competitive dynamic on both Miller's and Anheuser-Busch's margins and market shares is shown in Figure 3–12. Beginning in 1971, Miller's margins dropped dramatically, but by 1973 the strategy was working in terms of increases in market share. After 1973 margins began to recover and market share continued to grow, reaching a share of over 12 percent by 1976, and margins of over 9 percent, significantly better than their 1970 margins of 5.8 percent. Meanwhile, Anheuser-Busch's margins dropped. However, market share increased from almost 18 percent in 1970 to over 25 percent by 1975, but dropped back below 20 percent in 1976, due in part to a strike that kept the brewer's product off retail shelves during the peak summer season of 1976.

The dynamics of what was happening industry-wide are captured in the sector chart for the period in Figure 3–13. Anheuser-Busch was slightly below the industry growth rate of about 4 percent, but Miller is off the chart with a growth rate of 36 percent. They moved from a position of very low growth, approximately 2 percent per year and only 20 percent the size of Anheuser-Busch, to more than 30 percent growth at almost 70 percent the size of Busch.

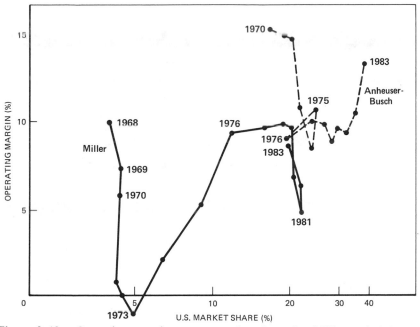

Figure 3–12. Operating margins versus market share for Miller and Anheuser-Busch, 1970–1983

SOURCES: Company annual and 10-K reports, *Beverage Industry* (various issues), Standard & Poors' COMPUSTAT, and *Modern Brewery Age* (various issues).

THE U.S. BEER MARKET, 1976–1979

Figure 3–14 shows that in the 1976–1979 period, Miller continued its aggressive growth, but at the expense of the smaller brewers rather than Anheuser-Busch. Busch responded to Miller's competitive thrust and began its own aggressive expansion. Miller's growth rate declined to less than 25 percent, but Busch's growth rate improved dramatically from less than 4 to above 16 percent in an industry whose growth rate remained at about 4 percent. Heileman is the only other large brewery that continued to grow faster than the industry—the others fell to below zero growth (Coors, Pabst, and Stroh), and Schlitz slipped off the chart with − 11 percent decline. Figure 3–14 shows the dramatic decline of the smaller brewers in the face of the Busch-Miller battle. When the elephants dance, the mice often get stepped on!

Margins over this period were about the same for Busch and

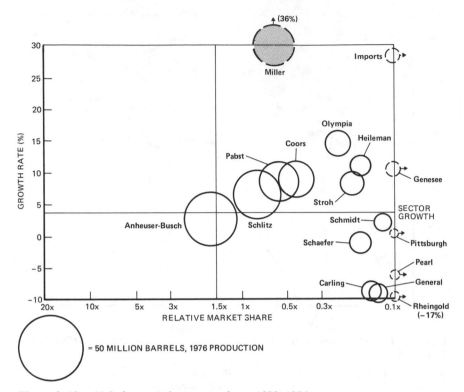

Figure 3-13.   U.S. beer market sector chart, 1972–1976

SOURCES: Company annual and 10-K reports, *Beverage Industry* (various issues), and *Modern Brewery Age* (various issues).

Miller—about 10 percent on an operating basis—as shown in Figure 3-12. This margin level was significantly lower than that enjoyed by Busch prior to the Miller challenge, but slightly higher than Miller's traditional levels. Busch's margins were still depressed from their 1970 high by the heavy advertising expenses demanded by the new competitive environment, together with no price relief. But Miller enjoyed improved margins due to its improved cost position consistent with its vastly increased scale.

THE U.S. BEER MARKET, 1979–1983

Clearly, Anheuser-Busch was no marshmallow competitor, unlike RMI and TIMET in titanium sponge. It rose to the competitive test of

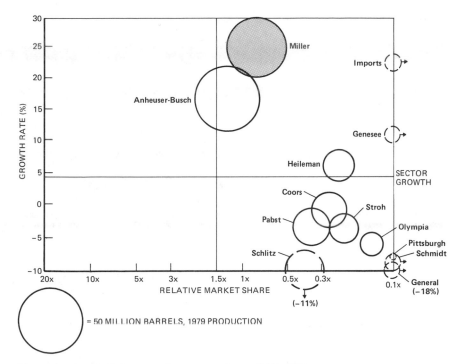

Figure 3-14.   U.S. beer market sector chart, 1976–1979

SOURCES: Company annual and 10-K reports, *Beverage Industry* (various issues), and *Modern Brewery Age* (various issues).

Miller and stopped the challenge as shown in Figure 3–15. By 1983 Busch had moved to more than 1.5 times the size of Miller by growing faster than Miller from 1979 to 1983. By 1983, as shown in Figure 3–12, Busch was able to restore its margins to almost the 1970–1973 level. Miller's margins deteriorated badly as Busch fought back, but once the game was over and it stopped gaining market share, its margins began to recover too. In 1983, Miller's margins were back to the mid-1970s level, but below Busch's.

Miller was not able to dislodge Busch from its leadership position—Busch has regained its relative market share. Indeed, the "Miller maneuver" resulted in a decline in profitability for the entire industry, with a rapid decline of regional breweries. The victims have been the small regional breweries, but it has been a blood bath for everyone in the industry. Of the 93 U.S. breweries in 1970, 50 have either gone out of business or been driven into the arms of stronger

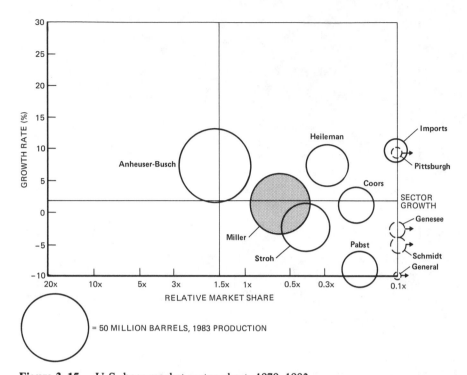

Figure 3-15. U.S. beer market sector chart, 1979–1983

SOURCES: Company annual and 10-K reports, *Beverage Industry* (various issues), and *Modern Brewery Age* (various issues).

partners by 1984.[3] Perhaps Miller picked the wrong target in Anheuser-Busch. The industry is not yet consolidated but it is fast becoming so—with Busch the clear winner. All that remains is for the competition among the minor brewers to sort itself out—Miller, Stroh, Heileman, Coors, and Pabst.

As of 1983, Anheuser Busch had 34 percent and Miller 21 percent of the market, with three of the strongest regionals, Stroh, Heileman, and Coors, having 14 percent, 10 percent, and 8 percent respectively. In the face of further intense price and market competition, it appears highly likely that there will be further consolidation, with Busch gaining market dominance.

By mid 1984, the shakeout had taken on a new dimension—a shrinking market and falling prices. Not only was installed capacity very large, but shifting demographic patterns were reducing the number of beer drinkers and the amount of beer drinking. The former growth of the 18 to 25 age group was declining, and this is the group that drinks the most beer. Also, stiffer drunk-driving laws and America's concern for fitness have had an effect on beer consumption.[4]

Summary

The value-added pattern illustrated by Figure 3–1 for the titanium industry is common in other industries in the sense that different firms in the same industry participate in the activities of the industry in quite different ways.

For example, in the consumer electronics industry, Japanese producers such as Sony, Panasonic, and Sanyo are heavily integrated backwards into component manufacture and assembly, but participate only to the extent of 60 to 70 percent in marketing, sales, and distribution, and do not participate in retailing at all. Two starkly contrasting patterns are found with Emerson and Radio Shack. Radio Shack is involved with no component manufacture and does about 40 percent of its own assembly, but performs all of its own marketing through retailing. Emerson is solely involved with its own marketing, sales, and distribution, and is not involved with any of the other activities.

The dominant firms in the industry are not necessarily integrated, witness Osaka in the titanium industry. But sometimes they are integrated, as with the Japanese consumer electronics firms. The strategic value in understanding the value-added activity structure is in exposing the relative strengths and weaknesses of the businesses in the industry.

The scanning of the other aspects of capacity/demand patterns, prices, relative growth rates, and margins helps fill out the picture of the industry and its participants, and contributes to an understanding of the market structure. It is in the analysis of the market structure that important additional strengths and weaknesses of firms become more clearly identified. Is the industry consolidated? If not, which firms have the best opportunities to take initiatives that could consolidate the industry? What are the kinds of outside influences that could destabilize the industry? Which firms would be helped or hurt most by various kinds of destabilizing events?

For example, the U.S. machine tool industry seems unconsolidated currently. Cincinnati Milicron is the largest producer in the industry, but it has only about 1.4 times the market share of the next largest, and there are an additional four or five firms that are more than half its size. The industry is fragmented. Furthermore, the leader and most other U.S. producers had negative growth during the 1979–1982 period. Cross and Trecker, and Giddings & Lewis have slightly positive growth rates, but the really high-growth companies are all Japanese. The destabilizing force may have already been put in place in the form of an aggressive move by the Japanese into lathes and numerically controlled machine tools, which industry experts say is the future high-growth market of the industry and the highest value-added product type.

If an industry is consolidated, what are the strategies left for the other firms? Could a direct attack on the leader possibly succeed? Usually not! What events could destabilize a consolidated industry? Steelcase has consolidated the office furniture industry. It is three times the size of its next largest competitor and is growing at 20 percent in an industry that is growing at only 7.5 percent as of 1982. While it is a privately held company, its profits have been estimated to be nearly as large as the sales of its closest competitor, Herman Miller. It is difficult to see how Steelcase could be attacked at this time. Successful competitors in the industry seem to do well with market segments, but there are no across-the-board competitors.

On the other hand, Union Carbide had the dry battery industry fairly well consolidated at one time with the carbon zinc cell, but the alkaline battery was developed and offered certain advantages (it provides more power at a smaller cost per unit). The two batteries require rather different plant facilities, so that substantial new investment is required to shift into alkaline battery production. Mallory challenged with the innovation, and by 1978 was growing at 25 percent in an industry growing at only 8 percent, with Union Carbide growing at 3 percent, emphasizing its carbon zinc product. At that point, Carbide was still 2.5 times the size of Mallory, but was shrinking rapidly with the prospect of losing its leadership position. Apparently, Mallory caught Carbide in a situation where it had other important needs for its investment cash, and did not or could not respond rapidly to the investment requirements to maintain its position in the industry by developing facilities for the alkaline product.

The entire thrust of industry and market analysis is to gain insight into the situations of competitors. Then, in strategy formulation, an attempt is made to counterpoise strength against competitors' weaknesses, rather than strength against strength. Each competitor wants to find a hill in the playing field and defend it.

Chapter 4

Productivity/Exchange-Rate Effects in Global Competition*

Some of the basic ingredients on which a firm can base competitive strategies are contained in the analyses of industries and markets discussed in Chapter 2. With the central objective of increasing long-term economic value of the firm, we try in some way to be better than our competitors. There are many ways to achieve this objective—better marketing and advertising, better images of products and the firm, new and better products, better technology, better employee relations and the nurturing of these assets through deeply-felt corporate cultures, organization values and structures that deal effectively with ambiguity and paradox. Many of these elements of success were identified by Peters and Waterman[1] in their recent best seller, *In Search of Excellence,* as being characteristic of the best managed firms in the United States.

But from a strategic point of view, many of these success components reduce to the operations advantage of being more productive than one's competitors. The advantages that accrue from experience, strategic advantages resulting from economies of scope and scale, technological innovation, the choices made concerning the activities in the value-added stream in which to participate, and the choice of business units that lend synergy and reinforce experience effects in ac-

*See Elwood S. Buffa and Marcus C. Bogue, "Productivity and the Exchange Rate," *National Productivity Review,* Vol. 5, No. 1, Winter 1985–1986, pp. 32–46.

tivities, all support the concept of increasing productivity leading to lower costs, and thereby being more competitive.

But does increased productivity in an industry lead to market growth, and vice versa, and ultimately to profitability? There is evidence that it does. For example, Figure 4–1 shows for a large cross

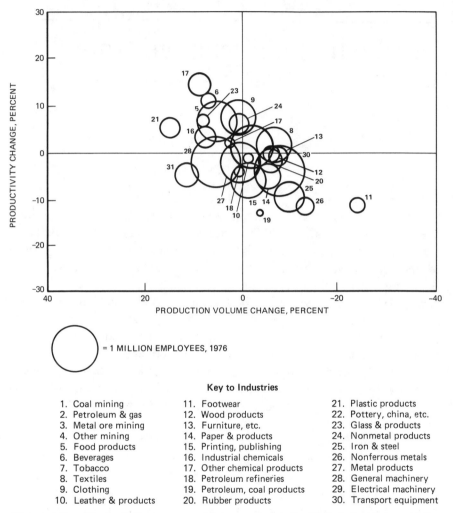

Key to Industries

1. Coal mining	11. Footwear	21. Plastic products
2. Petroleum & gas	12. Wood products	22. Pottery, china, etc.
3. Metal ore mining	13. Furniture, etc.	23. Glass & products
4. Other mining	14. Paper & products	24. Nonmetal products
5. Food products	15. Printing, publishing	25. Iron & steel
6. Beverages	16. Industrial chemicals	26. Nonferrous metals
7. Tobacco	17. Other chemical products	27. Metal products
8. Textiles	18. Petroleum refineries	28. General machinery
9. Clothing	19. Petroleum, coal products	29. Electrical machinery
10. Leather & products	20. Rubber products	30. Transport equipment

Figure 4–1. Productivity versus output growth for the U.S. industrial portfolio, 1972–1976

SOURCE: *United Nations Yearbook of Industrial Statistics,* OECD.

section of the U.S. industrial portfolio the relationship between productivity growth and output growth from 1972 to 1976, a period during which the U.S. was falling behind in productivity and growth. In general terms, the industries with higher output growth have had higher productivity growth—those in the upper left-hand quadrant, such as industrial chemicals, other chemicals, and beverages—and those with lower productivity change have had lower output growth, such as footwear, nonferrous metals, and iron and steel.

The experience curve suggests that growth is related to productivity; therefore, we should expect that high or low growth relates to high-or low-productive sectors. Whether productivity or growth is the primary generator is not the issue—a probable theory is that they feed on each other in a reinforcing cycle. In any case, we observe that there is a general relationship.

To carry the analysis one step further, there is also a general relationship between output growth and returns to stockholders equity, as shown in Figure 4-2. Other than petroleum, the group of industries that experienced the highest growth during 1978–1980 had the highest returns, and vice versa. Petroleum is the exception, with negative growth and high returns, but the reasons for the high-return/low-growth situation may be attributed to factors of slackening demand due to conservation and substitution, OPEC control of high prices, and other political factors.

The prescription seems straightforward—growth and productivity in a reinforcing cycle lead to increased profitability. Earlier in our history when our domestic markets were more secure and dominated the strategies of U.S. firms, the prescription seemed to work fairly well. International competition was not a vital issue—after all, the United States was the largest world market for most products. We tended to manufacture and sell for our own large markets, and by being productive we could compete in both domestic and international markets.

But that prescription is not sufficient to compete in international markets for firms not sheltered from foreign competition, and "if one considers potential exposure to import penetration, over 70 percent of our goods must now operate in an international marketplace."[2] Markets have become globalized, enhancing the significance of the benefits stemming from the experience curve and productivity increase.[3] A competitor in a given country could have significant advantages in factor costs such as labor, materials, and energy, and it could

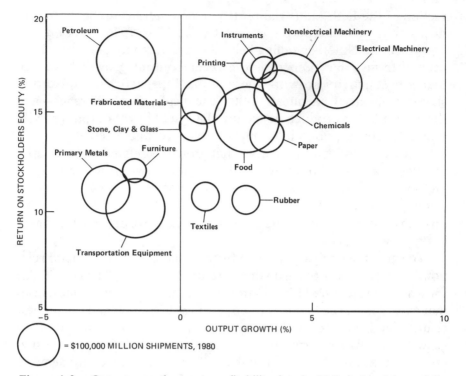

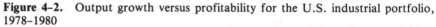

Figure 4-2. Output growth versus profitability for the U.S. industrial portfolio, 1978–1980

SOURCES: U.S. Department of Commerce, Federal Reserve Board, and Federal Trade Commission.

have a significant productivity advantage. Of course, the factor cost and productivity advantages can result in substantially lower manufacturing costs, and all add to the net effect of being productive within an industry. In addition, however, productivity enters into the international competitive equation through international exchange rates.

A company could be moderately successful in improving productivity. It could even have some factor cost advantages, resulting in relatively low costs and substantial growth, and could be in a position to compete effectively with domestic rivals. But exchange rates could still wipe out these advantages in international markets. To understand productivity effects in international competition, we must establish a broader framework—we must first understand long-term foreign exchange rate movements and their influence on foreign competition.

Exchange Rate Effects

In the short term, exchange rates are subject to a number of variations that probably cannot be predicted, and do not persist long enough to be converted to strategic advantage. This does not mean that such variations should be ignored, for they can be balanced off through hedging in foreign exchange, and through other activities designed to deal effectively with short-term movements.

But long-term (five to ten years) foreign exchange rate movements balance off the productivity differences of entire economies. Productivity increases and inflation in a country are offset by exchange rates. Therefore, the ability to compete with a foreign producer depends not only on how well a company does relative to that producer, but on how well the national economy competes with the foreigner's national economy.

PURCHASING POWER PARITY

Long-term equilibrium exchange rates are driven by "purchasing power parity," which relates the purchasing power of currencies in different countries.[4] If $100 would purchase a representative basket of goods in the United States, and 100 monetary units (MU) would buy a representative basket of goods in a foreign country, then the long-term equilibrium exchange rate between the two currencies should be 1:1. If the ratio were not 1:1, then there would be a flow of goods from one country to the other to take advantage of the bargain.

Now suppose that, in ensuing years, productivity increases and price changes due to inflation in the United States, when balanced out, reduced the cost of the representative basket of goods to $70, while in the foreign country productivity increases and inflation reduced the cost of a representative basket of goods to 90 MU. The long-term equilibrium exchange rate would then float from the previous 1:1 to 7:9, or $1 would exchange for 9/7 = 1.29 MUs of the foreign currency. The change in floating exchange rates is shown in Figure 4–3, reflecting the interacting effects of productivity and inflation.

The movement of exchange rates is controlled by the relative productivity improvement and inflation of the two economies, represented by aggregate price levels. For example, if the 1960–1980 average annual productivity improvement in the United States and

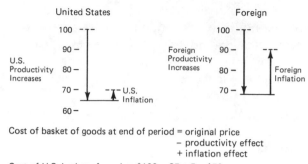

Original exchange rate = 100 MU/$100 = 1 MU per dollar

Change in the cost of a basket of goods

Cost of basket of goods at end of period = original price
                                        − productivity effect
                                        + inflation effect

Cost of U.S. basket of goods = $100 − 35 + 5 = $70

Cost of foreign basket of goods = 100 MU − 30 + 20 = 90 MU

New exchange rate = 90/70 = 1.29 MUs per dollar

Figure 4–3. Change in floating exchange rates based on changes in the cost of the same basket of goods in the U.S. and in a foreign country, reflecting productivity and inflation effects over a period of time

Japan of 3.0 and 9.4 percent respectively were compounded over that twenty-year period, aggregate U.S. productivity improvement would be 80 percent compared to 672 percent in Japan; that is, if the initial productivity indexes were both 100, the 1980 indexes would be 180 for the United States, and 672 for Japan.

The relative influence of productivity on prices in the two countries would be in relation to these productivity improvement achievements. If inflation were equal in both countries, then the *relative* price changes would reflect only the influence of productivity improvement. But if inflation averaged 4 percent in the United States, compared to 3 percent in Japan for the twenty-year period, compared to productivity increases of 3 and 9.4 percent, then the relative prices would reflect net inflation in the United States averaging 1 percent annually, while the Japanese would enjoy a net average deflationary effect of 6.4 percent. Over the twenty-year period, the relative price changes would be reflected in exchange rate adjustments, because the purchasing power of the two currencies would have changed. Of course, at any particular time, short-term policies may move exchange rates from their purchasing power parity values, but in the long run, the fundamental forces return the exchange rate to equilibrium values.

Empirical evidence of the validity of purchasing power parity as an explanation of long-term changes in exchange rates has been provided by studies in eight industrial countries (Canada, Great Britain, France, West Germany, Italy, Japan, Switzerland, and the United

States) for the 1900–1967 period,[5] studies of five South American countries (Argentina, Brazil, Chile, Colombia, and Peru) during 1954–1967,[6] and by studies of the mark/dollar exchange rate during the German hyperinflation in the early 1920s,[7] as well as by other studies focusing on both inflationary and noninflationary periods.[8] These studies have shown that in periods when actual rates were significantly different from expectations, there was a high tendency to return to equilibrium rates in the following period.

Now, where do the costs and prices of individual products enter the equation? In a large, diversified economy such as that of the United States, the effect of a single product on long-term exchange rates is miniscule. The product has an effect, of course, through the aggregation of prices in the representative basket of goods. However, in contrast, through the exchange rate, the productivity of our economy as a whole has an enormous effect on the prices of export products in foreign countries and on the prices of foreign goods in U.S. markets. An individual company's productivity achievements for a product, or even an entire industry's achievements, are dwarfed by the productivity progress of the economy as a whole. *To compete effectively in a particular international market, a company must be at least as productive in that field relative to the national economy as its international competitor is relative to its own economy,* rather than our traditional thinking of simply being more productive than the foreign producer directly.[9] Examples will help clarify this important concept of strategic analysis.

EXAMPLE 1—FOREIGN PRODUCER'S ADVANTAGE

If a firm achieved a 20 percent improvement in productivity over a ten-year period, for example, while the economy as a whole was achieving the same percentage productivity improvement, the firm might think that it had done very well in an absolute sense, but it would have just kept up with the national economy. If its *domestic* competitors had achieved only a 5 percent productivity improvement during the same period, the firm would have gained a 15 percentage point cost advantage in real terms. Much of the cost-competitive process in the domestic situation is under each firm's control, and depends on how the firm is managed internally, how technologically innovative it is, and so on.

However, if the firm had a foreign competitor that achieved only a 5 percent productivity improvement in an economy that was stagnant with zero net improvement, the foreign competitor would be better off than the domestic firm by 5 percentage points, because the competitor performed better than its economy. This may seem paradoxical, but it reflects the workings of long-term international monetary exchange.

In the context of the previous discussion, consider a product—a machine tool or an automobile—whose initial cost in both the United States and a foreign country is 5000 monetary units (MUs), reflecting parity initially; that is, a 1:1 exchange rate. Over ten years, the U.S. producer achieves a 20 percent productivity improvement (a $1000 cost reduction to 80 percent of the earlier cost) in an economy that improved by 20 percent, while a foreign producer achieves a 5 percent productivity increase (a 250 MU cost reduction to 95 percent of the earlier cost) in an economy that did not improve at all in the aggregate. The second row of Table 4–1 shows the domestic cost improvement for each producer.

/The long-term equilibrium exchange rate would reflect the productivity changes during the period, 80 (U.S.) to 100 (foreign), or 8:10. Thus, $1 U.S. equals 10/8, or 1.25 MU foreign (assuming equal inflation within the two countries). The last two entries in Table 4–1 indicate the cost of each product in the other country in its monetary units, not including transportation and import duties.

The $1000 cost improvement in productivity achieved by the U.S. producer relative to the 250 MU cost improvement achieved by the foreign producer has become a 5000 MU − 4750 MU = 250 MU *disadvantage* for the U.S. producer competing in the foreign country, before transportation and duty. On the other hand, the foreign producer has a $4000 − $3800 = $200 *advantage* in competing against the U.S. producer's product in the United States, before transportation and duty.

TABLE 4–1.   **Foreign Producer's Advantage**

	U.S. PRODUCER	FOREIGN PRODUCER
Initial cost (Exch. rate, 1:1)	$5000	5000 MU
Cost within each producer's country after productivity improvements	$0.8 \times 5000 = \$4000$	$0.95 \times 5000 = 4750$ MU
Cost of U.S. product in the foreign country after monetary exchange	$10/8 \times 4000 = 5000$ MU	
Cost of foreign product in the U.S. after monetary exchange		$8/10 \times 4750 = \$3800$

EXAMPLE 2—A STANDOFF

These effects are clarified and confirmed by calculations for a producer who improves productivity only to the extent that the national economy improves. Even if in absolute terms the U.S. producer has a far better record of productivity than the foreign competitor, the U.S. producer will not necessarily be better off. For example, if the U.S. producer achieves only a 20 percent productivity improvement during the period that the economy achieves 20 percent, and the foreign producer achieves zero percent improvement in a stagnant economy, both producers will do just as well as their economies. The calculations shown in Table 4–2 confirm that cost-price competition will be a standoff; the U.S. producer's 20 percent productivity improvement will receive no reward in the international marketplace.

EXAMPLE 3—U.S. PRODUCER'S ADVANTAGE

If the U.S. producer increases productivity by 30 percent while the economy improves by 20 percent, and if the foreign producer improves by only 5 percent in a stagnant economy, then the advantage is with the U.S. producer. The calculations shown in Table 4–3 confirm that the U.S. producer has the competitive advantage under these circumstances.

Of course, these examples assume that each producer had equal initial costs, and this is not likely to be true. Nevertheless, as the examples show, competitor productivity differences are strongly affected by national productivity differences over a period of time.

TABLE 4–2. A Standoff

	U.S. PRODUCER	FOREIGN PRODUCER
Initial cost (Exch. rate, 1:1)	$5000	5000 MU
Cost within each producer's country after productivity improvement	$0.8 \times 5000 = \$4000$	$1.00 \times 5000 = 5000$ MU
Cost of U.S. product in the foreign country after monetary exchange	$10/8 \times 4000 = 5000$ MU	
Cost of foreign product in the U.S. after monetary exchange		$8/10 \times 5000 = \$4000$

TABLE 4–3.   U.S. Producer's Advantage

	U.S. PRODUCER	FOREIGN PRODUCER
Initial cost (Exch. rate, 1:1)	$5000	5000 MU
Cost within each producer's country after productivity improvement	0.7 × 5000 = $3500	0.95 × 5000 = 4750 MU
Cost of U.S. product in the foreign country after monetary exchange	10/8 × 3500 = 4375 MU	
Cost of foreign product in the U.S. after monetary exchange		8/10 × 4750 = $3800

The result of these exchange rate effects is that a U.S. company competing internationally must generalize its notion of productivity; it must recognize that, in order to improve its competitive position, it must be more productive *relative* to the U.S. economy than its foreign competitor is *relative* to its own economy. Unfortunately, achieving that goal depends partially on many factors outside the firm's control, particularly on national policies that determine the support given some industries.

Comparative Advantage

Economists and business managers would probably agree that, today, the Japanese have a comparative advantage in certain manufacturing industries—for example, in steel and automobiles. But these two types of experts are probably approaching this appraisal from rather different viewpoints. Managers tend to think in terms of differential factor costs and productivities. The above examples showed that when cost and productivity differences are transmitted through international exchange rates, they are amplified to the advantage or disadvantage of a manufacturer. The resultant costs must be thought of as being relative to each other.

Economists think in terms of relative costs too, but their concept of relative costs is different. When economists analyze comparative advantage or disadvantage, they define costs in relation to producing another product, that is, the opportunity cost of using equivalent resources to produce something else. In these terms, country A may be more efficient in converting resource inputs for product X than country B, but B might be more efficient than A for product Y. Such a differentiation would lead to specialization in both countries. Even when one country is more efficient in producing both products, it may have a *comparative* disadvantage in one of the products when opportunity costs are compared. This difference would then still lead to specialization resulting in a net advantage. See the appendix to this chapter for an analysis explaining this point.

In the United States, the economics of comparative advantage would probably lead to the redeployment of our national resources from steel and, possibly, automobiles to electronics. But this type of national resource allocation is antithetical to managerial thinking. For example, one prominent economist lost his job as a corporate economist for advocating that the company become a supplier to Japanese auto producers rather than one of the big-three U.S. producers.

Managers, understandably, take a more local point of view, rather than one that considers national resource allocation. They choose to compete and try to change the balance, and if they have a current disadvantage resulting from poor productivity, they take it as their responsibility to improve productivity. If they have a factor cost disadvantage, they seek out ways to offset this disadvantage. These are admirable managerial characteristics. Nevertheless, in the future the economist's concept of comparative advantage and the effects of being less productive relative to one's own economy than a foreign producer may direct U.S. companies toward profitable and more comfortable niches in the international market.

National Industrial Portfolios

In Figure 4-1, which shows the productivity versus output growth for the U.S. industrial portfolio between 1972 and 1976, note that while productivity and growth varied from industry to industry during this period, the entire set of industrial sectors was "bunched" around an average output and productivity growth. There do not seem to be any big winners, nor any industries that are doing extremely poorly. Nevertheless, we know that our national productivity on an absolute basis is the highest in the world. Our national productivity is affected by productivity in sectors, such as agriculture. Productivity in these sectors boosts the average, and makes it difficult for individual companies to do much better than the economy as a whole.

When we compare ourselves with other economies, we find that they are characterized by much greater variation during a comparable period. Figure 4-4 shows plots of industrial portfolios for Japan,

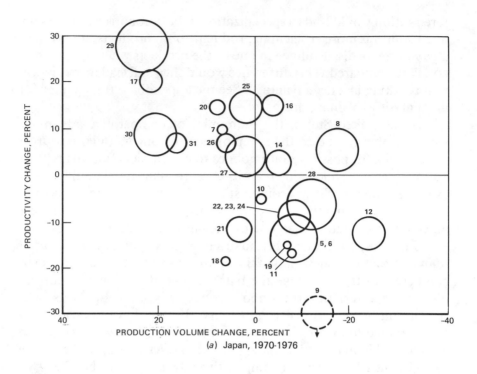

(a) Japan, 1970-1976

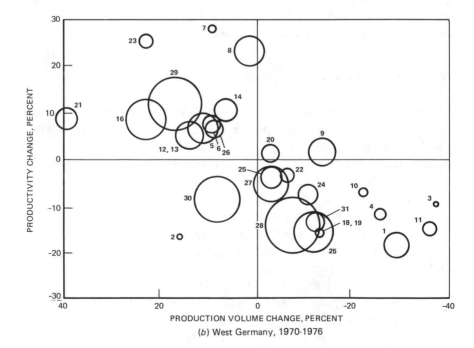

(b) West Germany, 1970-1976

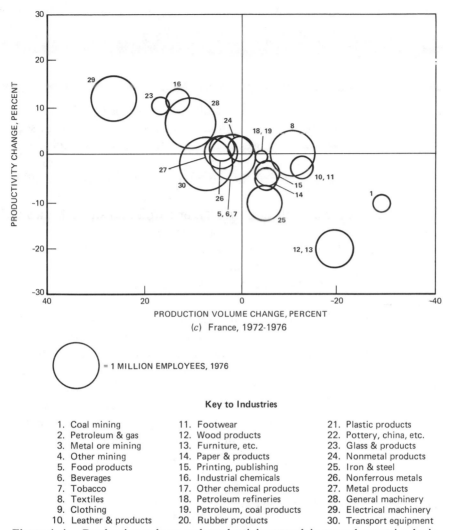

Figure 4-4. Production volume and productivity growth in several countries, by industry: (*a*) Japan, 1970–1976, (*b*), West Germany, 1970–1976, and (*c*) France, 1972–1976

SOURCE: *United Nations Yearbook of Industrial Statistics,* OECD.

West Germany, and France for the 1970–1976 period. The striking comparison indicates that the other countries all seem to have some industries that are experiencing high growth and productivity increase, as well as some industries that are real losers, and are pulling down the average. In addition, the several national portfolios represented in

Figure 4-4 lend further credence to the concept of a general relationship between productivity growth and output growth.

THE JAPANESE PORTFOLIO

Japan, the paragon of growth and productivity increase in the world's
eyes, has some industrial sectors that are doing very poorly. These sectors include footwear, wood products, food products, beverages, and
general machinery. What does this productivity and growth mean regarding the competitiveness of the sectors in which Japan excels, such
as electrical machinery, nonindustrial chemical products, transport
equipment, rubber and metal products, and iron and steel? It means
that the productive sectors are doing extremely well, both in an absolute sense, and *relative* to the Japanese economy as a whole. To be
sure, Japan's international competitive position for their low-growth,
low-productivity sectors is extremely poor, but they do not try to compete internationally in those sectors.

Through MITI (Ministry of International Trade and Industry) and
their banking system, the Japanese funnel resources to their high-
growth industrial sectors, thus increasing their growth and productivity, making them strong both in absolute terms and relative to the
Japanese economy.[10] This support provides these industries with a
double-edged sword in competing with foreign firms that have performed only as well as their own economies—Japanese costs are low
because of productivity improvements, and in addition have an exchange rate advantage that amplifies their cost advantage.

THE PORTFOLIOS OF WEST GERMANY AND FRANCE

The wide performance characteristics of the Japanese industrial portfolio are also found in the portfolios of France and West Germany.
Both France and West Germany have industries in the "winner" and
"loser" quadrants, with West Germany having more really high productivity winners such as tobacco, textiles, and glass, though these industries are relatively small.

THE U.S. PORTFOLIO

The U.S. portfolio of industries (see Figure 4-1) exhibits less variation
in both productivity and output growth than do other national port-

folios. For the 1972–1976 period, there were no productivity-growth industries in the 20 to 30 percent range, as was true for Japan, France, and West Germany. On the other hand, there were also fewer industries in the lower right quadrant, representing poor performance relative to the national economy.

The explanation for the U.S. portfolio pattern of low variance is largely political. We have supported our weaker industries through a network of subsidies at the expense of our stronger industries, while the Japanese and West Germans have followed the opposite pattern.[11]

Politically, it is perhaps easier to point to a few hundred jobs saved for the United States in some regionally depressed industry than it is to justify helping industries that are already strong. But for each 100 jobs saved in weak industries, there is a small penalty imposed on the international competitive strength of the growth industries in our portfolio. In the end, average U.S. productivity rises so that our strong industries are not doing as well compared with our economy as a whole as they might have done had the weak industries been allowed to wither. Accordingly, the growth industries suffer a disadvantage in the international marketplace because of the impact of the increased average productivity on exchange rates, as illustrated in the examples discussed.

NATIONAL INDUSTRIAL PORTFOLIO MANAGEMENT

There is a parallel between company portfolio management and national portfolio management. It is an accepted practice for corporate strategists to play to the strengths in the portfolio, and to harvest or divest their weak businesses. Resources are funneled to the strong, often coming from the divestment of the weak business units.

On a national scale, this process involves political factors that are somewhat more difficult to manage than intra-company ones, yet the recognition of the problem is growing in the outcry for the establishment of a national industrial policy. Such a policy should make the same kinds of hard choices made by corporate strategists, buttressing strength with greater support, and allowing weak industries to atrophy. It is not a question of whether or not we should have a national industrial policy—we already have one that supports weak industries. The issue is whether or not it should be changed.[12]

With this perspective on international competition, focused on productivity increase and exchange rates, we must extend our analysis to world industry and market structures. Part of that analysis must be focused on factor cost advantages, and the dual effect of productivity, directly as it affects product costs, and indirectly as it affects national exchange rates. We will first examine the world steel industry, and then draw some parallels in the world automobile industry, noting that steel is one of the major factor costs in automobiles.

The World Steel Industry

Since national monetary exchange rates are an important element in international competition in an industry, we turn to an examination of the structure of national participation in the world steel industry. One of the surprising facts about the world steel industry is that so many countries participate, since the minimum investment for facilities of economic scale is large. Figure 4–5 is a sector chart showing the growth during 1977–1982 and the relative market shares of 22 countries that participate in the industry.[13] One can speculate why so many

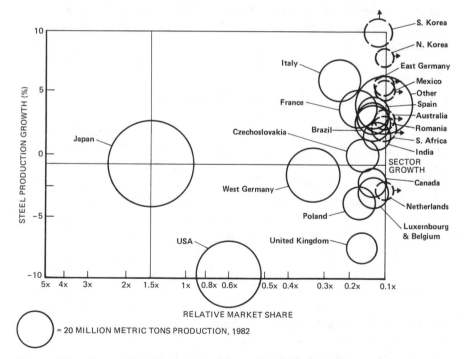

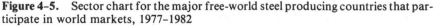

Figure 4–5.   Sector chart for the major free-world steel producing countries that participate in world markets, 1977–1982

Source: International Iron and Steel Institute.

countries participate in the steel industry, in many instances providing strong national support. Perhaps it is for reasons of national pride, because steel is a basic building block for industrialization and defense, but whatever the reasons, the result is huge world capacity in specialized facilities that have no alternate use, creating exit barriers. Since the facilities costs are largely sunk, marginal capacity tends to remain in use, creating a chronic world overcapacity and pressure for low prices.

In terms of production, the free-world industry shrank by about 1.5 percent per year during this period. Japanese production, the largest in the group, shrank at the sector rate. The Japanese steel industry was about 50 percent larger than that of its nearest national competitor, the United States, where production was shrinking by about 10 percent per year.

As shown in Figure 4-4, iron and steel is one of the industrial sectors in Japan that was substantially more productive than the Japanese economy as a whole. In the United States it is an industry that is somewhat less productive than the U.S. economy as a whole.

A number of countries have steel industries that are growing quite rapidly compared to the industry average, particularly Italy, France, Brazil, South and North Korea, East Germany, and Mexico.

Figure 4-6 narrows the focus to the competitive positions for the individual major steel companies for 1977-1982 in Europe, the United States, Asia, and developing countries. Nippon Steel in Japan, with −2.5 percent growth, is clearly the world leader with a world-market share about 2.4 times its nearest competitor. All the U.S. companies have negative growth. Were it not for the international political forces that keep many national steel companies operating, and the exchange/productivity effects, Nippon Steel would probably rapidly consolidate the world-wide market.

STRUCTURE OF THE U.S. DOMESTIC STEEL INDUSTRY

Finally, in terms of industry structure, it is useful to examine the competitive positions of our domestic steel industry, shown in Figure 4-7. The industry is not consolidated—U.S. Steel was about 1.1 times the size of Bethlehem in 1982, both with negative growth. The merger of Republic Steel into the Jones & Laughlin Division of LTV formed the second largest steel company in the United States.[14] There are several other companies that are large compared to the leader, having market

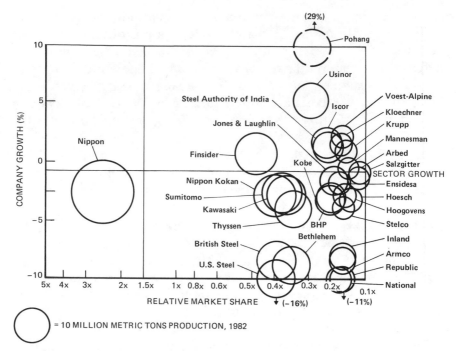

Figure 4-6. Sector chart for the major world-wide steel companies, 1977–1982
SOURCE: International Iron and Steel Institute.

shares that are about 45 percent that of U.S. Steel, presenting an unconsolidated unstable situation in the industry.

MINI-MILLS—A PROCESS INNOVATION

The highest-growth companies in the domestic steel industry are the nonintegrated producers that do not engage in the full range of steel making activities, such as Florida, Georgetown, Lukens, and North Star. They represent the impact of the technological change to electric furnaces—the mini-mills. Mini-mills melt scrap and tend to produce specialty steels. With mini-mills, smaller scale is economical, and since scrap occurs over a wide geographic range in the United States, the mini-mills can be more decentralized to supply markets at lower transportation costs.

Because there is a limited supply of scrap, there may be a burgeoning market to produce raw material for the mini-mills. These raw

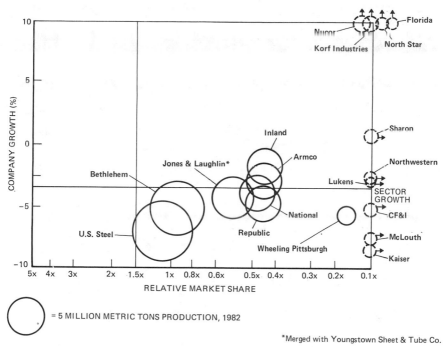

Figure 4-7. Sector chart for the U.S. domestic steel industry, 1973–1982

SOURCE: *Metal Statistics Annual Summary* (American Metal Market), Fairchild Publications.

materials are likely to be supplied by the lowest cost producers, perhaps on a world-wide basis. Currently, this producer would probably be Nippon Steel, with its low basic costs and exchange rate advantages. However, an aggressive domestic producer that specialized and reduced its costs could fill this role. The technological change to mini-mills represents a potentially potent challenge to the U.S. integrated producers that could destabilize the organization of the domestic industry.

PRICE-EXPERIENCE EFFECTS

There has been a long-term decline in the deflated price of steel in relation to accumulated production for both Japan and the United States from 1952 to 1972, as shown in Figure 4-8. Prices and costs should have been tracking fairly well, since a twenty-year record is included. Prices from 1973 through 1981 reflect the effect of substantially in-

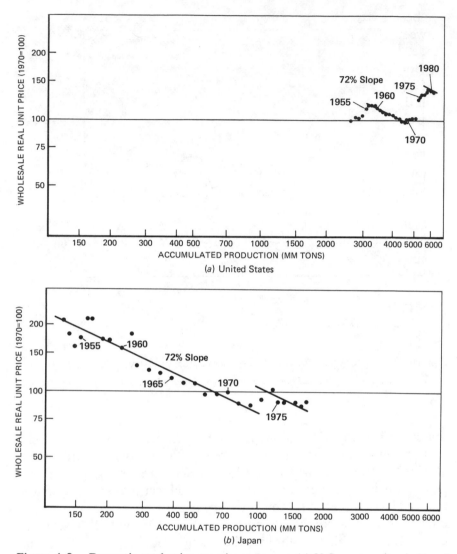

Figure 4-8. Domestic steel price experience curves: (*a*) U.S. companies, index of real dollars, and (*b*) Japanese imported steel, index of real Yen, 1952–1981 (1970 = 100)

SOURCES: U.S. Department of Commerce, and *Iron Age*.

creased energy costs in both countries resulting from the OPEC oil embargo and price escalations that followed. The prices for Figure 4–8*a* are expressed in a real dollar index, and for Figure 4–8*b* they are expressed in a real Yen index (1970 = 100). Therefore, the position of one against the other is not indicated by the curves; that is, they have not been adjusted for exchange rates or differences in starting points between the two countries, and direct price comparisons cannot be made.

Both national curves reflect a 72 percent price-experience curve; that is, an average 28 percent price reduction was being effected for each doubling of accumulated production. The Japanese seemed to have absorbed the energy-cost shock more quickly than the U.S. producers, and the stabilized level at which the 72 percent experience curve takes over again is higher for the United States. Another observation is that the accumulated experience for the United States was about 3.5 times that of Japan, even as late as 1981, but the Japanese were accumulating experience at a faster rate as they gained world market share in relation to the United States.

It is interesting to express the Japanese prices in dollars and to compare them year by year to the U.S. prices, as in Figure 4–9.

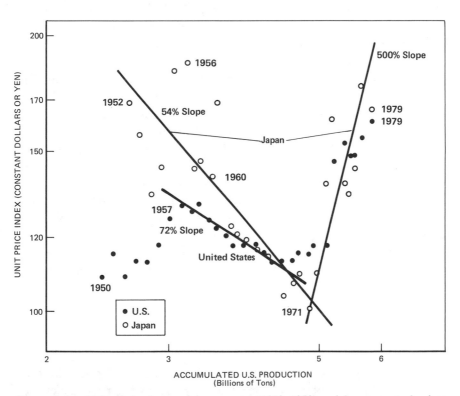

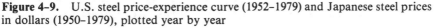

Figure 4-9. U.S. steel price-experience curve (1952–1979) and Japanese steel prices in dollars (1950–1979), plotted year by year

SOURCES: U.S. Department of Commerce, and *Iron Age*.

Remember that while Figure 4–8 showed that the price curves of both countries in their own currencies were averaging a 72 percent experience curve, the Japanese were gaining experience at a faster rate, even though the U.S. total experience was far greater. Therefore, when placed on the same year-by-year comparison in relation to the U.S. cumulative experience, the Japanese prices appear to be falling faster until about 1971, even though in relation to their own cumulative experience they were on a 72 percent price-experience curve.

From 1972 to 1979, the Japanese prices in dollars rocketed from $100 to about the $170 to $180 range in constant dollars. What happened to raise the price competition umbrella so dramatically? There was an oil embargo as we know, but in addition, the free world moved to floating exchange rates, and the yen went up in value tremendously in relation to the dollar, relieving competitive pressure on U.S. steel producing firms. There were a number of possible competitive responses open to the U.S. firms to this removal of price pressure in their domestic markets—wider margins, consolidation of market position, more liberal worker benefits and wages, and others. But it appears that U.S. producers chose to give a large fraction of the increased profitability to labor.

Figure 4–10 shows the average U.S. wage rates for production workers in constant 1967 dollars for several industries, including the steel and automobile industries. Two prominent features stand out. First, wage rates for both steel and automobiles are significantly higher than for the other four industries represented. Second, the slopes for the wage-rate curves for both steel and automobiles increase significantly beginning in 1972, representing the labor-management bargains made. It appears that the price discipline imposed by the Japanese had been effective until 1972 in ensuring cost discipline on U.S. producers. But the cost increases ensured by the labor agreements did not take account of the fact that the exchange rates would normalize again, and that the price pressure would be reapplied by the Japanese.

Factor Costs

Advantages and disadvantages in the factor costs of raw material, energy, and labor enter into the results of the cost-experience curve, helping to account for comparative performance. Pluses and minuses in factor costs can make the results of performance relative to one's

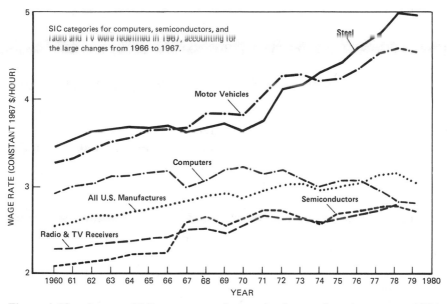

Figure 4-10. Average U.S. wage rates for production workers in constant 1967 dollars per hour

SOURCE: *U.S. Industrial Competitiveness: A Comparison of Steel, Electronics, and Automobiles,* Congress of the United States, Office of Technology Assessment, Washington, D.C., July 1981, Figure 5, p. 60.

economy a little better or a little worse, but they are unlikely to change that situation fundamentally. At issue is how these cost advantages and disadvantages pass through the monetary exchange rate to affect costs when exported to a foreign country or, comparatively, how the costs of a foreign competitor pass through to our domestic markets. An understanding of differences in factor costs between international competitors is important to understanding the competitive terrain, and characterizing it appropriately so that managers can take action.

Raw Material and Energy Costs. The United States has historically enjoyed an advantage in iron ore and coking coal resources. While the Japanese have no such resources and must import iron ore from Australia and Brazil, and coal from Australia, Canada, and the United States, they have offset this disadvantage by building very large ships that could transport large quantities of materials at a time to steel-making facilities located at deep water ports. Though the distances are great, the cost of shipping is low relative to overland transportation required for many U.S. facilities locations. The competitive terrain changed—what was once a U.S. advantage in having raw materials close at hand has turned into a disadvantage because of current transportation costs. Dynamic processes can grow new hills and erode old ones in the playing field. In addition, the costs of surface mining high-purity iron ore in Australia are lower than costs in Michigan and Minnesota, resulting in a net Japanese advantage in transportation and mining costs.

Japanese steel producers also have raw material advantages that stem from coal blending and blast-furnace technology that allow them to use lower grades of coal, and less coke per ton of pig iron than U.S. producers. In addition, improved techniques of materials recovery have had a positive impact on Japanese raw materials costs.

Energy costs increased dramatically for both the United States and the Japanese following the 1972 oil embargo. The Japanese are completely dependent on oil imports, while the United States has substantial domestic oil reserves that were under price control. Perhaps because of their dependence on imports, the Japanese had early success with conservation efforts. At any rate, the "oil shock" effects on steel prices that are evident in both the U.S. and Japanese price-experience curves of Figure 4–8 seem to have had a greater effect on U.S. producers than on the Japanese, and the Japanese seem to have absorbed the shock more quickly and returned to the previous slope of their price-experience curve sooner than the Americans.[15]

Labor Costs.   Hourly wage rates in the U.S. steel industry are the highest in the nation as shown so clearly by Figure 4–10. A gap between the wage rates for all manufacturing and steel can be rationalized to some extent by noting the skill requirements for many jobs in steelmaking, and the hot, dirty, dusty, hazardous working conditions found in steel plants. Similar wage gaps may be found in other countries, but are commonly of the order of magnitude of 30 percent above the average for manufacturing rather than the 70 to 90 percent premiums found in U.S. steelmaking.[16] It is this internal comparison of wage rates in steel and automobiles that penalizes these industries in the context developed in this chapter, making it more difficult in aggregate terms for an enterprise to be more productive than the U.S. economy. A foreign competitor whose wage rates are in line with the 30 percent premium standard will not face this handicap in striving to be more productive than its economy.

But wage rates are only part of the picture—benefits must be added to obtain total employment costs per hour, which in turn must be coupled with labor productivity in order to see the comparative labor costs in steel products.

Total hourly employment costs in dollars for 1982 in several steel-making countries were as follows:[17]

United States	$23.99
West Germany	$13.45
France	$12.37
Japan	$11.08
Great Britain	$9.32
South Korea	$2.39

The numbers speak for themselves—the United States has a significant disadvantage in employment costs, which it could make up only through significant advantages in productivity to produce a competitive labor cost in steel products. But in general, productivity in Japan is said to be 25 to 30 percent higher than in the United States.[18]

The reasons for the poor competitive position of our steel industry are commonly assigned to low productivity because of old process technology, and high factor costs including transportation and energy costs, wages and labor costs. Advantages and disadvantages in productivity and in the factor costs of raw material, energy, and labor enter into the results of the cost-experience curve, helping to account for comparative performance.

Table 4–4 shows the 1960–1970 period of steel productivity improvement in the United States, Japan, West Germany, and Canada. In 1960, U.S. productivity was the highest, at 66.7 tons per 1000 man-hours, followed by Canada, West Germany, and Japan, respectively. During the following ten-year period, U.S. steel industry productivity rose to 83.3 tons, an increase of 24.9 percent, and in 1970 the U.S. still had the highest productivity of the four countries. But Japanese productivity had increased by an astounding 203.3 percent. West Germany's and Canada's increases were 70.2 and 49.9 percent, respectively. Thus, during 1960–1970, productivity increases in the U.S. steel industry lagged behind the U.S. economy as a whole, while productivity increases of the steel industries in other countries had outpaced their own economies.

The 1970–1980 period demonstrates the same kind of general relationship; U.S. steel industry productivity lagged behind its own economy, with an aggregate ten-year productivity increase of only 15.4 percent. Meanwhile, Japan, West Germany, and Canada re-

TABLE 4-4.   Comparative Steel Productivity: The United States, Japan, West Germany, and Canada

	PRODUCTIVITY, TONS PER 1000 MAN-HOURS		
	1960	1970	1980
United States	66.7	83.3	96.1
Japan	24.6	74.6	136.9
West Germany	38.9	66.2	102.0
Canada	47.3	70.9	117.6

SOURCE: Presentation by Paul Marshall at the UCLA-AISI Conference on "Strategies for the U.S. Steel Industry in the 1980s," UCLA, February 24–26, 1985.

corded ten-year productivity increases of 83.5, 54.1, and 65.9 percent, respectively. By 1980, Japan had the highest productivity, 136.9 tons per 1000 man-hours, and was followed by Canada and West Germany. The United States had the lowest productivity of the group.

THE DECLINE OF THE U.S. STEEL INDUSTRY

There are many explanations for the decline of the U.S. steel industry, including "stodgyness," "a tired old industry," and poor management. If any of these characterizations are true, they probably reflect themselves in the slowness of the industry to deploy the available new technology such as continuous casting, the basic oxygen process, process automation, and so on.

Almost 200 U.S. steel producing facilities have already been closed. We still make a substantial proportion of our steel in inefficient open hearth furnaces, but virtually all the steel made in Japan and Europe is done in oxygen and electric furnaces. U.S. steelmakers have been slow to convert to continuous casting—a process that improves product yield, cuts energy use, and improves labor productivity; only 26 percent of the steel produced in the United States is continuously cast versus 86 percent in Japan and 61 percent in Europe. "The American Iron and Steel Institute estimates that the industry will have to spend $60 billion (in 1982 dollars) over the next decade to bring its facilities up to world-class levels. But last year [1982], U.S. steelmakers spent just $2.2 billion for modernization, and this year [1983] they will cut that to about $1.7 billion."[19]

The failure to invest in the modernization of plants has meant lower productivity increases in the steel industry relative to those of the U.S. economy as a whole, as we have discussed. But why did steel industry managers fail to reinvest? This issue is one that puzzles many people, since the U.S. industry was clearly the world leader, and at a time in the not too distant past had more accumulated experience in the industry than the rest of the world combined. How could they have failed to read their opportunities and combine them with strategies that would retain leadership?

The Automobile Industry

The automobile industry and steel industries face similar problems in international competition, and Japan is the nemesis for both. In addition, the two industries are interdependent. The auto industry is the largest single customer of the steel industry, and steel is a major factor cost for automobiles.

How does the U.S. auto industry perform relative to the U.S. economy, and how does Japan's auto industry perform relative to its economy? Figure 4-4 shows that in the United States, sector number 30, transport equipment—which includes the auto industry[20]—had negative growth and productivity change during the 1972–1976 period. This industry was one of the star performers during the 1970–1976 period in Japan. Therefore, we should not be surprised about the news reports that Japanese costs appear to be from $2000 to $2500 less per car than U.S. costs, when passed through the exchange rates to compete in the U.S. market.[21] These cost differences are partially real, as one would expect from the differences in productivity increase and factor costs of labor and raw material, and partially due to the fact that the Japanese automakers have been more productive relative to their economy than U.S. automakers relative to our economy.

We must remember that much of the delivered cost difference of a Japanese automobile reflects exchange rate effects that we have emphasized in this chapter. By supporting our weak industries, we handicap our strong ones, and the automobile industry has suffered beyond its due, for by any reasonable standard it is a highly efficient industry. We do not take the point of view that the industry has no internal problems—executives in that industry would freely admit that they do. But these internal problems are amplified in international competition by the exchange rate effects.

There are some important differences between Japanese and U.S. factor costs. For example, it is estimated that the U.S. auto industry pays about $8 per hour more than the Japanese in wages and benefits.[22] The other major difference in factor costs is the cost of steel. It has been widely held that the Japanese have at least a 10 percent material cost advantage in steel.[23]

Figure 4–11 presents a picture of U.S. automobile and steel prices that is informative on several counts. Both curves are plotted as indexes, with 1970 = 100. First, from 1946 through 1959, both industries were increasing real prices and, while we do not have deflated cost curves for comparison, both industries were probably increasing margins as well, since this period was not one of extreme inflation. The pattern may be similar to that shown in Chapter 2 (Figure 2–8) for Kodak's amateur photographic business. So when the two industries had a dominant world position, they appear to have widened margins, attracting competition into the industry as economic theory would predict. Recall the comparable situation presented in Chapter 2 concerning Kodak's widening margins during the 1952–1965 period. The steel industry's upward slope is greater than that of the auto industry, suggesting that auto industry margins may not have increased as much as steel margins.

Beginning in 1960, the price curves of both industries decline,

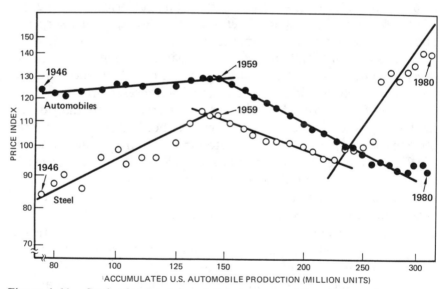

Figure 4–11. Steel price trend in relation to automobile price-experience curve, 1946–1980. Steel prices are plotted to align year-by-year with annual automobile prices

Sources: U.S. Department of Commerce, *Wards Automotive,* and *Iron Age.*

reflecting the price pressure of foreign competition as Japanese and European industry recovered from World War II. But, beginning in 1970, steel prices explode, resulting in an increased factor cost for the automobile industry. The steel industry's poor performance relative to the U.S. economy contributes to the auto industry's poor relative performance. Of course, automakers have bought some foreign steel in response to the domestic steel price increases.

Concluding Remarks

The principle of being more productive than one's economy helps to explain why an economy dominated by a single highly productive segment, as Norway's is by petroleum, is noncompetitive in manufacturing in international markets. "Today, petroleum accounts for 17 percent of Norway's gross national product and one-third of its exports. During 1981, oil levies brought in $4 billion—about $1000 per citizen."[24] One result of this bonanza is a death knell for manufacturing and other industries that operate in international markets. Oil, which dominates the economy, pulls the productivity average up very high, making it extremely difficult for Norway's other export industries to be more productive than the economy as a whole. Therefore, shipping, shipbuilding, forestry, and fishing—all dependent on exports— are currently depressed industries in Norway.[25]

The analysis of a company's industry and markets cannot stop with the domestic scene, unless the industry and its markets are domestic by their nature. Yet, competing internationally has the disturbing quality of fencing through a system of mirrors; the thrust and parry are confused by multiple reflections. It is uncommon for businesspeople to think in the "relative-to-one's-economy" mode, yet that is the reality of international competition. It is important to grow and to increase productivity in order to drive costs down, but that progress may be drained off by an unfavorable exchange rate in international markets.[26] A broader framework is therefore essential in the formulation of corporate strategy.

Finally, when a producer realizes that it must be more productive than its own economy to be globally competitive, there is a reemphasis on improving productivity. We have always known that productivity improvement was important, but now with global markets we have a new and dominating reason to believe it.

Appendix

While the advantages of specialization in the production of goods between countries is straightforward when each country has absolute advantages in different products, it is not so obvious that specialization
is advantageous when one country is more efficient in the production
of all products.

Assume a two-product, two-country situation, where country A is
more efficient in the production of both products (assume no transportation costs, perfect factor mobility between the production of the
two products in both countries, and constant average costs as output
is increased). The output per period for the two products for equal
resource input in each country is

	Country A	Country B
Product X	50 Units	10 Units
Product Y	10 Units	5 Units

Country A is more efficient than country B in the production of
both products, with five times the output of product X and twice the
output of product Y using the same resource inputs. The reasons for
the absolute superiority may be many and varied—our interest is only
in the fact of superiority.

Comparative advantage is demonstrated when we convert the
above figures into opportunity costs within each country. The relative, or opportunity costs represent the quantity of product X that
must be foregone in order to produce an additional unit of product Y.
For example, for country A, since resource inputs are equal, we have
$50X = 10Y$, or $X = (10/50)Y = 0.2Y$. That is, the opportunity cost in
country A of producing an additional unit of product X is to forego
the output of 0.2 units of product Y. Similarly the opportunity costs
for all product-country combinations are

	Country A	Country B
Product X	0.2Y	0.5Y
Product Y	5.0X	2.0X

While country A has an absolute advantage as the efficient producer of both products, when we compare the opportunity costs, it has a *comparative* advantage in the production of only product X. It has a comparative disadvantage in the production of product Y because it must forego more of product X to produce an additional unit of product Y than does country B, 5.0X versus 2.0X. With this comparative advantage in product Y, country B can compete effectively in that product market with country A even though A has an absolute advantage.

In the initial situation, presumably in the absence of trade, if each country used one unit of resources for the production of each product, total production would be 60 units of product X and 15 units of product Y. However, if the two countries specialize according to their relative advantages, total production can be increased with the same total resources. If country A uses 1.5 resource units to produce product X, and 0.5 resource units for product Y, while country B uses 2.0 resource units to produce only product Y, total production increases as follows:

	Country A	Country B	Total
Product X	$1.5 \times 50 = 75$	0	75
Product Y	$0.5 \times 10 = 5$	$2 \times 5 = 10$	15

Suppose for a moment that the United States is more efficient than Japan in both steel and in agricultural production. Of course, we presume that this is not true for steel, but it certainly is true for agriculture. If comparable resources in the steel industry produced 50 units compared to 30 agricultural units, while the same resources produced 40 steel and 10 agricultural units in Japan, Japan would have a comparative advantage in steel in terms of marginal opportunity costs since one unit of Japanese steel costs only $10/40 = 0.25$ the cost of agricultural product, while in the United States steel costs $30/50 = 0.6$ the cost of agricultural products. Of course, all public information indicates that the U.S. steel producers do not have an absolute advantage in steel production, so conventional wisdom would suggest that each country specialize on the basis of its absolute advantages.

Corporate Analysis

Chapter 5

Product and Activity Structures

Corporate analysis provides a slightly narrower focus than industry or market analysis, with an emphasis on individual firms. Using the background of insights into industry and market structures (national and international) provided by Part II of the book, corporate analysis magnifies internal dynamics so we can see their competitive effects. In Part III, we will be interested in competitive effects of the relationships between products and activities, the goals and impact of diversification and acquisition, and in the evaluation of the financial impact of strategies. In all these analyses we cannot ignore our competitors, for seldom can we take independent action without considering what they are doing and what their perceived strategic objectives are—we must know who is doing what to whom.

Strategic strengths and weaknesses can be revealed by an analysis of the product structure—how the products are related in the product/process technological sense and in the market. The business units in a product portfolio may be independent of each other in marketing or manufacturing, but if so, we may not be taking advantage of potential economies of scope that could provide competitive strengths.

It is the complex interlinking among products and activities that belies the simplicity of the prescriptions of traditional portfolio analysis—making it naive to consider managing a portfolio on the basis of simply investing in high-growth/low market share SBUs, driving them to star status, and letting them mature to be milked. We must look inside an SBU to see the interrelationships and relate what we find to other SBUs, and to analyze our competition in a similar way. Examining the scope of operations may reveal common activities from which we can accumulate combined experience, leading to low activity costs and competitive strength.

For example, a substantial portion of Eastman Kodak's 1978 product portfolio shown in Figure 5-1 is related to the technology of thin film coating, especially when viewed as a fraction of sales. Business units that have their technological base in thin film coating are crosshatched in Figure 5-1. Kodak is reaping the benefits of the *economics of scope;* that is, the scope of their activities in thin film coated products accumulates in certain activities to give them low cost—they are far down the experience curve in these activities.

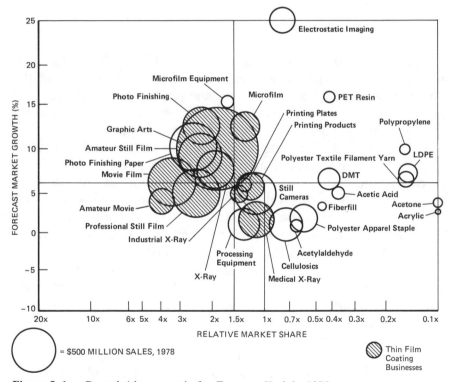

Figure 5-1.   Growth/share matrix for Eastman Kodak, 1978

SOURCES: Company annual and 10-K reports, analysts' reports, conversations with industry experts, *Directory of Chemical Producers, Chemical Economics Handbook,* SRI International (various editions), and *The Kline Guide to the Chemical Industry,* P. Noble, editor, 2nd ed., C. H. Kline & Co.

Medical X-ray film is in the low-growth, low relative market share quadrant. Given traditional product portfolio prescriptions, it should be considered for divestment. But close relationship to the technological base adds to the experience accumulated for certain activities, and medical X-ray film is probably a profitable product line. Similar questions might be raised about Kodak's industrial X-ray and printing plate and product businesses. A decision to divest cannot be made solely on the basis of a business unit's position on the growth/share matrix.

Other companies have product portfolios that share common technologies. Chemical companies usually have a central technology from which many of their products are developed, partly because of the by-product nature of chemical processing. For example, the nature of petroleum refining provides a broad base of related products from which petroleum companies can derive cost-competitive advantages.

But the central-technology concept is not limited to chemical companies: Texas Instruments has a central technology in chip manufacture that gives them advantages in consumer electronics products; IBM's marketing and field service strength enabled them quickly to gain a significant position in office copiers; Dupont's commanding position in Nylon fiber is related to the fact that they dominate the textile, industrial, and carpet Nylon fiber markets; Procter & Gamble's strength in a variety of consumer products results from their strength in consumer marketing.

Strategic analysis motivates us to look for these relationships and to take advantage of the strengths they provide. For example, engines are an important component in the value-added stream for farm tractors. Who has the greater experience on which to draw in engine manufacture, Caterpillar Tractor, Deere & Co., Ford Motor Company, or International Harvester?

Shared Activity Structures

The activity structures that we have used for illustration to this point have been linear in form, that is, they dealt with a single product or product type. We made no attempt to link the activity structures of several products, other than to show the close relationships of thin film products for Kodak's product portfolio in Figure 5-1, and to discuss some of the implications of activity relationships. Through an example in consumer electronics, we will now discuss the implications of reenforcing effects in activity experience that can result from shared-activity structures.

Figure 5-2 shows the activity flow of the three products of a hypothetical firm making AM table radios, FM table radios, and FM portable radios. The three products share common activity bases: all three use the same acoustical components (manufactured in a central location) and the same type of assembly process, such that on a given day the same workers may assemble any of the three products; AM and FM table radios also share the same component manufacture and the same wood housing manufacturing processes, and are distributed through the same sales force and wholesalers.

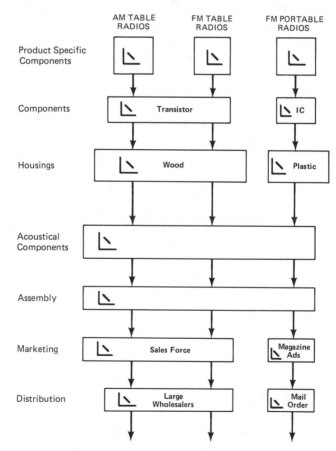

Figure 5-2. Activity flow for three products of a hypothetical firm

Because of these interrelationships, treating the products independently would understate their combined strength and the fundamental value of the portfolio to the firm. Some of the implications of this interdependence are suggested by the reminder that each activity is subject to the effects of a cost-experience curve—there is a symbolic experience curve inserted in each activity box in Figure 5-2. The experience accumulates at the activity level, not at the product level. True, we have demonstrated that products also seem to have cost-experience curves, but these effects are derived by summing the costs incurred by each activity—the product did not learn, but the activities did.

Now what are the growth/share characteristics of the three products in the firm's portfolio? Figure 5-3 shows that FM table radios have excellent relative market share but slow growth, the traditional cash cow. FM portable radios have star status with very good relative share and high growth, and AM table radios are the typical dog with poor relative share and low growth, and in traditional portfolio theory might be a candidate for divestment.

Now we develop an activity-based growth/share matrix for the company, plotting the major activities on the grid. Circle areas are

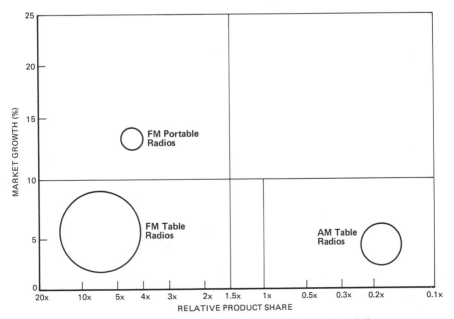

Figure 5-3. Product-based growth/share matrix for a hypothetical firm

proportional to the total costs for each activity, and are plotted at the intersection of the market growth and the relative market share for the *activity*. Market growth and relative market share are calculated based on the generic activity, summing for all products, whether or not the company makes those products. The activity-based matrix shown in Figure 5-4 indicates, for example, that the market growth of plastic housings is nearly 25 percent, while the company use of plastic housings in Figure 5-3 is only 12 percent, because they are used only in FM portable radios, which has an expected marked growth rate of 12 percent per year.

The company's activity strength is especially in acoustic components, where it dominates with large volume, and more than four times the relative activity share in the industry, compared to its nearest competitor. The company is also in an excellent position in the assembly activity, with a relative activity share of more than 1.2 times its nearest competitor. Both activities are used by all three products. The market growth in both activities is 5 percent, closely matched by the company growth rates of FM and AM table radios. Finally, the company has very good activity position in wood housing, used in both FM and AM table radios. Its relative activity share is about 10

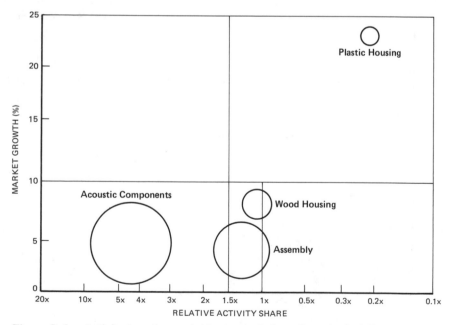

Figure 5-4. Activity-based growth/share matrix for a hypothetical firm

percent larger than its nearest competitor, in a market growing at 8 percent. But it has a poor position in the high-growth plastic housing activity.

The experience accumulation for three of the activities is reenforced by the interrelated nature of the product-activity requirements. They must not be treated as if they are independent of each other, for the cost positions of the three products are affected by their interdependence. The plastic housings are used only for FM portable radios and the activity is fueled solely by this product volume.

With this perspective, we can see that the rapid growth of FM portable radios will influence the cost positions of all three products, because experience will be accumulated more rapidly in the accoustical components and assembly activities. Of course, this same principle operates in the Kodak example cited near the beginning of the chapter—the rapid growth of amateur still film influences the cost positions of medical X-ray and printing plates and products.

Similarly, if the hypothetical firm decided to divest itself of the AM table radio line, the other two product lines would be affected by the reduced rate of experience accumulation in six of the seven activities shown in Figure 5-2. Depending on the magnitude of the reduction in an activity, its scale could be affected, making it uneconomic to continue to use certain equipment. Of course, the effects are not limited to the manufacturing phases—a smaller sales force to serve only FM table radios might be stretched more thinly and be less efficient, and shipping costs to wholesalers would not benefit to the same degree from combining shipments for both product lines.

Interestingly, with respect to the FM portable radios, we can see from the activity growth/share matrix a potential problem for the future. Our position in plastic housings is related solely to the FM portable line. While we have a good position in FM portable radios, we have a poor position in plastic housings. How can this be? Some of our competitors must be doing something else with plastic housings—making all their radios with plastic housings, or making some other product with plastic housings, or both. The plastic housing activity is growing very rapidly, faster than any of the radio markets, so in making other products with plastic housings, some of our competitors are fueling their plastic housing volume. If we grow with the FM portable market, we will fall behind in our plastic housing cost position. Even by growing at the market growth rate, we will fall behind in cost position in this key activity. To the extent that the cost associated with that activity is an important part of the total, we may fall behind in total cost for FM portable radios. The "star" could easily become a shooting star.

The technological base is one way of looking more closely at a product portfolio—other ways include segmentation by product or by geographic markets.

Product Structure and Markets

Figure 5-5 shows the sector chart for an industry in which there are seven main competitors. Competitor 1 with annual sales of about $300 million is the market leader, having about twice the market share of Competitor 3, its nearest rival. Although the business is growing, Competitor 1 is losing share dramatically to Competitors 3, 4, and 5. The obvious question is, Why?

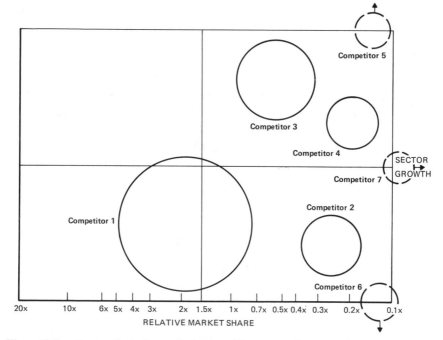

Figure 5-5. Sector chart for an industry with seven main competitors

SOURCE: Based on client study.

SEGMENTATION BY PRODUCT LINE AND GEOGRAPHY

The industry is an international one, so segmentation by product family and geography is a logical step, to see if there are systematic differences in market position and attractiveness on either or both of these bases. The business represented in Figure 5-5 was divided into five broad product lines, and further into the sales of each product line in the eight major markets of the world and a few minor ones, or 43 combinations of product line and market area. To reduce complexity, Figure 5-6 shows only three product lines for Competitor 1. For example, each circle labeled A represents the sales of product line A in a geographic market—the U.S., Japan, Europe, the Far East, etc.

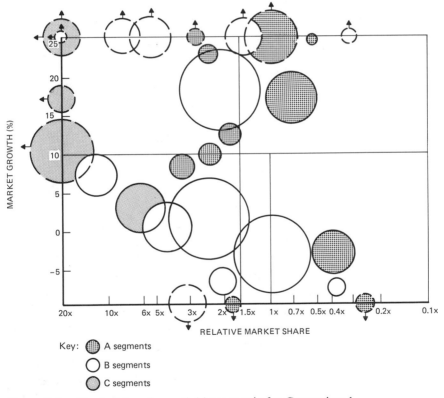

Figure 5-6. Product-based growth/share matrix for Competitor 1

SOURCE: Based on client study.

Therefore, for Competitor 1's single large circle in Figure 5-5, we have 27 circles in the simplified product-based growth/share matrix in Figure 5-6, each representing a major or minor product-geographic segment.

Consistent with our overall view of their business, examining Figure 5-6 indicates that Competitor 1 has a strong relative market position with positive average growth, but there are some high and low growth segments of the business. Note that in most segments, Competitor 1 dominates, having larger relative market shares than their nearest competitors, however, many segments are low-growth. In C business Competitor 1 is particularly dominant. In order to examine this issue more closely, we analyze Competitor 1's growth versus market growth by means of a share/momentum chart.

Share/Momentum for Competitor 1.   Recall from Chapter 2 that the share/momentum chart is a plot of market growth on the vertical axis versus company growth on the horizontal axis, and shows clearly which segments are gaining market share and which are losing, a measure of the momentum that each segment has for positive or negative growth. In Figure 5-7, each of the segments in the previous growth/share matrix is plotted at the point of its market growth and Competitor 1's growth, so that all segments that fall above the 45 degree diagonal line are losing market share and all those below the line are gaining market share; This is true all along the diagonal line, including the negative-growth quadrants of the chart.

Analyzing Figure 5-7, we see that Competitor 1 is losing in most of the market segments; that is, most of the circles are above the diagonal line, and many are substantially above it—a broad retreat from the markets, the circle sizes indicating that the retreat dominates company sales. But in low-growth markets, those growing at less than 10 percent, Competitor 1 does well. In fact in the negative growth segments, it does even better—"the last one to turn out the lights." In high-growth segments, Competitor 1 is weak.

Of course, what Competitor 1 would like to see is exactly the reverse pattern—some segments in the upper right hand part of the share/momentum chart, exiting some of those markets in the lower left. We would like to establish some hills in the playing field, and exit from the valleys, recognizing that perhaps we do not have the right structural configuration to compete in those businesses. Examining the share/momentum chart for Competitors 3 and 5 provides some insight into what is happening.

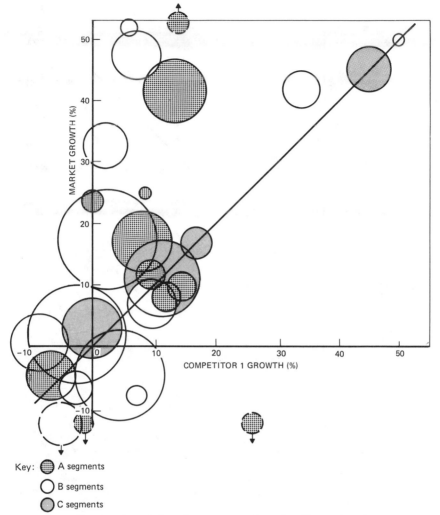

Key: A segments
B segments
C segments

Figure 5-7. Product-based share/momentum chart for Competitor 1
SOURCE: Based on client study.

Share/Momentum for Competitors 3 and 5. Figure 5-8 shows the share/momentum chart for Competitor 3, a Japanese producer. Obviously, Competitor 3 is doing extremely well in A market segments, in most instances growing at 60 percent or more in markets that are also growing in the range of 20 to 50 percent. On the other hand, Competitor 3 seems to be exiting B segments. Competitor 3 seems to have

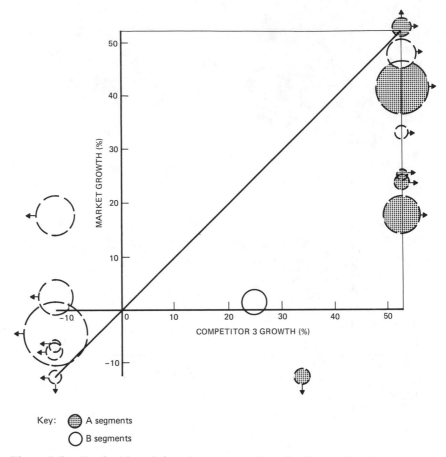

Figure 5-8. Product-based share/momentum chart for Competitor 3
SOURCE: Based on client study.

made a conscious decision to be dominant in A and exit B segments, and does not compete in C at all.

If we were to examine the share/momentum chart for Competitor 5, another Japanese producer, we would see the exact reverse pattern—dominance in B segments and exiting A segments. Now far be it from us to suggest collusion between Competitors 3 and 5, but the results of this analysis are extremely important to Competitor 1, who now has a better understanding of what is happening within the product/market structure. If Competitor 1 attempts to build strength in either segments A or B, it will run head on into the dominance of Competitors 3 or 5—disaster will often overtake a competitor who attempts to build hills where other competitors have already done so. Understanding the perceived strategies of competitors is part of our purpose in these analyses—exposing what competitors seem to be telegraphing to the market.

Competitor 4. All competitors may not be following a product-based strategy, and that was the case with Competitor 4, who seemed to be emphasizing a geographic strategy. When its product portfolio was segmented into "made and sold in Europe," and "made and sold in the United States," two very different patterns emerged, as shown in Figure 5-9. Made and sold in Europe (Figure 5-9a) represents a strong portfolio of high relative market share, low-growth business units—this portfolio was generating a great deal of cash.

On the other hand, made and sold in the United States (Figure 5-9b) presents an entirely different portfolio, one emphasizing high-growth businesses financed by the cash generated in Europe. Competitor 4 seemed to be moving from Europe to the United States—an "anywhere in the U.S." basic strategy. As a matter of fact, Competitor 4 was British, and investment in the United States was very attractive at the time of the study, because of the strength of the pound versus the dollar. But Competitor 4's U.S. initiative was so strong, and investment in its European markets so small, that the move to the United States seemed to be a long-term strategy.

Competitor 1's understanding of its own portfolio and share/momentum, and of what seemed to be the strategies of Competitors 3, 4, and 5, provides important insight. Attempting a strong thrust into product lines A and B will face strong opposition by the Japanese Competitors 3 and 5, but these competitors are not so strongly entrenched in C products (and some other product lines not shown). Also, perhaps a market thrust in Europe would not be strongly opposed by Competitor 4, since its cash was being used to build a base in the United States.

The farm equipment industry provides additional insight into the relationship between market segments and activity strengths and weaknesses and the importance of value-added streams in activity analysis.

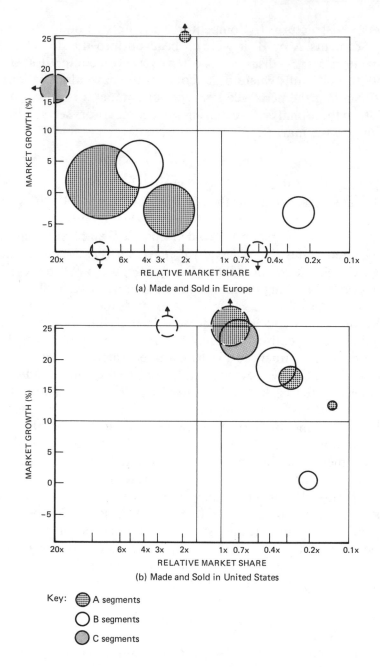

Figure 5-9. Product-based growth/share matrixes for Competitor 4: (*a*) made and sold in Europe, and (*b*) made and sold in the United States

Source: Based on client study.

Analysis of Deere & Company in Farm Tractors

We select Deere & Company from within the farm equipment industry for analysis because it is the leader, producing farm equipment across the board in combines, harrows, haying equipment, planters, plows, and tractors. Figure 5-10 shows Deere's product portfolio for 1979–1982, with the farm tractor businesses crosshatched. Tractors represent a significant portion of the company's sales—there are four SBUs in farm tractors alone, under 40 horsepower (hp), 40–99 hp, 100+ hp, and four-wheel drive (4-WD). Therefore, a segmentation based on farm tractors seems useful.

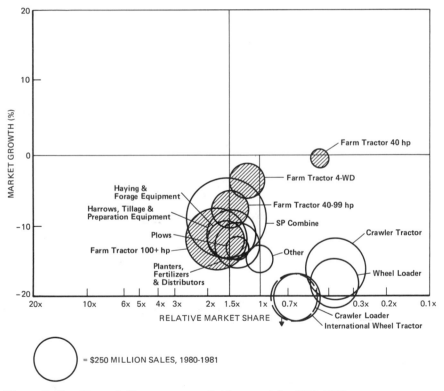

Figure 5-10. Deere & Company growth/share matrix, 1979–1982

SOURCES: Company and competitors' annual reports, 10-K reports, financial analyst's reports, *Truck and Off-Highway Industries* (various issues), Frost and Sullivan, and conversations with industry experts.

Looking at farm tractors in relation to their markets in the sector chart of Figure 5-11, we see that Deere is the leader with market share about twice that of its nearest competitors, International Harvester and Ford. Furthermore, Deere is growing faster than the industry, though the sector growth rate is negative during the 1979–1982 period. So the initial observation is that Deere & Company is strong in the farm tractor business, which represents a large fraction of their portfolio, but we will look into the four segments of that business.

SEGMENTS OF THE FARM TRACTOR BUSINESS

First, we examine the total North American sales of farm tractors sold, to see the percentages of the total units accounted for by each of

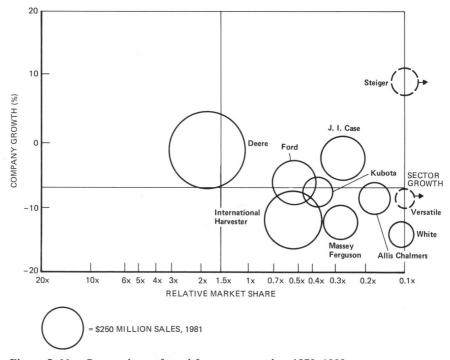

Figure 5-11. Sector chart of total farm tractor sales, 1979–1982

SOURCES: Company and competitors' annual reports, 10-K reports, financial analyst's reports, *Truck and Off-Highway Industries* (various issues), Frost and Sullivan, and conversations with industry experts.

the four sizes in Figure 5–12, and which segments of the market are growing. The most attractive market segment is small tractors (under 40 hp). The four-wheel drive tractor market is also attractive in terms of growth but currently represents a somewhat smaller percentage of total volume. Both are gaining against the larger tractors, which dominate current sales but represent no-growth segments. The large 100 + hp tractors represent the least attractive sector which is shrinking rapidly. The next question, of course, is which segments represent Deere's strength?

The further segmentation of tractors into the four sizes is shown in Figure 5–13. Here, each tractor size is examined as a sector, and Deere's position vis-à-vis its competitors is rather different in the four markets.

In the under 40-hp market shown in Figure 5–13*a*, Deere has a

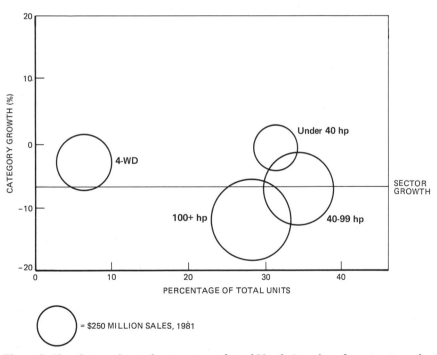
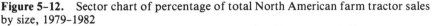

Figure 5–12. Sector chart of percentage of total North American farm tractor sales by size, 1979–1982

SOURCES: Company and competitors' annual reports, 10-K reports, financial analyst's reports, *Truck and Off-Highway Industries* (various issues), Frost and Sullivan, and conversations with industry experts.

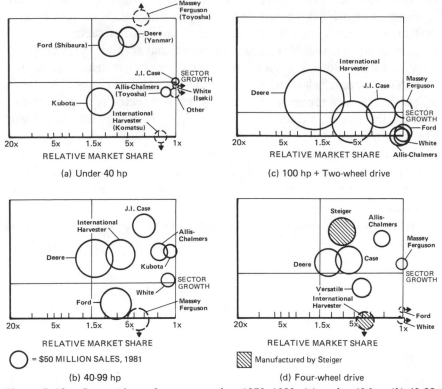

Figure 5-13. Sector charts for tractor sales, 1979–1982: (*a*) under 40 hp, (*b*) 40-99 hp, (*c*) 100 + hp, and (*d*) four-wheel drive

SOURCES: Company and competitors' annual reports, 10-K reports, financial analyst's reports, *Truck and off-Highway Industries* (various issues), Frost and Sullivan, and conversations with industry experts.

somewhat smaller market share than both Kubota and Ford, though it is growing rapidly. Massey Ferguson is the fastest growing company. But note something significant about all the U.S. firms—each has a Japanese name following it in parentheses. No firm in the United States is manufacturing tractors under 40 hp, the fastest growing segment in the business; they are all distributors of Japanese tractors. In fact, both Allis-Chalmers and Massey Ferguson are distributing the same Japanese tractor, Toyosha. So even though Deere's sales are growing fast in the under 40-hp market, it is developing no activity experience in engineering design or manufacturing terms.

Deere's great strength in medium and very large tractors is shown in Figure 5-13*b* and *c,* but as we noted, these are the least attractive segments of the market. Medium tractors are at the sector growth rate in Figure 5-11, and the 100 + hp tractors are somewhat below the sector growth rate. While Deere & Company is the leader in these segments, the market dynamics are not in their favor.

Finally, Deere holds a good position in four-wheel drive tractors, but Steiger is growing more rapidly, and seems likely to overtake Deere. Steiger and International Harvester are crosshatched in the Four-Wheel Drive sector chart of Figure 5-13*d* because they are not independent—Steiger is a specialty producer of 4-WD tractors, and manufactures what Harvester sells under its brand name. In fact, in 1982, "after International Harvester balked at accepting $10 million of Steiger tractors it had ordered, Steiger won the right to sell its tractors through about 100 Harvester dealers. . . ."[1] Late in 1984, Harvester sold its farm equipment business to J. I. Case, making it No. 2 in the industry.

We will now look to see where in the process value is added in farm tractors, and which activities are of the greatest significance. What are the implications that Deere (and other U.S. manufacturers) are only distributors in the most attractive sector of the farm tractor business?

VALUE-ADDED STREAM AND ACTIVITIES

Recall that we discussed value-added streams in Chapter 3 in connection with industry and market analysis as a mechanism for comparing different players in an industry and how each participated in the broad range of possible activities. Figure 3-1 showed that rutile, the basic raw material, was inconsequential in the value-added stream for several titanium firms. On the other hand, sponge, ingot, mill products, and fabrications had great importance, because they all added significant portions to the value of titanium end-products. Examining the value-added stream for farm tractors provides important insights to an analysis of Deere & Company.

Figure 5-14 shows the value-added streams for typical four- and two-wheel drive farm tractors. What stands out is that distribution represents one of the smaller value-added components—tires and wheels are approximately as important as distribution in 2-wheel drive tractors, and more than twice the value added in 4-wheel drive tractors. Given the fact that Deere and the other U.S. manufacturers of farm tractors are only distributors in the fastest growing segment, a manufacturer's strategy based on distribution of the products of others seems questionable.

The largest single proportion of the value-added stream for two-wheel drive tractors is engines. Though a smaller proportion of the

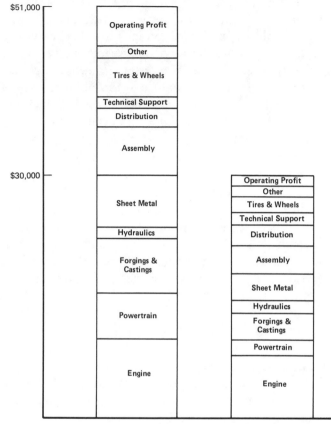

Figure 5-14.   Typical value-added streams for four- and two-wheel drive tractors

SOURCES: Company and competitors' annual reports, 10-K reports, financial analyst's reports, *Truck and Off-Highway Industries* (various issues), Frost and Sullivan, and conversations with industry experts.

total, engines also represent the largest single component in the four-wheel drive stream. Therefore, a further segmentation on the basis of the activities in the stream should provide further insight. Where are Deere's activity strengths within the value-added stream, and what are their weaknesses?

ACTIVITY-BASED ANALYSIS FOR DEERE & COMPANY

By combining value-added information and market share data, activity-based growth/share matrixes can be developed for Deere as

well as its competitors. Figure 5–15* shows that Deere is well positioned in the key activities of the industry. They are first in distribution,
forgings and castings, and hydraulics, and strong but not dominant in
engines.

Some of the tractor manufacturers with which Deere is competing
are manufacturing engines for products other than tractors, thereby
gaining experience in that central activity. For example, Ford makes
engines for cars and trucks, Harvester for large trucks, and Caterpillar
for earth moving equipment. Therefore, though Deere dominates in

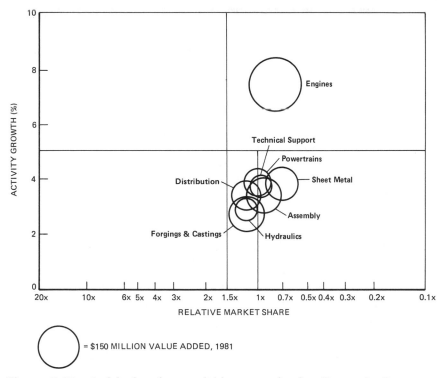

= $150 MILLION VALUE ADDED, 1981

Figure 5–15. Activity-based growth/share matrix for Deere & Company,
1981–1984

Sources: Company and competitors' annual reports, 10-K reports, financial analyst's reports,
Truck and Off-Highway Industries (various issues), Frost and Sullivan, and conversations with
industry experts.

*This activity-based growth-share matrix is slightly different than previously de-
scribed. While the relative market share reflects the company's (e.g., total engine
value-added compared to competitors' total engine value-added), the circle sizes
represent that portion of the value-added in the tractor business only, i.e., nontractor
business activity is not included.

tractors, they do not dominate the most important underlying activity, and this may be a point of vulnerability. Of course, the situation is not as crucial as when Bowmar had no position at all in chip manufacture, which was an activity that dominated the consumer electronics valued-added stream somewhat more than engines dominate the farm tractor stream. Both Caterpillar and ailing Harvester have stronger positions in engines, and a linkup between them could be a destabilizing force for Deere, as could the entry of General Motors into the farm tractor business.

Decentralized operations invariably pose questions of which activities to centralize, and in general how to take advantage of transportation cost/economy-of-scale tradeoffs. These issues have a special significance in international operations because of the complications of local content rules and exchange rates.

International Activity Bases—Rationalized Exchange

Activity analysis is important in competitive analysis of international operations. Different forms for organizing production facilities have been proposed, and we will discuss three: central location, multidomestic, and rationalized exchange.

The *central structure* establishes one basic location for production and ships the product from it to all markets. Boeing Aircraft is an example—an order for a 747 is made in Seattle and flown to the customer, wherever the destination. Similarly, if a foreign customer wants Dupont Nomex or Kevlar, new high-tenacity fibers, they are made in the United States and shipped overseas. Centralizing facilities yields scale advantages, and permits the accumulation of experience at the system rates for all activities. The disadvantages are in dealing with local content rules in many countries, and in dealing with the problems of monetary exchange and short-term exchange rate movements.

The *multidomestic* form is illustrated by Massey-Ferguson in farm equipment. They have set up a microcosm of operations in each of the countries in which they compete. There are marketing advantages in having a presence in a country, easily meeting local content rules, and in providing service. The disadvantages are in fluctuating exchange rates, the cost position of small-scale plants, and the fact that experience curve effects are restricted by the multiple plant organization—while the total volume may be large, experience is accumulated at the lower activity levels of each plant.

Rationalized exchange is a third form that is illustrated by the Ford Motor Company and IBM in Europe. Rationalized exchange is particularly applicable to complex assembled products, by allocating component manufacture among the countries in which business is done. Therefore, transmissions may be made in one country, engines in a second, bodies in a third, assembly in a fourth, and so on. By carefully designing the system of inputs and outputs, local content rules are satisfied and the monetary flows are also in balance as completed autos are shipped back to each country for sale. The operating advantages are of considerable importance: each specialized plant is of large scale for efficient operations, experience is accumulated at the activity level for the total volume for each component, and each plant is focused on a limited set of activities for manufacturing as well as management. However, in addition to the advantages in operations, there is a balanced foreign exchange exposure—much of the problem of dealing with exchange rate fluctuations is eliminated through the balancing of monetary inputs and outputs. Rationalized exchange then seems to combine all the advantages, where the nature of the business makes it an appropriate alternative.

Concluding Remarks

Traditional portfolio analysis makes the assumption that the individual SBUs and products in the portfolio are independent of each other. But an analysis of the activity bases and product structures may reveal important interdependencies that can be exploited. Experience is accumulated at the activity level, and the cost positions for products are affected by the impact of related products through the increased volume in activities. Segmentation on the basis of product line and/or geography can provide insight into the competitive dynamics of markets—which competitors are following a geographic strategy and which a product strategy, for example. These interrelationships can produce situations where a dog may have characteristics more akin to a cash cow in many instances, as was demonstrated on a statistical basis by the study of dogs reported on in Chapter 2.[2]

The value-added stream for products can provide important insights into strategic activities in which a company may participate. Finally, alternate strategies for organizing physical facilities can have important scale and experience-curve effects on activities that affect cost position.

These analyses of the interdependence of the costs of activities and product lines demonstrate that the firm functions as a system. As Lord Acton stated with elegant simplicity, "You cannot change just one thing," there may be unintended effects. We must anticipate the interactive effects, and either find ways of counterbalancing them, or analyze in advance if the benefits will outweigh the negative side effects.

Chapter 6

Diversification and Acquisitions

The drive to diversify corporate portfolios continues, and as the United States emerged from the 1981–1983 recession, there was a jump in merger and acquisition activity. While many are mega-mergers, such as Dupont/Conoco, LTV/Republic Steel, and Texaco/Getty, the post-recession activity in the acquisition of smaller firms whose shares are not publicly traded has also been intensified.[1] In 1984 alone there were 2543 mergers and acquisitions for a total of $122 billion.[2]

There are many reasons for firms to merge with and acquire other firms. Diversification for its own sake can be a major concern, and acquisitions may be unrelated to present core activities. For example, American Can bought G. Tsai & Company, a small brokerage firm.[3] But the move was a part of a broad diversification into financial services that involved buying insurance companies and a mutual fund group within the previous two years. Within the same month, American Can led a group of investors to buy most of the assets of Southern Pacific's Ticor Insurance unit in a $271.3 million leveraged buyout, extending American Can's expansion into financial services which accounted for nearly half its first-half 1983 profit.[4]

Access to additional markets in the same field is another reason for acquisition. For example, AT&T recently bought 25 percent of Olivetti for $260 million to give it a distribution system in Europe,[5] and Cigna Corp. agreed to buy AFIA for $215 million, an association of

U.S. insurance companies doing business overseas—the acquisition would provide Cigna with access to markets in about 23 countries where it is not currently licensed.[6]

Major Acquisitions by Sector

Figure 6–1 shows graphically the pattern of major acquisitions during the 1975–1980 period. A major acquisition was defined as one involving an acquired firm with sales of $100 million or more, and the circle sizes indicate the number of such firms involved during the period.

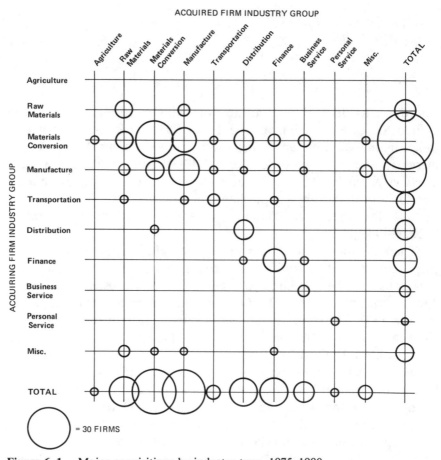

Figure 6–1.   Major acquisitions by industry type, 1975–1980

SOURCE: *Mergers & Acquisitions: The Journal of Corporate Venture,* 1975–1980 annual surveys.

The industry types of the acquiring firms are listed in the right column, and the acquired firms' industry group across the top.

There are two important trends indicated in the acquisition activities of firms, represented by the "total" column of circles at the right. First, the major trend was that firms acquired what they already knew—most of the activity is within the same industry group, as indicated by the dominance of the diagonal line of circles and the size of the circles that fall on the diagonal. The move by Cigna cited previously falls in this category, where they extended their markets into foreign countries in the insurance field.

The second discernible trend in Figure 6-1 is for firms to diversify, particularly basic industries—metals conversion and manufacturing. But on closer examination, we see that the diversification was directed into service sectors—transportation, distribution, finance, and business service, all the service sectors except personal service. The diversification of American Can into financial services cited previously is illustrative.

The "total" row of circles across the bottom of Figure 6-1 summarizes the industry groups being acquired. Since the dominant pattern of acquisition was for firms to acquire within their industry groups, materials conversion and manufacturing dominate. But acquisition activity is strong in seven of the nine identified industry groups.

Objectives of Diversification and Acquisitions

The central business objective of diversification and acquisitions is to enhance the economic value of the firm, the focal point of strategy as discussed in Chapter 1. We want to diversify and acquire in patterns that will increase the value of assets in the long term over and above what was paid for them.

Recall that the four factors that contribute to economic value discussed in Chapter 1 and summarized in Figure 1-3 were scale, returns, growth, and sustainability. Scale refers to the size of the opportunity—the larger the scale, the greater the potential increase in economic value. Returns refer to the ability of the opportunity to earn returns in excess of the cost of capital—those with positive returns add value, and those with negative returns are subtracting economic value. Growth refers to the magnitude of the potential increase in the size of the opportunity, and sustainability refers to the short- or long-term nature of opportunity, that is, the greater the duration over which the returns and growth can add value, the greater the total value increase.

UNRELATED DIVERSIFICATION AND ACQUISITIONS

The objective of diversification and acquisitions, then, is to find combinations of expansion opportunities or firms that will add value—acquire assets that in themselves enhance value, by virtue of their scale, returns, growth, and sustainability. These assets could be unrelated to the present core activities, but may *add* value becuse they earn at higher rates than present activities.

An example of a company that added value through diversification into new lines of business unrelated to its former lines is NL Industries, which we discussed in Chapter 1 in connection with economic value. Recall that NL Industries was originally in metals—principally lead products and some titanium through its 50 percent ownership of TIMET—with a heavy investment in paint, before it moved strongly into petroleum services. Analysis of NL's return on assets (in excess of the cost of capital) in Figure 1–4 in 1981 showed that the paint business was subtracting value and growing slowly, while petroleum services loomed large in their sales revenue, was adding value, and was growing rapidly. Metals (principally TIMET), while growing slowly, were adding value to the firm through high returns in excess of the cost of capital. NL Industries had diversified into lines of business that earned substantially more than its traditional lines, and had divested many of its former SBUs that were subtracting value—it had redeployed its assets in ways that increased their value resulting in an improved market-to-book ratio as of 1981. Subsequently, however, the downturn in petroleum services resulted in a strong negative impact on NL.

RELATED DIVERSIFICATION AND ACQUISITIONS

On the other hand, diversification and acquisitions may have relevance to present activities. Such combinations may include diversification into related activities in vertical or horizontal integration, or activities that are complementary or supplementary to current lines of business.

Vertical integration moves forward or backward in the activity stream, that is, the materials conversion, manufacturing, marketing, and distribution of the product. Vertical integration is also an activity view of related businesses, raising issues of improving cost position or securing a source of supply. It deals with the activities of marketing, manufacturing, and distributing the product, and whether or not buying materials from suppliers will offer improved cost or supply, or if selling the product to distributors will provide better access to markets and lower costs than integrating these functions within the company. The basic issue is whether or not the company can be strengthened and obtain a better cost position by performing more activities itself.

Horizontal integration is a marketing view of the world, raising issues of access to markets, or the attractiveness of new markets for a product or new products for existing channels. What other products can be sold through existing channels? Where else can the product be sold? What other markets offer potential for the same or modified products? Expansion of existing markets, or expansion into new markets will provide experience curve benefits within the marketing, manufacturing, and distributing activities.

Whether or not diversification and acquisitions should be related or unrelated is an issue. The record indicates that relatedness is important. "Stick to the knitting," that is, do what you know best, is one of the admonitions that comes from the experience of the best-run American companies, as reported by Peters and Waterman in their best-selling book, *In Search of Excellence.*[7] Furthermore, empirical evidence is provided by a broad study of diversified companies by Richard Rumelt, a UCLA colleague.[8] He found that companies that enter only those businesses that build on, draw strength from, and enlarge some existing central strength were the best performers. These firms did not indulge in unrelated diversification.

Pacific Power and Light provides an example of the results of a mixture of backward integration into coal, and diversification into telecommunications (purchase of RCA's telecommunications business in Alaska). Our objective will be to trace the effects of these moves through to their impacts on economic value. Certainly on the basis of the sales record from 1977 to 1981 shown in Figure 6–2a both coal and telecommunications were adding significantly to the increasing total sales for the period (the sales scale is log of sales). The original electric business represents a declining portion of sales.

The margins earned by these businesses during the 1978–1981 period, however, were flat in the aggregate. Figure 6–2b shows that coal margins were declining during the period, telecommunications

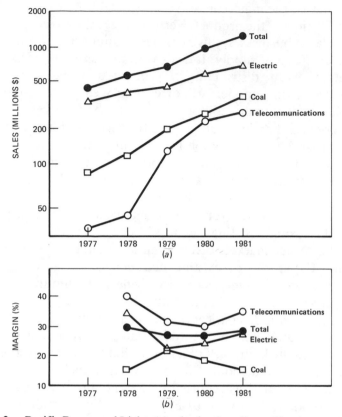

Figure 6–2.   Pacific Power and Light: (*a*) sales for three lines of business, 1977–1981, and (*b*) margins, 1978–1981

SOURCE: Company annual and 10-K reports.

declined with a recovery in 1981, and electric margins increased, all resulting in fairly level total margins. The telecommunications business had much higher margins than the base electric or coal businesses, with coal margins decaying rapidly. But it appears that Pacific Power and Light was now in some low- and some high-earning businesses.

Examination of the returns on assets (ROA) of the three lines of businesses confirms that the ROAs for both coal and telecommunications are higher than for the basic electric business. Figure 6–3 shows that returns on assets for the 1979–1981 period for electric operation was about 6 percent, while telecommunications was 11 percent and coal about 12 percent. Coal had the highest ROA results because while

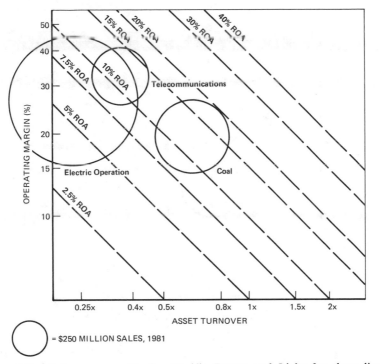

Figure 6–3. Returns on assets for Pacific Power and Light for three lines of business, 1979–1981

SOURCE: Company annual and 10-K reports.

the margin is the lowest of the three businesses, the asset turnover is the highest with the net result of a higher ROA.

Therefore, it appears that, like NL Industries, Pacific Power has converted its asset base from one involving low returns to one earning higher returns. But the real issue centers on whether or not these businesses are earning returns in excess of their costs of capital, and which cost of capital applies to which business units. The cost of capital for an electric utility is vastly different from that for a telecommunications business. In fact all three businesses had negative returns compared to their costs of capital, and were subtracting value that would decrease their market-to-book valuation.

This unhappy picture is shown in Figure 6–4—all three lines of business are subtracting value with negative returns. Returns here are defined as ROA minus the cost of capital for each line of business,

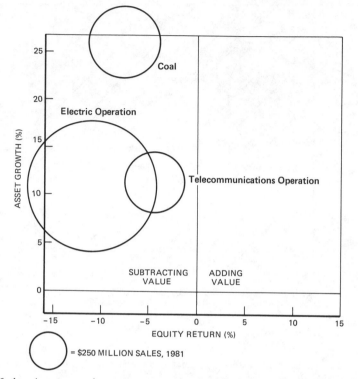

Figure 6-4. Asset growth versus returns for Pacific Power and Light, 1981
SOURCES: Company annual and 10-K reports, and *Value Line*.

assuming 100 percent equity financing. Each line of business falls into a separate risk class; therefore, the cost of capital for each is different.

The effects of the decline in economic value can be read in the changes in the market-to-book valuations during the 1975–1981 period. Figure 6–5a shows that while return on equity actually increased, particularly from 1977 to 1981, market to book ratios declined to less than 1.0. The reasons for the decline in market to book are more clearly shown in Figure 6–5b, because returns above the cost of capital for Pacific Power went negative after 1977 even though returns on equity were increasing.* Note that the measures of returns

---

* Though Pacific Power's return on equity was rising throughout the 1977–81 period, it was not rising as fast as the cost of capital—which was rising principally because of increasing inflation. Therefore, the equity return was actually declining throughout the period.

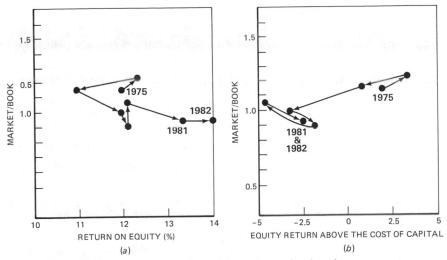

Figure 6-5. Pacific Power and Light: (*a*) market-to-book ratios versus returns on equity, 1975–1981, and (*b*) market-to-book ratios versus returns above the cost of capital, 1975–1981

Sources: Company annual and 10-K reports, and *Value Line*.

on the horizontal scales of Figures 6–4 and 6–5*b* are different, that is, returns for each line of business in excess of the cost of capital for that business are shown in Figure 6–4, while Figure 6–5*b* shows a weighted average for the company as a whole.

We have summarized two case examples, NL Industries and Pacific Power. NL Industries was able to redeploy its assets successfully into petroleum services and titanium from lead and paint, increasing the value of the firm, though hindsight has shown sustainability to be an issue as the petroleum services business turned down. On the other hand, Pacific Power's redeployment into coal and telecommunications did not achieve these objectives. With such widely differing results of diversification moves, the question is, How does one tell a good move in advance—what should we look for in diversification and acquisitions?

Hallmarks of Effective Acquisitions

When the search for an acquisition is begun, it may be natural to want a good financial performer—good sales growth, good earnings growth, good margins, and a low price-earnings (PE) ratio. But on sorting thought the reams of available financial data, it soon becomes apparent that this combination of delightful characteristics does not exist. The companies that have high growth in sales, earnings, and good margins typically have high PEs, as we should expect. For example, we showed the sector graph for the manifold business forms industry in Figure 3-9, indicating that Moore had consolidated the industry, having a relative market share more than five times that of its nearest competitor. Would Moore be a good acquisition? Unless we were simply looking for an excellent asset, the answer would be no. Even then, the price for the asset would be very high, reducing the relative returns—it would not add value because of the high price. In addition, there is no obvious way to grow faster than the market, since Moore is such a large fraction of the market.

Indeed, if we were to find the delightful combination with low PEs, the company is probably being milked, and would be the worst acquisition possible since it would soon fall apart. So buying good past and current financial performance is doomed either because it is too expensive and future performance in relation to a high purchase price will be poor, or because a low purchase price may be indicative of a poor future performer even though the past performance has been good.

What we must ferret out is the candidate for acquisition that has good future prospects for growth, where the underlying trends are attractive, where the competitive dynamics are positive, where there may be complementary strengths in activities, and where the strategic direction is compatible with acquisition. These four dimensions of acquisition analysis provide the basis for finding diversification and acquisition candidates that will add value to the combined organization. These are the predictors of *future* good financial performance as opposed to past and current performance. We must pay dearly for past and current performance, because it is essentially the purchase of an asset. Buying a growth opportunity, however, that has

- positive underlying trends,
- positive competitive dynamics,
- complementary activity structure, and
- good strategic direction

has the hallmarks of a good acquisition. We will discuss each of these four dimensions of acquisition analysis.

UNDERLYING TRENDS

What are the attractive sectors in the economy? That is, which sectors have growth potential, and which are shrinking? For example, without analysis we know that electronics-related businesses are growing, and steel is receding. What are the demographic trends that may be a harbinger of sectors for future growth? What demographic trends represent sectors that are likely to have poor or even negative growth? Diversification and acquisition analysis of these underlying trends can help position a company to take advantage of positive trends and avoid being in harm's way.

Sector Output Growth Trends.   A macro-screening of output growth trends in the industrial sectors of the U.S. economy in relation to other industrialized countries is shown in Figure 6-6. The U.S. output growth between 1976 and 1980 is shown on the horizontal axis, and the growth during the same period for other industrialized countries is shown on the vertical axis. Therefore, circles representing the volume of shipments in 1980 (in 1976 constant dollars) that fall on the diagonal line indicate sectors where U.S. and foreign growth has been the same. In most of the industry sectors shown, the U.S. output growth trends were approximately the same as for other industrialized countries.

On the other hand, there are some important exceptions to the general parity of output growth. Basic metals is a sector in the United States that has been shrinking while the other nations have shown positive growth. Recall that in our discussion of free-world steel markets in Chapter 4, Figure 4-5 showed the position of steel-producing countries in terms of relative market share and steel production growth, with the United States shrinking at almost 10 percent in an industry that was shrinking at only 1 percent. To the extent that productivity increase and growth are linked, as we argued in Chapter 4 (see Figure 4-1), this means that we have not been achieving productivity gains in basic metals that were as high as the economy as a whole, while foreign producers have been more productive than their own economies. The result has been that the lower productivity increases affect the comparative product cost directly *and* these cost disadvantages are amplified through the international exchange rates as we demonstrated in Chapter 4. Transportation equipment, textiles, clothing and leather, and wood and wood products are industrial sectors that share this disadvantageous position.

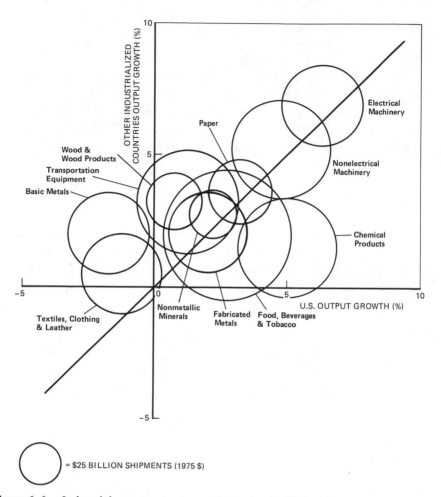

Figure 6-6. Industrial sector output growth trends, the United States versus other industrialized countries, 1976–1980

SOURCE: *Indicators of Industrial Activity*, OECD (various editions).

On the other hand, the expansion of the U.S. chemical products industry during 1976–1980 has completely outpaced foreign producers, and the food, beverages, and tobacco sector has also grown faster in the United States. Both are very large industrial sectors as represented by their circle sizes. We are strong in these industries and growing faster than our counterparts in other industrialized countries. The underlying trends provide general guidance—other things being equal, we would like to be in industrial sectors that are growing faster in the United States than their counterparts abroad, to be in markets of the future rather than the past.

Linking the concepts of Chapter 4 on international strategic issues with our objectives here, it is important to know in which sectors the United States may have a comparative advantage. Output growth and productivity growth are positively correlated. A business in an industrial sector that is experiencing growth may also be experiencing productivity growth that outpaces our economy.

Since exchange rates balance out aggregate productivity increases of entire economies, it is desirable to select businesses where we can outpace the productivity increases of our own economy. It is not good enough to think only about being in good growth sectors. Rather, where an international market exists, we must be in good growth sectors relative to our economy compared to international competitors relative to their economies. Therefore, a macro screening of the type provided by Figure 6–6 helps direct our focus toward broad classes of businesses, while isolating other sectors as areas for further study. This does not mean that there are not opportunities within sectors such as basic metals. There are undoubtedly profitable niches, or new products that could be exploited. But like oil drilling, the cost of drilling urges one to look for the larger pools. Panning for gold is less likely to be profitable than attempting to find larger veins of the yellow metal.

Positive Demographic Characteristics. Demographic trends are of importance in future markets. For example, it is fairly obvious that because of the growing Hispanic population in the United States, targeting products toward that market segment could take advantage of this underlying trend. But a more systematic scanning of possibilities is useful in diversification and acquisition analysis. We need to look inside such a trend to see how various products and businesses might be affected.

Focusing on one demographic trend that is well known: women have been entering the labor force at a high rate (see Figure 6–7). The percentage participation of women in the labor force has grown steadily from about 37.5 percent in 1960 to about 52.5 percent in 1982, and forecasts indicate that this trend will continue as indicated by the dotted portion of the curve to 57.5 percent by 1990. What is the significance of this important trend for various products and businesses in the U.S. apparel industry, for example?

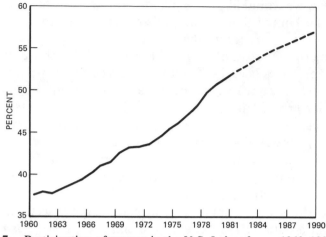

Figure 6-7.   Participation of women in the U.S. Labor force, 1960–1982

SOURCE: Data and projection by the U.S. Department of Commerce.

In order to help answer this question, let us examine the dynamics of output growth in relation to the share of industry sales for a variety of products in the U.S. apparel industry. Figure 6–8 shows a graph of the situation for the 1972–1981 period, the circle sizes being in proportion to shipments in 1981. The industry as a whole grew at a modest 1 percent during this ten-year period; however, the demographic trend of increasing participation of women in the labor force shows strongly in the high-growth products.

Women's suits and coats are items that might be worn to the office; women's blouses are items that might be worn to the office; and other women's outerwear are office garb. The only other product group that registers a growth rate above the industry average is men's work clothes, at a growth rate of 2 percent compared to the higher-growth women's work clothes rates of about 6 percent. So even in the mature apparel industry, an examination of the demographic dynamics reveals products with strong underlying trends. In choosing a business within the apparel industry, it would certainly be preferable to select one with strong demographics as an underlying trend.

ADVANTAGEOUS COMPETITIVE DYNAMICS

One of the delightful aspects of diversification and acquisitions is that for once you can choose your competitors, at least at the time of the

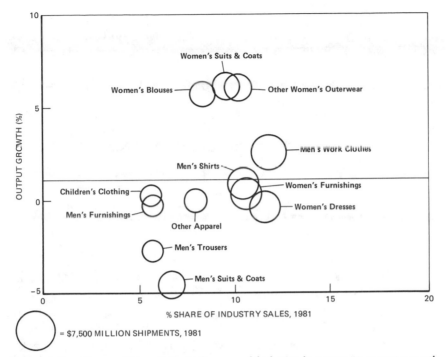

Figure 6-8. Composition of the U.S. apparel industry in terms of output growth versus market share for various product lines, 1972–1981

SOURCE: U.S. Department of Commerce.

acquisition. This being the case, it is important to choose them wisely. An analysis of the industry and its competitors can reveal its market structure, who if anyone dominates, and the logical future direction of competition. Recall that in our discussion of market structures in Chapter 3, we identified two broad types of market structures, those that were consolidated by a dominant leader, and those that were not consolidated. Figure 3-7 further subdivided unconsolidated structures into fragmented, unconsolidated stable, and unconsolidated unstable.

From the point of view of advantageous competitive dynamics in choosing candidates for acquisition and areas for diversification, we can label one group as desirable and the other not desirable as in Figure 6-9.

Undesirable Sectors. It is often true that one producer has consolidated its industry, having established an impregnable position that

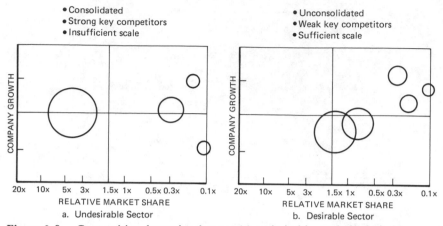

Figure 6-9. Competitive dynamics that are (*a*) undesirable, and (*b*) desirable

cannot be attacked successfully unless something destabilizes the industry. This situation is shown in Figure 6-9*a* where one competitor has consolidated the industry. To come into such an industry with the intention of attacking the leader is most often suicidal. The leader has large scale and experience that should give it basic cost and market advantages. Entry by way of acquisition of an existing player might not provide sufficient scale to compete effectively with the leader.

A good example of such a consolidated position is that held by Steelcase in the U.S. office furniture industry, shown in Figure 6-10. Steelcase is more than 2.5 times the size of its nearest rivals, Herman Miller and Hon, and is growing faster than either.

Steelcase's successful competitors tend to be in market segments. For example, Hon concentrates on file cabinets instead of a broad line of office furniture, selling through smaller dealers and through Sears. On the other hand, All-Steel attempts across-the-board competition with Steelcase, but with poor results—it has slightly negative growth compared to Steelcase's 20 percent growth rate, and is only 20 percent as large.

Other examples of consolidated markets are Moore in the manifold business forms industry discussed in Chapter 3 and illustrated by the sector chart of Figure 3-9, and IBM in mainframe computers, and more recently in personal computers.

Desirable Sectors.   An unconsolidated sector provides opportunities simply by virtue of the fact that no one has yet locked it up. The competitors within such an industry are relatively weak, and because no

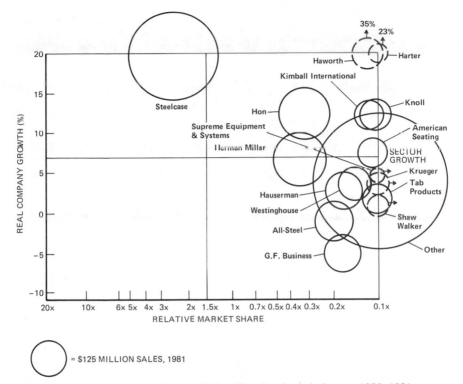

Figure 6-10. Sector chart for the U.S. office furniture industry, 1979–1981

SOURCES: Annual and 10-K reports, and analysts' reports, and conversations with industry experts.

one really dominates, entry may be possible with sufficient scale to be viable. The situation shown in Figure 6-9*b* indicates the dimensions of a desirable sector.

While fragmentation within an industry is not a requirement, it does indicate that many opportunities may exist. For example, the U.S. pharmaceutical industry is fragmented, as shown in Figure 6-11. No one dominates—American Home Products is only slightly larger than Lilly, its nearest rival. But several other producers are of nearly the same size—Merck, Smithkline, Johnson & Johnson, Bristol Myers, and Warner-Lambert. In addition, many competitors are non-pharmaceutical, being chemical companies such as American Cyanamid and Dow, consumer products such as most of the leaders, or a variety of other basic industry groups such as 3M and American Hospital Supply. Of the purely pharmaceutical companies, only

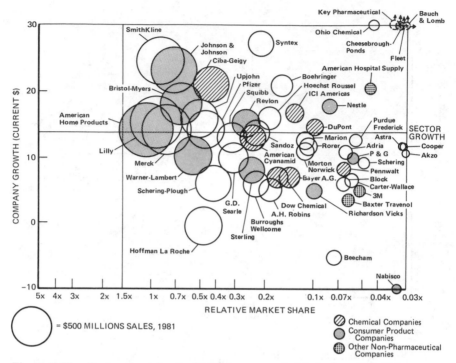

Figure 6–11. Sector chart for the U.S. pharmaceutical industry, 1978–1981

SOURCES: Company annual and 10-K reports, analysts' reports, COMPUSTAT, *Prescription Drug Industry Factbook* (Washington, D.C.: Pharmaceutical Manufacturers Association, various issues).

Smithkline is one of the leaders—the others, such as Hoffman La Roche, Schering-Plough, and Upjohn are rather smaller. The market seems to be filled with many comfortable niches and cracks—this does not imply unprofitability. These niches are commonly protected through patent rights for drugs.

The U.S. production of machine tools presents a fragmented picture with many firms of similar size and relative market share, as shown in Figure 6–12. But Figure 6–12 presents only the main competitors. The U.S. industry is composed of about 1340 businesses, mostly small and family-owned. The 1977 Census of Manufacturers found that about 65 percent of machine tool firms surveyed employed fewer than 20 employees.

Of course, the Japanese threat in the machine tool industry is now well known, but in 1977 the percentage of our domestic market held by imports was only 15.5 percent, mostly Japanese. But that market incursion has progressed rapidly to about 36 percent in 1983.[9]

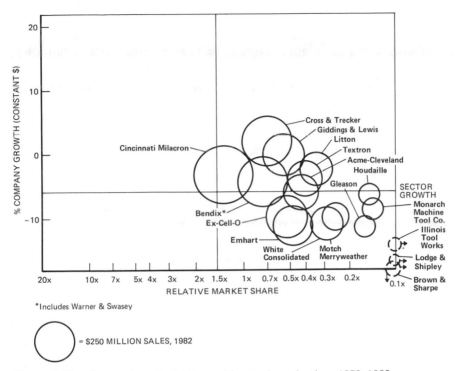

Figure 6-12. Sector chart for U.S. machine tool production, 1979–1982

Sources: COMPUSTAT, company annual and 10-K reports, and analysts' reports.

The Japanese have chosen a very effective way to compete in the machine tool business. They have chosen to emphasize the high-tech numerically controlled machine tools in their exports—the future markets—rather than to compete strongly with conventional tools. The Japanese have targeted certain sectors of the industry through the extensive introduction of more sophisticated products—they invested heavily in technologically advanced machines along with computer controls, and these sectors have proved to be the strong ones. Machining centers, lathes, and milling and boring machines have been developed to run with computerized instructions, and often with little human involvement. If anyone is to consolidate the machine tool market, it is likely to be through these markets of the future.

But beyond being unconsolidated, whether fragmented or stable, the unconsolidated unstable situation is one that may provide unique opportunities to penetrate a market and possibly dominate it with a new and winning strategy. Diversification and acquisition moves in unstable market situations are perhaps riskier, but contain the possibility of large enhancements of economic value. We discussed some of the situations that might destabilize an existing market in Chapter 3, such as deregulation, the introduction of a dramatically different product of process technology, or the withdrawal or neutralizing of an important producer in the industry.

COMPLEMENTARY ACTIVITY STRUCTURES

In Chapters 2 and 5 we discussed the significance of product and activity structures and how their interrelationships can have important strategic implications, particularly concerning activity experience and cost position. In examining potential acquisitions, we wish to know whether or not the candidate business unit draws on or adds to existing raw material sources, R&D capability, manufacturing activities, or marketing and distribution systems. These relationships can have important effects on the attractiveness of the proposal. This does not mean that only acquisitions with complementary activity bases should be considered, for diversification moves may involve new business units that add value to the company by virtue of their characteristics of scale, high returns, growth, and sustainability—the four factors that contribute to increased economic value.

When an SBU is independent of others in the portfolio—that is, there are no shared activities—there is a relationship between product volume and cost position through cumulative experience. Cost position is improved through experience, but there is no reenforcement from other product volume.

On the other hand, when SBUs are interrelated through shared activity bases, related product experience adds to the low cost position of other products, and vice versa. There is the added dimension of attractiveness of an acquisition that would share activities.

We referred in Chapter 5 to the activity flow of three products of a hypothetical firm making AM table radios, FM table radios, and FM portable radios, summarized in Figures 5-2, 5-3, and 5-4. The three products shared common activity bases in that they all used the same acoustical components, the same type of assembly process, and two of the products were distributed through the same sales force and wholesalers. Each activity is subject to the effects of the cost-experience curve, and the firm enjoys cost advantages because of the interdependence. If another SBU were to be acquired that shared some of the same activities, both the existing products and the newly related products would benefit from the increased experience. Or, given the weakness of the plastic housing activity, acquiring a product that could significantly fuel this activity could be useful.

We referred to the Eastman Kodak product portfolio in Chapter 5 (Figure 5-1). By relating many of their products to the core technology of thin film coating, Kodak benefits from the economics of the scope of their activities. Since experience really accumulates at the activity level, Kodak has cost positions in these fundamental activities that both benefit from related product volumes and contribute to the cost positions of the related products.

STRATEGIC DIRECTION

In what strategic direction would a given acquisition take the company? If the market is consolidated by a dominant producer, is the intention to challenge the leader, or is it to establish a niche within the broad market? A good example of a consolidated market is in soaps, detergents, and household cleansers, that is, the household products business. As one would expect, Figure 6-13 shows Procter & Gamble as the market leader in a consolidated position with more than five times the market share of its nearest competitors, Colgate Palmolive, Lever Brothers, and S. C. Johnson. The chart is at an aggregate level—it is important to recognize that some of the firms shown do not compete head-on with others. The sector chart shows a growth rate of about 7 percent, with P&G at this rate, since it dominates so completely.

Colgate and Lever Brothers tend to compete directly with P&G, while others, such as Purex and Clorox, found comfortable niches in the market that were profitable. The relative profitability of P&G, Colgate, Lever Brothers, and Purex is shown in Figure 6-14, with P&G having ten-year average margins of about 15 percent. P&G's direct competitors had much lower margins of about 10 percent for Colgate, and only 2 percent for Lever Brothers. But Purex, a niche player, was really doing quite well with an average margin of more than 11 percent. The highest margins, however, were initially recorded by Clorox, which had 1966 margins of about 28 percent.

Clorox was in a very profitable niche by themselves as a bleach company, though they were only a small fraction of the size of P&G. But Clorox chose a strategic direction that was disastrous. They decided that growth was good, and their annual reports indicate that they decided that their strength was distribution in supermarkets.

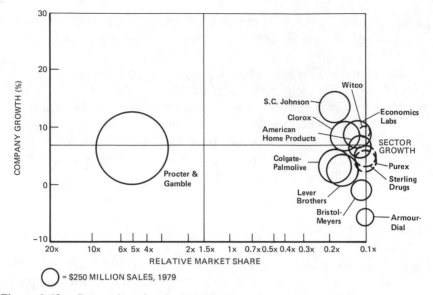

Figure 6-13. Sector chart for the household products business, 1977–1979

SOURCES: COMPUSTAT, company annual and 10-K reports.

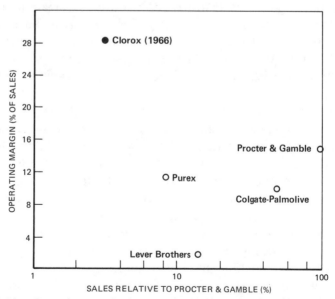

Figure 6-14. Operating margins in percent of sales, versus sales relative to Procter & Gamble, 1966–1975 average

SOURCES: Company annual and 10-K reports, and *Value Line.*

They decided to become a household products company, acquiring B&B Mushrooms, Formula 409, Tilex, and other products, backed by product managers. As the products were added, market share compared to P&G grew, until they were about the size of Lever Brothers by 1975, but their margins had also declined drastically, year by year, as shown by Figure 6-15—they were now competing with P&G, but with the resources, costs, and experience approximating that of Lever Brothers, and with similar results.

The strategic direction chosen by Clorox took them inexorably into the margin valley of death, that margin/market-share region where lack of scale and experience result in high costs and low profits. There are high margins for the market leader and for niches, but Clorox had neither the scale nor the accumulated experience to challenge P&G. While they were able to gain market share, their costs could not match P&G's. To cross the valley of death is bound to be risky at best.

We do not mean that one never takes on the industry leader, for there are examples of a challenger winning. But the challenger needs a focus, activity strength, or some other inherent structural advantage. For example, Texas Instruments had a dominant activity strength in

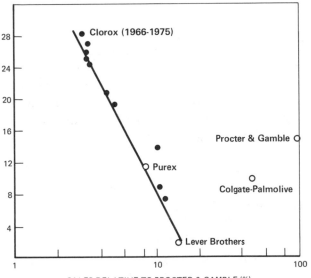

SALES RELATIVE TO PROCTER & GAMBLE (%)

Figure 6-15. Clorox operating margins, 1966-1975, compared to 10-year averages for several competitors

SOURCES: Company annual and 10-K reports, and *Value Line*.

integrated circuits in winning against Bowmar in hand-held calculators.

Concluding Remarks

The objective of diversification and acquisition is to increase the economic value of the company. We can do this by finding candidates that are of sufficient scale to result in a large value increase, that have the potential to earn returns in excess of the cost of capital, that can provide growth so that there is a large potential for value increase, and where the duration or sustainability of the opportunity results in long-term returns.

The diversification moves by NL Industries and Pacific Power provide two contrasting examples. In one case, economic value was increased because assets were redeployed toward those that had higher returns above the cost of capital, and in the other, new assets did not earn such returns.

In uncovering acquisition candidates, we look for positive underlying trends, positive competitive dynamics, complementary activity structure, and good strategic direction. Though not all need apply for a given situation, these are the hallmarks of good diversification and acquisitions.

But, "in an era of ever-increasing and even-larger mergers, a remarkable number—somewhere between a half and two-thirds—simply don't work," and one-third are later undone. Some notable recent examples of major marriages that did not work out are: Coca-Cola and Wine Spectrum, Fluor and St. Joe, Mobil and Marcor, Schlumberger and Fairchild, and Wickes and Gamble-Skogmo. Some of the often cited reasons for failure were:[10]

- Paying too much
- Assuming a boom market won't crash
- Leaping before looking
- Straying too far afield
- Swallowing something too big
- Marrying disparate corporate cultures
- Counting on key managers staying

Or put another way, the hallmarks of good diversification and acquisitions were not observed.

Chapter 7

Financial Implications of Strategic Positions

If strategy does indeed make a difference in financial performance, then we should be able to measure the financial effects of alternate strategies. But the measurement process itself is not the thrust of this chapter. There are many books that deal with the appropriate techniques for comparing financial alternatives.[1] Our purpose is to focus on important financial implications of strategic positions such as the time relationship of margins between competitors that we call the margin paradox, the effects of alternate corporate financial structures, financial leverage, price/return structures, reinvestment economics, the components of required returns within a firm, and the financial impact of overall generic strategies.

Cost/Price Experience Relationships Among Competitors

The two cost-experience curves shown in Figure 7-1 represent the cost curves of two real competitors, and were developed by Company A. Company A knew its own costs, of course, but how did it know Company B's costs? The product was undifferentiated—that is, basically a commodity—and the nature of the business was such that the equipment used in production set the basic cost structure, and was manufactured by a common European supplier. It was large heavy equipment, and using aerial photographs of Company B's plant, Company

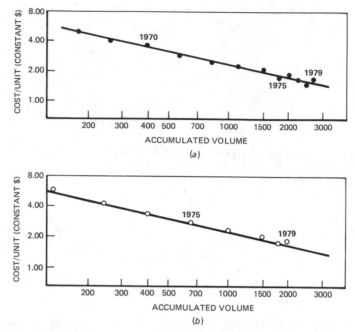

Figure 7-1. Cost-experience curves showing (*a*) average annual costs for Company A, 1968–1979, and (*b*) average annual costs for Company B, 1972–1979

A counted the number of production units in B's plants. Because there was an industry-wide labor contract, an estimate of total labor costs was extrapolated from a study of aerial photos showing the number of cars in plant parking lots.[2] It seemed, in fact, that Company A spent so much time and effort on determining B's cost structure, that they may have had better information on it than on their own cost structure.

The relationship between these cost-experience curves for two companies and the industry price curve can produce an anomalous situation. In Figure 7-1, Company A, the industry leader, enjoyed unit costs in the early 1970s that were much lower than those of its competitor Company B, which was just entering the business. Added experience in the 1970s drove Company A's unit net cost down according to the experience curve shown in Figure 7-1*a*, where each dot represents average costs for a year. However, Company B's volume growth through the 1970s exceeded Company A's. As shown in Figure 7-1*b*, Company B's unit net cost followed an experience curve with virtually the same slope[3] as Company A's. But because of its much higher volume growth in the 1970s, Company B's unit net cost had been reduced to the point that it was almost on a par with Company A's unit net cost.

THE MARGIN PARADOX

The changing year-by-year margins of the two companies (difference between price and cost curves) are shown in Figure 7-2, where the two cost curves are plotted in relation to A's cumulative volume. The markedly steeper slope of B's cost when plotted against A's experience is due to B's faster growth relative to A. Industry prices, indicated by the dashed line in Figure 7-2, were declining faster than A's costs, but slower than B's. (Note that the price line is not an industry price-experience curve, since it is plotted in relation to A's accumulated volume.) Company B built a new plant and cut prices to fill it, thus applying price pressure on A who tried to maintain prices, even though B's costs were higher than A's. Prices followed B's costs more closely than A's. In the early 1970s, Company B's margins were negative and Company A's margins were quite large. But by 1980 the situation had changed dramatically, as shown by Figure 7-2, where each point represents an average annual cost, plotted in relation to Company A's cumulative volume. Company A's margins declined while Company B's increased, because of its fast rate of growth and increase in accumulated experience relative to *A*.

By the late 1970s, Company B appeared to be an attractive business; it was inclined to invest in new capacity and was prepared to continue to grow and reduce its unit costs even further. On the other

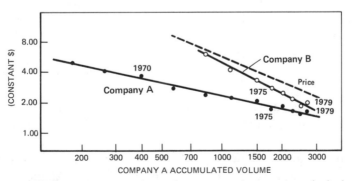

Figure 7-2. Difference between price and cost curves shows progressively decreasing margins for Company A, while margins increase for Company B

hand, Company A seemed to be an unattractive business with decreasing margins, though it still had lower costs than B. Company A had an incentive to deploy its resources elsewhere, foregoing capacity additions, and eroding its once strong position in the business.

Company B's margins doubled in five years, while Company A's margins were cut in half. The changing relationship between the margins of the two companies is not dependent on their two experience curves crossing. Rather, it is dependent on the rapid year-by-year improvement of Company B's costs paced by its accumulating experience, and the fact that it is able to put on price pressure. One of the most common misconceptions in the business world is that the competitive situation is the same for everyone. While in the late 1970s business was "good" for Company B, it was "bad" for Company A, just the reverse of the early 1970s.

Margins for different competitors will not necessarily be the same. In fact, a given business may be increasingly profitable for one company, but increasingly less profitable for another. Different companies may see a given business as being either "good" or "bad," rather than see their particular position in the business as good or bad. They often do not understand why their margins are shrinking while a competitor's are growing. But the reason here is clear—B's margins were growing because it was improving its productivity faster by virtue of a faster growth rate, not because of a steeper experience curve slope. B was growing faster and gaining market share, improving its cost position more rapidly.

The scenario can be easily imagined. When B begins to pose a threat, A goes to its board stating that funds are needed to fight B, the aggressive new competitor. The board responds, "Wait until you get your margins back to where they used to be; we have many uses for funds." Of course, given the situation, this is exactly the reverse of what is needed—A needs the funds to fight B now, not later. On the other hand, with its growing success, B says to its board, "We have had growth in sales, margins, and earnings; give us more expansion funds and we will make more gains." Both actions seem to involve self-fulfilling prophesies.

Given the situation in the mid 1970s, a logical question would surely be that if B had been pursuing this course for several years and still did not have margins as large as A's, what other factors were affecting investment behavior of the two companies? A common answer to such a question would be, "Well B was being strategic. Like the

Japanese, it was buying into this market."* A better answer can be found by tracing the composition of both A's and B's margins and their differing financial structures.

MARGINS VERSUS ASSET TURNOVER

Figure 7–3 shows a plot of operating margins versus asset turnover for the 1977–1979 period for Companies A and B. Confirming what we have observed, A's margins are 38 percent and B's only about 17 percent. But there is also a difference in the asset turnover ratios between A and B—A's asset turnover is about 0.45, resulting in a pre-tax

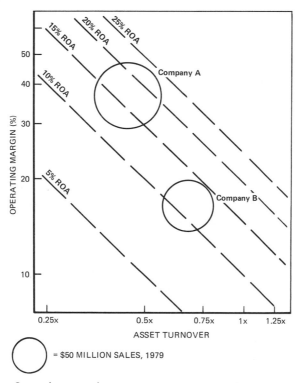

Figure 7–3. Operating margin versus asset turnover for Companies A and B, 1977–1979

---

*Proponents of this attitude excuse such uneconomic behavior by calling it "strategic." True strategic behavior is always economic in our view.

return on assets (ROA) of about 38 × 0.45 = 17 percent, while B's lower margin is combined with an asset turnover of about 0.7 to produce a 17 × 0.7 = 12 percent ROA. An important subsidiary issue, then, is how B is obtaining its higher asset turnover—better asset turnover in the same line of business is in some sense a measure of the quality of management. But asset turnover does not explain the differences—B still has lower ROA, even with higher turnover.

Effects of Corporate Financial Structure

Translating the pre-tax ROAs back through the two companies' capital structures reveals that B's after-tax return on equity (ROE) exceeds A's, because B has greater leverage in its financial structure. The concept is straightforward—if debt has a lower capital cost than equity, then the returns to the proportionately smaller equity base are higher, and these effects can be enhanced by a lower effective tax rate. Company A's pre-tax ROA of 17 percent, from Figure 7-3, results in an after-tax return on equity (ROE) of about 16 percent, while B's slightly more aggressive capital structure translates its 12 percent ROA to an after-tax ROE of 18 percent (see Figure 7-4). B has a little more leverage in its capital structure than A, less corporate overhead, and a much lower effective tax rate.* Which company is performing better? A's margins are still higher, but B's returns to equity are better. The reasons why the two boards of directors reacted differently to expansion proposals is now even more logical—compared to the individual costs of capital, both boards were probably making responsible decisions.

We too often view our competitors through our own eyes. Company A's managers might say, "We ran the numbers on B's new plant and we know his costs. He is not earning enough to justify plant expansion." But they would be looking only at B's manufacturing costs compared to their own lower costs, and comparing these numbers with what *they* had to earn to meet *their* own cost of capital. But because of B's more aggressive capital structure and lower effective tax rate, its cost of capital is lower. Therefore, the earning rate required to satisfy corporate goals for A is greater than for B. We must

---

*The lower effective tax rate is due to investment tax credits, depletion allowances, and interest deductions resulting from the use of leverage. Some of the investment tax credit is related to the business which is the subject of the example, but the majority is related to other businesses in which the corporation operates.

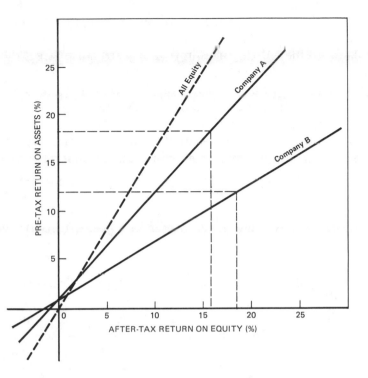

Figure 7-4. Pre-tax return on assets versus after-tax return on equity for Companies A and B, 1979

evaluate each competitor's performance in relation to its cost of capital, not our own. In this instance, both A and B are divisions of larger corporations, so that the strategic decisions concerning corporate and capital structure are not discretionary, they are told what hurdle rates are required to obtain funds from the parent. So it is useful to examine strategic effects resulting from target hurdle rates.

WHEN HURDLE RATES ARE SET

Assume a 15 percent after-tax return on equity, and that this corporate target is general within this industry. Within the industry group, there are differences in the amount of leverage employed by different companies, each with their own risk profiles. Therefore, we might have two firms such as our example companies with Company

B having a little more financial leverage than A, and both targeting a 15 percent return on equity.

How do these differences in financial structure affect the operating hurdle ROAs in the two firms? In the example situation of Figure 7–5, Company A, with less leverage, translates the 15 percent after-tax return on equity to a 26 percent pre-tax operating return on assets, while the more leveraged Company B translates it to only 14 percent. These pre-tax operating rates are the hurdle rates that must be met or exceeded for internal investments in capacity, market development, and other reinvestments, because they represent the internal costs of capital. The firm with lesser leverage has a higher cost of capital which becomes a part of the product cost and affects the price that must be charged, or conversely, given a market price, affects the company profitability.

PRICE/RETURN STRUCTURE, AND REINVESTMENT ECONOMICS

Recall that due to its greater accumulated experience, Company A had the lower cost position in terms of variable manufacturing cost—it was further down the experience curve. But the effect of a higher cost

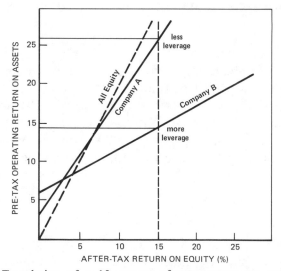

Figure 7–5. Translation of a 15 percent after-tax return on equity to pre-tax operating returns on assets for two firms with different degrees of leverage in their capital structures

of capital can result in the need for a higher required price, as shown in Figure 7–6, which expands the Figure 7–5 analysis. Figure 7–6 traces the 15 percent target return on equity through the differing financial structures, pre-tax operating ROAs, and manufacturing costs, to required price per unit. Company A's 26 percent hurdle ROA translates through the low variable manufacturing cost line to require a higher

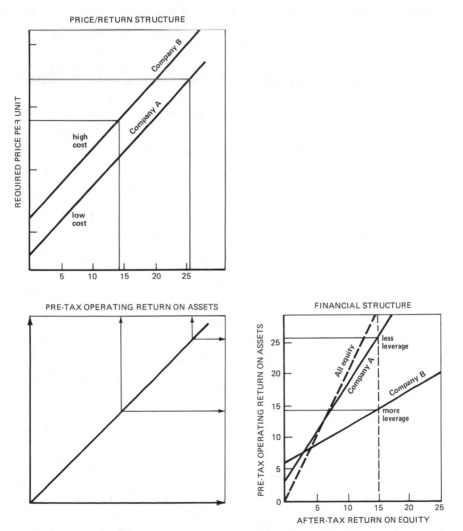

Figure 7–6. Price/return structure for two companies with different degrees of leverage coupled with different manufacturing costs

price, while Company B's 14 percent ROA translates through to require a lower price. Which company is actually the low-cost producer? Company A looked at that question only in terms of variable manufacturing cost. But costs must include the cost of capital, and in these total terms, Company B is actually the low-cost producer. This is not an anomalous result, it is perfectly logical, but commonplace practices lead us to look at cost in a narrow context.

Now, when each company is examining proposals to reinvest in the business by expanding facilities or exploiting new markets, they may find themselves in differing positions in terms of manufacturing costs, but because of different financial structures their costs of capital may also be different. Therefore, the same capital expansion proposal providing perhaps a 20 percent pre-tax operating ROA would be acceptable to Company B but rejected by Company A. The reinvestment economics for B would lead it to be more aggressive and expand, while A would find expansion uneconomic. The relative positions of the two companies in the business are not the same, and in this example instance, the combination of lower manufacturing cost and higher cost of capital for A actually results in a higher required price in the marketplace.

Adding to the concept of the margin paradox, not only does A see shrinking margins for that reason, but it sees unattractive opportunities for reinvestment in the business because of the higher cost of capital. Finding internal investment relatively unattractive also has an effect on manufacturing costs, since productivity-enhancing equipment becomes more difficult to justify. A's logical course is to seek out investment opportunities that exceed *its* cost of capital, which could ultimately mean divesting from its current business. Alternately, A could seek out ways of decreasing its cost of capital. Obviously, the relative importance of manufacturing costs and the cost of capital changes with the individual situation, depending on the complexity and labor/material intensity of the product, and on the capital intensity of the industry. The Company A/B example involved a capital-intensive industry.

When debt is fairly low in cost, the idea of offsetting some manufacturing cost disadvantage with a financial cost advantage works fairly well, but what are the effects during periods of high inflation? To gain insight into the way companies have used leverage in recent times and gauged the resulting risks, examining the components of required return is then useful.

Components of Required Return

During the double-digit inflationary period of the late 1970s and early 1980s, researchers looked at the components of return on equity in the previous low inflation period of the 1960s.[4] They found a real interest rate of about 3 percent that had to be covered, plus a risk premium that ranged from 3 to 9 percent, depending on the business—a total spread of 6 to 12 percentage points including the real interest rate. Typically, a utility was expected to earn 6 percent, and a hot high-tech business 12 percent after tax, but with high associated risks.

But during the late 1970s an additional component had to be added to cover high inflation. Interestingly, researchers estimated that the component attributable to the real interest rate remained almost the same, about 3 percentage points, and the risk premium component and spread also remained about the same, from 3 to 9 percentage points. But because of the addition of 9 to 10 percentage points to the level of returns to cover inflation, the risk premium as a proportion of the average level of returns was much smaller.

This interesting observation—that the risk premium remained about the same—means that the riskiness of a leveraged financial structure in the 1978–1980 period was a much smaller percentage of the total equity return than it was in the 1960s. Hence differences in capital structure were less important in determining the firm's overall cost of capital in the late 1970s than in the 1960s, so strategic use of debt to offset disadvantageous cost position was easier to achieve.

The Japanese steel industry is commonly cited as one that has greater leverage than the U.S. steel industry. Figure 7-7 shows a plot of pretax operating margin versus asset turnover for four major Japanese and six major U.S. steel producers for 1980–1981. The Japanese companies have higher margins and lower asset turnover than the U.S. companies, but with the exception of National Steel, the returns on assets of all the companies seems to fall in the 7.5 to 11 percent range. The operating margin advantage of the Japanese is not surprising based on what we know about their application of advanced steelmaking technology and high productivity, but the low asset turnover engenders wonder. The reasons for the differences in asset turnover are not entirely clear—perhaps the Japanese with newer less depreciated facilities have higher asset bases than the older more depreciated U.S. plants. At any rate, the observation is valid.

But 1980–1981 was still a period of high inflation in the United

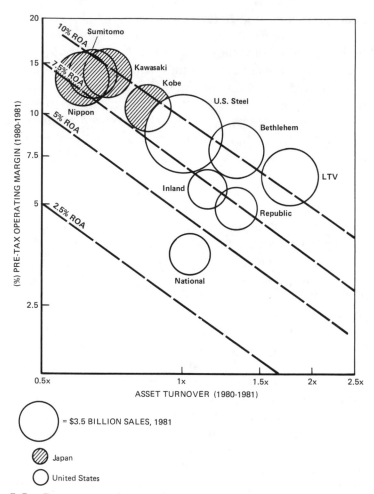

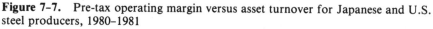

Figure 7-7. Pre-tax operating margin versus asset turnover for Japanese and U.S. steel producers, 1980–1981

SOURCE: Company annual reports.

States, and substantially less inflation in Japan—we trace the pre-tax ROAs through to after-tax returns on equity (ROE), and decompose the result into real returns and inflation. Figure 7–8 shows the relation between pre-tax ROA and after-tax ROE. In general, the Japanese firms have translated their 8 to 10 percent ROAs to ROEs in the range of 15 to 24 percent, averaging about 18 percent. The U.S. companies are in the 3 to 23 percent ROE bracket, but LTV is a great exception at 23 percent—most U.S. companies fall in the 3 to 13 percent range, and the entire U.S. group aggregates to an average 11.5 percent ROE. Ac-

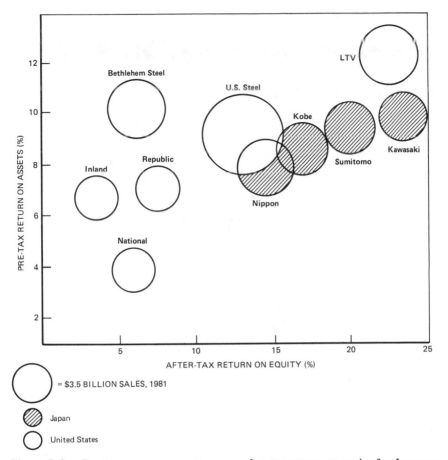

Figure 7-8. Pre-tax return on assets versus after-tax return on equity for Japanese and U.S. steel producers, 1980–1981

Source: Company annual reports.

counting for differences in ROE by differences in leverage is not necessarily a good argument—National Steel is highly leveraged but with very low ROE. LTV has both a high ROA and a high ROE. (Of the U.S. companies, LTV and National were the most levered.) The startling differences are in the "real returns," net after inflation.

The U.S. average after-tax ROE of 11.5 percent in Figure 7-9 covered mostly inflation of almost 10 percentage points, leaving only a small real return. On the other hand, the higher Japanese ROE of approximately 18 percent was mostly real, with only about 2.5 percentage points for inflation. At least during this period of high inflation, the Japanese advantage of 18 percent versus 11.5 percent in

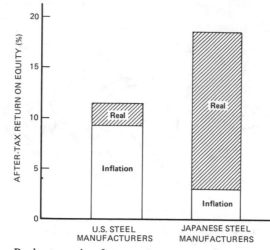

Figure 7-9. Real returns in after-tax return on equity for U.S. and Japanese steel producers, 1980-1981

terms of total ROE is even more dramatic in real terms, net after inflation. But, the argument that the Japanese advantage was solely due to the use of high leverage seems questionable at best.

The margin paradox shows how important differing growth rates can be in the assessment of the future potential of markets—widening margins encourages continuing investment, narrowing margins encourages a producer to look elsewhere for future profits. But in addition, differing financial structures affect product costs, even though direct manufacturing costs are equivalent—the low-cost producer is the one whose combined direct plus capital costs are advantageous. But differences in financial structure also affect the required returns on assets for new investments in process technology, which in turn affects productivity and therefore direct costs. Finally, it appears from the experience of the past twenty years or so, that risk premium remains about the same in periods of low and high inflation. Therefore, differences in capital structure between competitors in times of high inflation can be used strategically to counterbalance manufacturing cost disadvantages.

A Capacity Expansion Example

One of the most common reinvestment projects for a manufacturing firm is capacity expansion. A disguised example of a real situation will serve as a vehicle to illustrate the effects of differing amounts of leverage, the resulting hurdle ROEs for the important competitors, the price/return structure, and a new dimension, relative price versus capacity.

There are four dominant players in the industry, Companies C, D, E, and H, plus two small producers in niches, as shown in the sector chart of Figure 7–10. Company D is the market leader, with C nearly as large. Company H is the aggressive producer and has gained market share against C, D, and E. Both C and D have grown slightly faster than the market, with E seemingly backing out of the picture. The strategic competitive question is, can H continue its aggressive behavior? The industry itself produces an undifferentiated commodity-type product and is very capital intensive, where the cost to bring new capacity on line is quite high. In addition the plants are highly specialized, and once installed are of no use to anyone else, save another competitor. Furthermore, a unit of economical scale is very large. Finally, manufacturing cost is a large part of value added; raw materials are a small part, and the raw materials are available to everyone.[5]

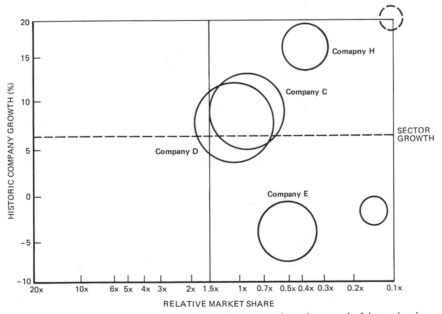

Figure 7–10. Sector chart showing four main competitors in a capital-intensive industry, 1978–1980

FINANCIAL STRUCTURE

The four main competitors have differing financial structures, ranging from E, with nearly an all-equity position, to H which was fairly
highly leveraged, with C and D falling in between. The 1980 period
was one of hope, with the expectation of an end to high inflation and
the prospect of an improved business environment. A 15 percent target after-tax ROE seemed appropriate.

The environment led H to be very aggressive in its capital structure, and to need only about a 12 percent pre-tax ROA for internal
projects, as shown in Figure 7–11. Because of its nearly all-equity
structure, on the other hand, Company E needed more than 26 percent for internal investments to at least equal its cost of capital, with
higher tax rates and lower asset turnover. Companies C and D fell in
between, requiring 19 and 23 percent respectively.

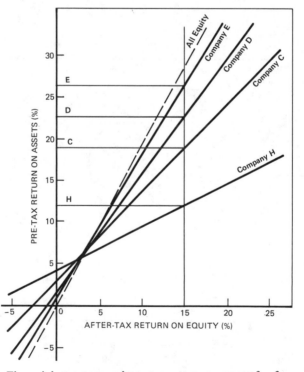

Figure 7–11.   Financial structure and pre-tax return on assets for four competitors
requiring a 15 percent return on equity, 1980

EXPANSION ALTERNATIVES

Looking at expansion alternatives competitively, D would be advised first to compare its alternatives with the best estimates of what H would do, since H was the aggressive challenger to D's rather insecure leadership position. D had the greater experience, and had manufacturing costs that were lower than H's. But because of differing financial structures H required a lower return and hence smaller profit margin to justify an expansion. Figure 7–12 shows for H and D the price required, as compared to the actual price, to generate various pre-tax returns on new assets for several expansion alternatives.[6]

H has two expansion alternatives, a new plant and a process improvement to its existing plant that would increase "throughput," both resulting in the same manufacturing costs but requiring different investments per unit of output. To achieve the 12 percent return on new assests, H requires that prices must rise by approximately 9 percent to justify a new plant, but only by 1 percent to justify its process

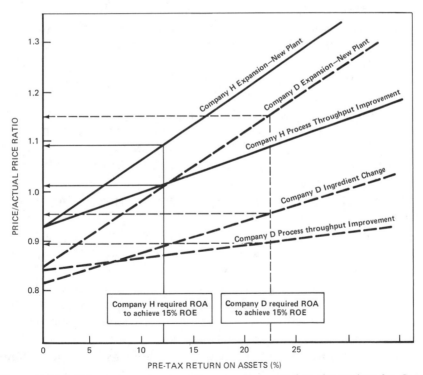

Figure 7–12. Price/return structure for capacity expansion alternatives for Companies D and H

throughput improvement. D has three expansion alternatives, a new plant, a process throughput improvement, and an ingredient change. The first two expansion alternatives result in the same manufacturing cost, while the third results in somewhat lower manufacturing costs. All require different investments per unit of output, with the new plant requiring the largest investment per unit and the process throughput improvement the least. To achieve the 23 percent return on assets, D requires that prices must rise by approximately 15 percent to justify a new plant, more than for H. However, current prices yield returns that more than justify the process thoughput improvement and the ingredient change.

The resulting situation is that if prices do not rise, neither competitor can justify a new plant. At current price levels D can justify the process throughput improvement and ingredient change expansions, while H's process throughput improvement expansion is marginal. Therefore, we would expect a halt to H's aggressive expansion behavior. If prices were to rise, however, H could justify a new plant expansion with a smaller price increase than D, because of H's lower required return on assets target, even though D has lower manufacturing costs. To rule out completely H's continued aggressive expansion behavior the possible level of future prices must be considered.

The long-run price level that prevails balances supply and demand. Capacity sets an upper limit on supply and will determine it in a growing capital-intensive industry such as the one in our example. But capacity depends on the price level, since at a given price only certain expansion alternatives are justified. By examining the expansion alternatives of all the major competitors, as in our example, the increments of capacity that are justified by the various competitors can be determined, depending on the price level.

Figure 7-13 shows the incremental units of capacity for the competitors, the industry capacity depending on the price level. If the expected level of demand at the expected prevailing price is in line with—approximately the same as—the level of justifiable capacity, then the price level should remain stable and future aggressive expansion by H will cease. Of course, it is possible for someone to misforecast and build a new plant or expand an existing one when it is not economically justified. But it is always more difficult to compete with a competitor that is not behaving rationally.

The procedure for competitive capacity-expansion analysis is as follows:

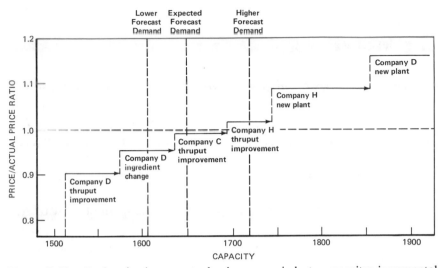

Figure 7-13. Ratio of price to actual price versus industry capacity: incremental units of capacity for the competitors, industry capacity depending on price level

- Examine expansion alternatives for *all* competitors as a function of prevailing price level—what expansions can be justified in terms of return on assets given their differing cost positions and required returns on assets?
- Add expansion alternatives for all competitors to obtain an industry capacity supply curve.
- Check to see if the industry capacity at the forecast (prevailing) price level is in line with demand.
- Determine which competitors can justify expansion at the forecast (prevailing) price level.
- Determine the strategic implications of the results.

Financial Implications of Generic Strategies

Michael Porter[7] classifies what he calls three broad generic strategies: overall cost leadership, differentiation, and focus. We will use these terms for the first two, but we will substitute the term "segmentation" for focus. The strategies are:

- Overall cost leadership
- Differentiation
- Market segmentation

The first two strategies are industry wide. The third, by definition, applies to only a portion of the market. Normally only one of these generic strategies can be employed in a particular business unit. That is, a mix of the strategies is not appropriate. However, different strategies can and should be employed in different business units within the same company. The test of whether or not business units are really in different industries is that the industry analysis results in a different assessment of such competitive forces as the threat of new competitors entering the industry, the rivalry among industry competitors, the threat of substitute products, bargaining power of suppliers, and bargaining power of customers.

OVERALL COST LEADERSHIP

This strategy requires a concentration in the production system on all the elements that make low cost possible: in-line operations; fabrication and assembly lines; equipment dedicated to a restricted mix of products; capital intensity in the form of specialized equipment, mechanization, automation, and robotics, all especially designed for the specific manufacturing problem; and usually highly specialized jobs.

Usually the cost leadership strategy also involves production to stock, since part of the strategy is to make the product available on demand, or off-the-shelf. Where economies of scale are possible, they are used in this strategy, as are the benefits that come from cumulative organizational learning, and the experience curve. In interrelated businesses attention must be given to issues of economies of scope as well as scale. Products are designed for producibility, so that experience curves can take off from a completely different point than for competitors who follow alternate strategies. The organizational structure places emphasis on cost control and on getting product out the door so that sales are not lost because the product is not available when demanded. Specialization also makes cost minimization possible in other functional areas, such as R&D, service, sales, advertising, and personnel.

DIFFERENTIATION STRATEGY

In this strategy, the firm attempts to differentiate itself from the pack by offering something that is perceived by the industry (and its customers) as being unique. It could be the highest quality (Rolls Royce or Mercedes Benz), innovation (Hewlett Packard), or innovation coupled with the willingness to be flexible in the product design (Ferrari or Maserati). All these examples of quality, innovation, and flexibility have extremely important implications for the production system and the way it is designed and managed. In the general sense, the requirement is to be flexible in order to cope with the demands on the system. Brand image is important to this strategy. There may be other ways that an organization differentiates itself—for example, a strong dealer network (Zenith), an extremely well designed distribution system (Gillette or Hunt Wesson), or excellent service.

MARKET SEGMENTATION

This strategy attempts to meet the special needs of a particular market or to provide lower costs for that market segment, or both. While the first two strategies are industry-wide, market segmentation means that we focus on a particular customer group, a segment of the broad product line, a geographic portion of the market, and so on. It selects a market segment on some basis, and tries to do an outstanding job of serving that market. Part of the rationale is that the industry-wide leaders cannot serve all segments of the market equally well, so there are important niches for specialists. Actually, nearly everyone but the industry leaders should be looking for a comfortable but viable niche.

Thus the segmentation strategy could take an approach that combines one of the first two strategies with it. For example, the supplier of a particular appliance to Sears must undoubtedly adopt a low-cost substrategy in order to meet the requirements for such a mass retailer.

Another example is the firm that limits itself to small special orders within an industry dominated by giants who cannot serve this market niche very well, and indeed, do not want to serve it. Yet there may be a substantial market for small special orders. In order to serve this segment of the market, manufacturing facilities must be flexible to handle all types and sizes in small volume. There must be frequent changeover of machines for the many different types of orders that flow through the shop. The equipment must be flexible to handle this variety. There is little application for automation and robotics here, though CAD/CAM (Computer Aided Design/Computer Aided Manufacturing) may change that situation in the reasonably near future.

Therefore, while segmentation can emulate either of the first two strategies in a more limited way, it is unlikely that it could ever achieve the market share of those in the industry that are attempting industry-wide strategies. The segmented firm is likely to be smaller, perhaps lacking the financial resources to attempt an industry-wide strategy.

The V Curve

The three generic strategies that were discussed briefly above each provide defenses against the forces in the economic environment. The firms that develop strategies within the framework of one of these strategies will earn higher than average returns in their industries. The implication is that firms that do not develop one of the basic strategies will earn lower than average returns in their industries.

Porter[8] calls this being "stuck in the middle." Such a firm lacks the market share, capital investment, and resolve to use the low-cost strategy, the industry-wide differentiation necessary to obviate the need for a low-cost position, or the segmentation to create differentiation or a low-cost position in a more limited sphere.

If some of the firms in an industry follow one of the three basic strategies and earn higher than average returns, then some firms in the industry must be earning lower than average returns—not all firms can be above the average. The in-between firms lose all the high-margin business. They cannot compete well for high-volume business from customers who demand low prices, for the high-margin business of the differentiated firms, nor for the segmented business that is either low-cost or differentiated.

The high returns are earned by the industry-wide firms with large market share (the low-cost and differentiated firms) and the segmented firms with small market share. Those firms in between, in terms of market share, earn the lower than average returns. The result is the V-curve, an example of which is shown in Figure 7–14 for agricultural equipment industry firms. Deere & Company is the industry leader and earns high returns. However, small specialty manufacturers such as Hesston and Sperry-New Holland also earn high returns. Massey Ferguson and J. I. Case are trapped in the valley,

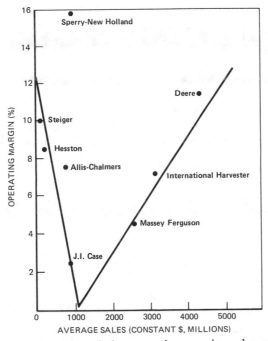

Figure 7-14. The V-curve for relating operating margin and market share in the agricultural equipment industry, 1978–1981

Source: Company annual and 10-K reports.

and International Harvester has a substantial market share, but earns low returns.

In the auto industry, for example, Toyota (low cost) and Mercedes Benz (differentiated) earn above average returns, while Chrysler, Ford, and Fiat are in the valley. Porsche is segmented with a small industry market share, and American Motors has attempted to establish a segmented position.

The V-curve seems to characterize companies within a wide variety of industries; for example, Figure 7–15 is a V-curve for the chemical industry. Dupont, with the largest market share is the overall cost leader, producing a tremendous variety of chemicals and chemical products including fibers (nylon, polyester, acrylic, aramid), commodity and specialty chemicals, pigments and resins, elastomers, films, plastic products, and so on.

Then, of course, our discussion of Figure 6–14 in Chapter 6 was focused on the strategic direction of Clorox, emerging from its strong

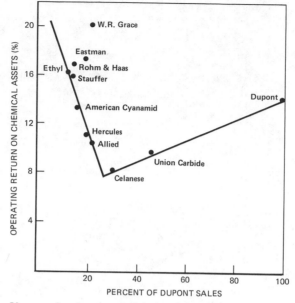

Figure 7-15.   V-curve for the chemical industry, 1981

SOURCES: Company annual and 10-K reports, and *Value Line*.

position with a segmented strategy. But by fitting two straight lines to the data presented, we have a V-curve for the household products business.[9]

Concluding Remarks

The competitive situation is not necessarily the same for all players—the playing field is not level. The rapid growth of one competitor can put price pressure on an existing leader, even though that leader has lower costs and better margins, applying the concepts of the margin paradox. Differences in financial leverage can produce different costs of capital that must be added to the manufacturing costs to determine who in the industry is in fact the low cost producer. These effects are reflected in the reinvestment economics of competitors, affecting them differentially in their application of productivity-enhancing technology. Particularly in capital intensive industries, the cost of capital can tip the balance of costs in favor of a higher variable cost producer. Some companies pride themselves in having virtually no debt, as did Eastman Kodak until recently, still revering the principle laid down by its founder rather than examining its strategic position vis-à-vis its competitors in today's world. We are not necessarily recommending higher leverage with its attendant risk, but are pointing out the resulting competitive differences among firms with different degrees of leverage.

We think that a current example of the margin paradox is the integrated steel industry in the United States. The aggressive and efficient producers in West Germany and particularly Japan were on experience curves that were similar to the U.S. companies', similar to those shown in Figure 7–1, and they gained experience at a very fast rate. Seeing widening margins, the aggressive foreign competitors invested even more heavily in improved process technology and in markets to exploit the ever improving situation, which simply reenforced their developing advantage. On the other hand, U.S. steel companies saw narrowing margins that were less attractive for further investment, and they moved slowly into important technologies such as continuous casting and automatic process controls, thus fulfilling their dim view of the future. Combine the concept of the margin paradox with the exchange rate disadvantages discussed in Chapter 4 and we have a reenforcing degenerative cycle that produces the present situation for the U.S. steel industry.

Part IV

Scenario Analysis and Implementation

Chapter 8

SCENSIM for Strategic Scenario Analysis

Strategic analysis examines the contours of the playing field to find the structural strengths and weaknesses of a company and its competitors. It seeks to know the competitors almost as well as the company itself, and certainly would know them as well if it could. As we have noted, the information available in public sources is extensive if one knows what to look for and where to look—knowledge of competitors can be extensive. The process of analysis distills the information available into more useful forms that allow comparisons between the players: comparative value-added streams, comparative experience curves, the growth/share matrix, sector charts, share/momentum charts, margin/turnover charts, activity analysis, and other analytical tools, each especially suited to particular situations.

In previous chapters we developed ways of analyzing a firm in relation to its competitors. We first took an industry view, examining the participation of competitors in the activities of the value-added stream, and examining capacity demand patterns, prices, and competitive dynamics. Then we examined market structures, particularly with respect to the degree of consolidation, and international aspects of the market, always focusing attention on the relative position of the competitors.

Finally, focusing on the individual company, we showed how strategic strengths and weaknesses can be revealed by an analysis of the product structure and how the products are related in the technological sense, and in the market. The characteristics of related and unrelated diversification and acquisitions, and desirable and undesirable sectors were analyzed, and analytical techniques were developed to show which business units were adding value to the firm and which subtracting value. We developed techniques for analyzing the financial implications of strategic positions, showing how the cost of capital can have important cost-price effects on competitive position, and how differential inflation rates for competitors in different countries can have startling effects on the required return on equity.

By the process of careful analysis, the structural strengths and weaknesses of a firm and its competitors can be exposed. Once these strengths and weaknesses are understood there are never more than a few viable strategic alternatives, and scenarios can then be developed to achieve the goals of these alternatives.

Strategic Scenario Analysis

Analytical techniques can also help in comparing the desirability of alternative strategic scenarios. Such scenarios should be developed by the managers themselves, for they must ultimately implement them. The role of analysis should be to assist the managers in determining and representing the strategic impact of the alternate directions they wish to consider so that they may make a more informed choice.

The impacts and responses can be complex and detailed, laying out in some detail the competitive responses to a chosen strategy. And not only the competitive responses, but the factors that affect the outcome must be considered, be they environmental, technological, political, or managerial. Traditional "what if" analysis can be very useful, but a more organized approach is really needed. The potential competitive responses and other factors must be characterized and quantified, and their impacts considered, both individually and together.

The methodology for analyzing scenarios presented here, called SCENSIM (*SCEN*ario *SIM*ulation), simulates the returns or other variables and displays the results graphically in such a way that managers can appraise the alternatives and decide. We will describe the technique in both general and specific terms, and then provide the results of real examples at the level of the business unit, and at the corporate level.

SCENSIM

The essense of SCENSIM is to present the risks associated with strategic scenarios in a visual manner so they can be easily comprehended and compared. The unique part of SCENSIM is not in the mathematical concepts or the computational techiques, rather it is in the way management's scenarios and concerns are presented, providing a different way of looking at the strategy planning world. When the risks associated with different scenarios are viewed in this graphic way, one gains an insight into the nature of risks faced that the equivalent word statement fails to capture.

We start with a simple example where management has isolated two different ways of achieving strategic objectives. For simplicity assume that both have the same level of capital intensity so that sales and earnings are a fair measure of performance. In the absence of other knowledge about the forecast performance of alternatives A and B shown in Figure 8–1a, most individuals would choose B over A. Alternative B shows higher sales and earnings than A, and thus, given the capital intensity assumption, provides "more bang for the buck."

But what about the uncertainties? The one thing that the managers know for certain is that B's and A's sales and earnings are only

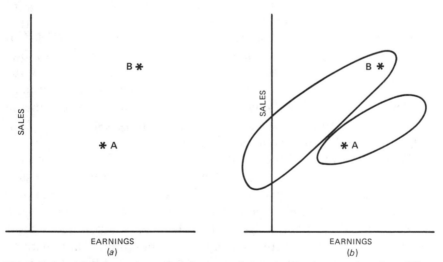

Figure 8–1. (a) Sales and earnings forecasts for two strategic scenarios, A and B as point estimates, and (b) as clouds of possible outcomes

* = Forecasts as point estimates.

forecasts—for a variety of reasons the actuals could be higher or lower. The SCENSIM technique involves eliciting from managers the issues or events that might affect the outcomes of sales and earnings for A and B. What are the key issues—the critical events that may determine whether or not forecasts are met? We seek the issues that provide the stimulus for "knots in the stomach," or the dreams of what could make the business blossom. Not simply whether or not prices will increase or decrease, but the strategic generators of such results, such as the installation of a competitor's new plant, the shutting down of a plant by the Occupational Safety and Health Administration, the introduction of a revolutionary new process or product by a competitor, or the effects of increased competitive intensity. The issues on which traditional "what if" analysis would focus. Not the large number of details associated with a business, but the dozen or so critical issues of strategic importance.

Managers know the key issues that will affect their businesses—they live with them on a daily basis. Analysts need to sit with them, encouraging them to articulate these issues and to specify the degree to which these events may occur. In these sessions with managers, analysts need to be good sparring partners and to force specificity. It is important that managers' descriptions of events be carefully articulated so that analysts can quantify the impact of the key issues on the performance variables. It is usually the analysts rather than managers who are best able to quantify these impacts.

The next step is to calculate the impact of the managers' list of critical events on prices, volumes, and costs—that is, on the variables that determine sales and earnings for this example. Accounting for the occurrence or nonoccurrence of each of the critical issues, as well as the level of occurrence, singly and in combination, determines a "cloud" of possible outcomes for sales and earnings estimates, shown in Figure 8-1b for the two alternatives.*

When the impact of the events is considered, it is no longer clear that B is better than A—the risks inherent in each alternative raise new issues. While B has the higher sales-earnings point forecast, the impact of critical events indicates a considerable downside risk—it could be a loser. On the other hand, the result of the events impacting A show small downside risk, but considerable upside potential. Though many of A's outcomes are not as good as those forecast for B, its minimum

---

*A more detailed example indicating this computational procedure is presented in the appendix to this chapter.

returns are a relatively sure bet. The potential outcomes for the two strategic scenarios do not dictate the decision. They do, however, provide managers with information concerning the risks in a comprehensible form that is of considerable value in making the decision.

In the preceding general example, sales and earnings were a valid representation because of the simplifying assumptions, but the nature of the technique does not limit the variables to sales and earnings. Scenarios can be presented in terms of whatever variables best represent them. For example, the relevant variables in high capital intensity situations might be measures of return and payback, and are discussed in one of the examples shown later in the chapter.

With this general background regarding the SCENSIM approach, we now develop the concepts more fully, and add controllable uncertainty in scenario analysis.

Sensitivity Analysis with SCENSIM

Following the analysis phase, profiling our competitors, gaining insight into the competitive dynamics of the industry and activity streams, and so on, management has selected two or three scenarios of particular interest, but we will concentrate on only one of them.

In the process of eliciting the events that could impact this scenario, management has focused on four events: (1) possible changes in economic conditions, (2) the possible development of a new product by the company in line with the strategic scenario, (3) the possibility of increased competition, and (4) the possibility that manufacturing costs do not decline as fast as projected. The four events impact prices, volumes, and costs in different ways, as follows:

	IMPACTS		
EVENTS	PRICES	VOLUMES	COSTS
Economic conditions	X	X	X
New product introduction		X	
Increased competition	X	X	
Increased manufacturing costs			X

Given the occurrence or nonoccurrence of these four events, possibly at different levels, the impacts on prices, volumes, and costs are quantified to produce impacts on sales and earnings, so the cloud of sales-earnings uncertainty shown in Figure 8-2 can be drawn. The

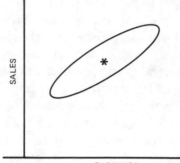

Figure 8-2. Sales/earnings cloud of uncertainty for a company, reflecting the impact of four events

∗ = Company sales/earnings forecast, and sales/earnings mean for the cloud of uncertainty.

star in the middle of the cloud represents the company forecast, and also represents the mean of the cloud in this instance. (Methods for accomplishing this task are shown in the appendix to this chapter). The cloud represents both the occurrence and nonoccurrence of the events at different levels, as well as the likely combinations.

The cloud of uncertainty shown in Figure 8-2 includes the effects of all four of the events. But what happens to the cloud if we assume that the new product is successfully developed? The shaded area of the cloud in Figure 8-3*a* represents the situation under the assumption that the new product is successfully developed, but with all other uncertainty remaining. In that situation the size of the cloud is decreased and the mean value of sales and earnings has increased. We see that in this example, the cloud of uncertainty is very sensitive to the new product development. If we could be sure of success with the new product development, the strategic scenario looks excellent, even with the other uncertainties. Unlike simple "what if" analysis, we are not simply comparing the expected outcome if we successfully develop the new product with what we expect if we do not. Rather we are comparing the expected outcome *and* the cloud of uncertainty around it depending on the other events, with what we expect and the cloud of uncertainty around it if we do not develop the new product.

We can perform sensitivity analyses on the other events in the same way. Figure 8-3*b* shows the effect of assuming that competition does in fact intensify, eliminating that uncertainty from the cloud. As we

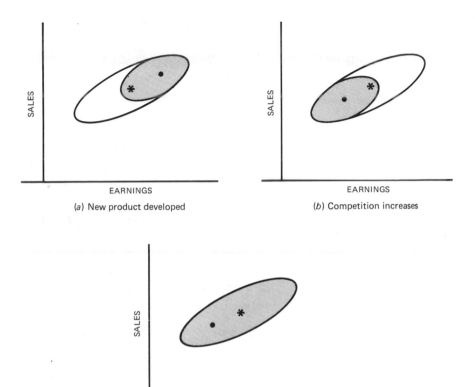

(a) New product developed   (b) Competition increases

(c) Manufacturing costs do not decline

Figure 8-3. Sensitivity analysis on cloud of uncertainty when (a) the new product development is assumed successful, (b) competition is assumed to increase, and (c) manufacturing costs do not decline as expected

* = Company sales/earnings forecast. • = Sales/earnings mean for cloud of uncertainty.

would expect, mean sales and earnings decline, and the remaining cloud of uncertainty is smaller.

On the other hand, if manufacturing costs do not decline as fast as predicted, the effects on the size of the cloud of uncertainty are small, for all practical purposes affecting only the mean values slightly, as shown in Figure 8-3c. The basic uncertainty associated with the scenario has not changed. This happens because of the effect that manufacturing cost has in the particular example chosen. In other situations, it could have important effects, but in this example manufacturing cost is not of great strategic importance.

CONTROLLABLE AND UNCONTROLLABLE UNCERTAINTY

*Dear God, give us the strength to accept with serenity the things that
cannot be changed. Give us the courage to change the things that can
and should be changed. And give us the wisdom to distinguish one
from the other.*

Management can influence the occurrence of some events, but
may have little or no influence over others. For example, the uncertainty associated with economic conditions is largely uncontrollable
by managers—they must deal with it as it happens, unfortunately remaining largely in reactive modes. But other events such as new product development can definitely be influenced. Managers can be proac-
tive and make the new product development a success. So this is
another dimension of sensitivity—in a strategic scenario, what portion of the uncertainty is controllable and what portion uncontrollable? Is the strategic scenario largely subject to perverse winds of
chance occurrence, or can managers have an important influence in its
achievement?

Segregating the uncertainty cloud into areas that are controllable
and uncontrollable is useful. Again, the managers concerned are the
ones to indicate the degree of control they feel they have over the
events they have developed. Given that information, an uncertainty
profile such as Figure 8–4 can be generated for the uncontrollable
uncertainty by considering only the uncontrollable events; that is, by
assuming all the controllable events occur as forecast.

Figure 8–4 shows the cloud of uncertainty for two scenarios A and
B. While the expected earnings for scenario B are higher, scenario A
has greater upside potential with lower downside risk, making it
perhaps more desirable. While most of B's uncertainty cannot be influenced by managerial action, A's can be influenced, providing
another powerful reason to favor A over B. On the other hand, all A's
uncontrollable uncertainty represents downside risk.

The fact that some of the uncertainty is uncontrollable does not
mean that management has no role. We can divide management activity in this regard into the following matrix:

	Controllable Events	Uncontrollable Events
Strategic Impact	Strategic Plans	Strategic Contingencies
Operational Impact	Tactical Plans	Tactical Contingencies

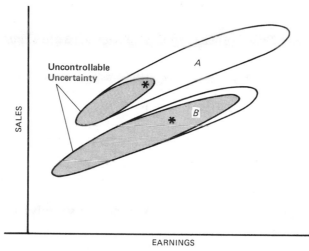

Figure 8-4. Uncertainty clouds for two strategic scenarios with different areas of controllable uncertainty

* = Company sales/earnings forecast.

Management can develop strategic and tactical plans for the controllable events that should have impact at these levels. But while management cannot control some events, they can think in terms of strategic or tactical contingencies—"If the economy takes a downturn, we would make the following changes to the plans."

Applications of SCENSIM

We now turn to actual examples of the application of SCENSIM in business unit and corporate environments. The appropriate measures of strategic plans and uncertainty vary with the application, but in each instance, the representation of the cloud of uncertainty for alternate strategic scenarios contributes an important dimension for appraising alternatives that was important to the strategy selection process.

A Product-Line Example

A common strategic issue is centered on the mix of products in a line, how they are related in cost, capacity requirements, profitability, and so on. Following is an analysis of the product line of a major SBU within a large corporation. The product line was industrial in nature; that is, it was sold to other manufacturers for use in their products, and in some applications it accounted for virtually all the cost and value of the final product while in others it represented a minor cost. The product was "structural" in that it was used to build things in a variety of end-use products—ranging from high-tech (aircraft and aerospace) to low-tech (automobiles)—that had very different market growth rates.

The product was made from unique ingredients manufactured only by the SBU, and with virtually no other use. There was limited "in kind" competition in Europe and Japan, and these competitors also made their own ingredients for internal use only. In addition, there were many functionally equivalent competitive products based on a very different technologies. The SBU's product and production process was protected by patents, but the strength of this protection was questionable, particularly in foreign countries.

Finally, the production process was very capital intensive, and a significant capacity expansion was about to be completed. The expansion required three years to build, and was a major, almost "bet the company" investment.

Strategic Events. The strategic events for the product line example are shown in Table 8–1, grouped into 18 major categories. The im-

TABLE 8–1. **Definition of Events and Their General Impacts for the Product Line Example**

Event	General Impact
1. ECONOMIC ACTIVITY	
GNP growth 2 percentage points more than forecast	• Approximately 3 percentage points higher volume growth in commodity end-use markets.
	• 4 percentage points higher volume growth in industrial and leisure end-use markets with slightly higher prices.
	• 5 percentage points higher volume growth in high-tech and marine end-use markets with moderately higher prices.
	• Prices in military end-use markets moderately higher.
GNP growth 2 percentage points less than forecast	• 2 percentage points lower volume growth in commodity end-use markets with slightly lower prices.
	• 2 percentage points lower volume

TABLE 8-1.   **Definition of Events and Their General Impacts for the Product Line Example, Cont.**

EVENT	GENERAL IMPACT
	growth in industrial end-use markets.
	•3 percentage points lower volume growth in leisure end-use markets with moderately lower prices.
	•1 percentage point lower volume growth in high-tech markets.
2. INFLATION	
Inflation 3 percentage points more than forecast	•Wage and material costs 3% more than forecast.
	•Prices in commodity markets 2% more and prices in specialty markets 3% more.
Inflation 2 percentage points less than forecast	•Wage and material costs 2% less than forecast.
	•Prices 2% less in all markets.
3. DOLLAR EXCHANGE RATES	
Dollar appreciates 10% against European currencies	•Foreign nonmilitary market prices 5% lower, volumes 20% lower.
Dollar depreciates 15% against European currencies	•Foreign nonmilitary market prices 5% higher, volumes 10% higher.
4. PRODUCT DURABILITY	
Insufficient for continuous duty applications in commodity market	•Commodity market volume down 40%, but average price up slightly due to mix change.
5. LOWER PRICES FOR FUNCTIONAL EQUIVALENT IN COMMODITY MARKET	
Moderately lower prices for functional equivalent	•Commodity market volume down 10%, prices down 5%.
Substantially lower prices for functional equivalent	•Commodity market volume down 20%, prices down 10%.
6. PREMIUM END COMMODITY MARKET PRODUCT	
Market exceeds expectations	•Premium end commodity market volume up 65% and commodity market prices up approximately 2% due to mix change.
Market does not develop	•No premium end commodity market volume and commodity market prices down approximately 3% due to mix change.
7. WORLD OIL PRICES	
Very much higher	•Commodity market demand lower in all segments by approximately 12%.
Moderately higher	•Commodity market demand lower in all segments by approximately 6%.

TABLE 8-1.   Definition of Events and Their General Impacts for the Product Line Example, Cont.

EVENT	GENERAL IMPACT
Slightly lower	•Commodity market demand higher in all segments by approximately 2%.
8. MARINE MARKETS	
Product acceptance high	•Marine market volume 100% above forecast.
Product acceptance moderate	•Marine market volume 50% above forecast.
9. HIGH-TECH MARKETS	
Faster growth than expected	•Volume in high-tech end-use markets grows 10 percentage points faster than forecast and prices up by 5%.
Slower growth than expected	•Volume in high-tech end-use markets grows 5 percentage points slower than forecast.
10. MILITARY PROCUREMENT PROGRAMS	
Substantial increases in programs using product	•Volume in military end-use markets up 80%, prices up 20%.
Moderate increase in programs using product	•Volume in military end-use markets up 30%, prices up 10%.
11. PRODUCT FAILURE IN MILITARY APPLICATIONS	
Occurs	•Volume in military end-use markets down by 90% and volume in high-tech end-uses down by 35%, from potential product liability fears.
12. INCREASED PENETRATION IN HIGH-TECH AND END-USE MARKETS	
Some increased penetration	•Volume in high-tech end-use markets up by approximately 20% and prices up by approximately 7%, mostly due to mix change.
Greatly increased penetration	•Volume in high-tech end-use markets up by approximately 38% and prices up by approximately 14%, somewhat due to mix and somewhat due to demand.
13. PRODUCT ACCEPTED IN CONSTRUCTION INDUSTRY	
Faster than forecast	•Volume in construction market up by 25%.
Much faster than forecast	•Volume in construction market up by 40%.

TABLE 8-1. **Definition of Events and Their General Impacts for the Product Line Example, Cont.**

Event	General Impact
14. INCREASED PENETRATION IN TRANSPORTATION MARKET	
Accepted for vehicle surface cover or skin	•Volume in transportation end-use market up by 40%.
Accepted as structural member as well	•Volume in transportation end-use market up 90% and prices up by 5%, due to mix changes.
15. INCREASED PENETRATION IN INDUSTRIAL MARKETS	
More than forecast	•Volume in industrial end-uses up by 15%.
Much more than forecast	•Volume in industrial end-uses up by 25% and prices up 5%.
Very much more than forecast	•Volume in industrial end-uses up by 40% and prices up 10%.
16. IN-KIND COMPETITOR BUILDS PLANT IN EUROPE	
Small plant	•Military end-use market in Europe closed off. Volume in all other end-uses in Europe drops by 40% and prices drop by 15%. Volume in Far East drops by 15% in all end uses except high tech.
Medium plant	•Military end-use market in Europe closed off. Volume in all other end-uses in Europe drops by 65% and prices drop by 20%. Volume in Far East drops by 25% and prices by 5% in all end uses.
17. COST REDUCTION PROGRAM	
Ingredient cost reduction target missed	•Ingredient cost decreases 1 percentage point slower per year.
Ingredient cost reduction not achieved	•Ingredient cost does not decrease at all.
18. LABOR COST	
Labor rates increase faster than inflation	•Labor costs rise 1 percentage point faster than inflation.
Labor rates increase much faster than inflation	•Labor costs rise 2 percentage points faster than inflation.

NOTE: The number of combinations of the preceding set of events is approximately 306 million.

pacts listed are those indicated by the managers involved, and reflect their major concerns and best estimates. The truly quantitative impact of events on sales and earnings was prepared by the analysts, and

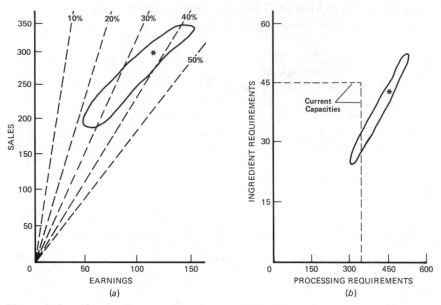

Figure 8-5. Clouds of uncertainty for (*a*) 1987 sales and earnings and (*b*) 1987 related ingredients and processing requirements

NOTE: Rays emanating from the origin are constant margin lines.

represents an analytical level below the ones shown, and the managers were not involved in that step.

When translated into sales-earnings impacts, these strategic events produced a cloud of uncertainty shown in Figure 8-5*a,* aggregated for all products. Although the degree of uncertainty was fairly high, since sales could vary from $190 million to $350 million and earnings from $50 million to $150 million, margins were in the 20 to 45 percent range. The company forecasts for sales and earnings of $300 million and $110 million respectively were only slightly less than the mean sales and earnings estimates based on the cloud of uncertainty of $280 million and $105 million. But these sales-earnings scenarios did not reflect needed coordination with capacity requirements.

Different combinations of strategic events may lead to the same dollar volumes of sales, but different product mixes may lead to different capacity utilizations. The mapping of event impact on capacity utilization is shown in Figure 8-5*b.* The ingredients represented a precursor or raw material for processing, and were produced in a separate plant. The cloud of uncertainty for ingredients versus processing requirements shows sufficient ingredients capacity for most of the outcomes, falling short of the possible maximum requirements.

However, the processing capacity falls somewhat short of even the forecast and cloud mean, and could not meet many of the goals.

Sensitivity Analysis. With the capacity imbalance between ingredients and processing, an analysis of various aspects of the product mix was examined through the SCENSIM technique. What impact would changes in the product mix have on sales, earnings, and margins, as well as the capacity constraints? First, we deal with the effects of not offering the low-contribution items in the product line. Figure 8-6a shows the effects on sales, earnings, and margins, and Figure 8-6b the effects in relation to the current capacity constraints. The sales-earnings cloud is lowered, the forecast reduced, and margins lowered to some extent. These overall effects are not large. But while the processing capacity is brought under control, the elimination of low-contribution items creates a very large excess capacity in ingredients—solving one capacity-imbalance problem but creating another.

Next, the business was divided on the basis of markets served. The commodity products had always been regarded as the "flywheel" of

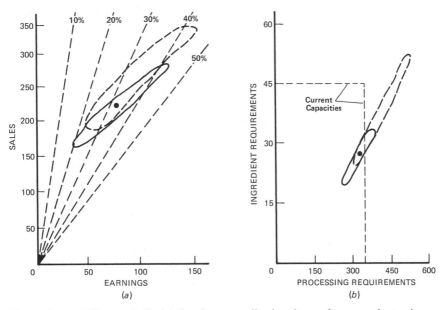

Figure 8-6. Effects of eliminating low-contribution items from product mix on clouds of uncertainty for (*a*) 1987 sales and earnings and (*b*) 1987 ingredients and processing requirements

Note: Rays emanating from the origin are constant margin lines.

the business. Earlier in the product's history, the commodity items were predicted to account ultimately for virtually all the demand. But in fact, commodity demand had become a smaller and smaller portion of the total, and the so-called "tag ends" seemed to be growing. The tag ends were aggregated, renamed a more respectable "specialty products," and analyzed as a group. Figure 8–7 shows the effects. Note that in Figure 8–7a, contribution has been substituted for earnings in the horizontal scale, to avoid the problems of allocating overhead costs to the two groups of end-use markets for the products.

In terms of sales and contribution in Figure 8–7a, specialty products have become the new flywheel of the business, accounting for most of the sales, but more important they command high contributions averaging $150 million. They were high-margin products, but they required much more processing capacity per unit of output than the commodity products.

Commodity products not only account for a smaller portion of sales, but contribution is forecast to be $50 million, and the mean of the cloud is only about $40 million. As shown in Figure 8–7b, the existing processing capacity was ample to accommodate the specialty products, though excess ingredients capacity was still an issue.

The information from the commodity-specialty SCENSIM analy-

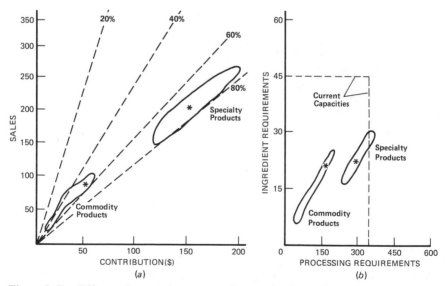

Figure 8–7. Effects of separating commodity and specialty products: (a) 1987 sales and contribution and (b) 1987 ingredients and processing requirements

NOTE: Rays emanating from the origin are constant contribution lines.

sis was very important in the managers' thinking regarding which portions of the business were really important, and led to the desire to see which portions of the clouds of uncertainty of each of these pieces of the business were controllable and which uncontrollable. Figure 8-8 shows this analysis. It had been assumed that managers were more in control of things in commodity products, but conventional wisdom was overturned by the results. Most of the risk in commodity products was uncontrollable. On the other hand, a very large fraction of the risk in specialty products could be influenced by management.

Since one of the critical issues was the allocation of sales, engineering, and other technical assistance in the most effective way, Figure 8-8 clearly showed that it did not make a great deal of sense to pour more resources into commodity products, especially since by the assessments anything they could do, including allocation of more resources, would have very little influence on outcomes. When commodities were clearly regarded as the flywheel of the business, backing them with more resources had seemed logical. But if the impact of these resources was minimal, a reallocation was a more acceptable, though "gut-wrenching," action.

The scenario analysis did not help redress the capacity imbalance problem, but it led to a restructuring of resources to put them where managers could make things happen, and a recognition that there was a new core to the business.

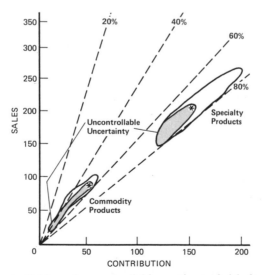

Figure 8-8. Controllable and uncontrollable portions of risk for commodity and specialty products, 1987

AN OIL FIELD DEVELOPMENT STRATEGY

One of the strategies for oil field development is to employ secondary or enhanced techniques in the waning years of a field's life to speed up or further recover the remaining oil. One such technique is called waterflooding. In simple terms, water is injected into the field to increase pressure. This *may* make it possible to recover oil faster or obtain additional oil from the field. Employing this technique requires additional investment, in an attempt to achieve higher returns earlier, but at the cost of lower returns later. The cash flow forecasts with successful waterflood are shown in Figure 8-9. The field had already been developed, so the base case (solid line) represents the positive cash flow without waterflood, and the cash flow with successful waterflood is the dashed line. The difference between the two lines represents the incremental investment required between 1979 and the middle of 1985, and incremental cash returns from the investment beyond that time.

Strategic Events.   The cash flow forecasts assume that waterflood is successful. While the technique is well known, however, results are not always predictable. In this instance, not everyone within the company thought that it would be successful. The only way to be sure of success or failure is to do it, and this is expensive and irreversible. Even though the investment decision itself is controllable, once made, the outcome becomes uncontrollable. In addition there were other important events that contributed to the uncertainty of the financial outcomes, such as well-head pressure changes, the amount of the reserve in the ground, oil prices, the demand for oil, and so on.

Given these inputs, the SCENSIM technique was applied to calculate the clouds of uncertainty for the base case and for incremental waterflood, as shown in Figure 8-10. Since the major strategic scenarios involved widely different investments, we use a measure of return (discounted cash flow) on the vertical axis, and a measure of risk (year of payback*) on the horizontal axis.

The time of the analysis was 1979, so the base case reflects variations in return resulting from all the uncertain events other than waterflood. The basic investment in the field had already been made, so payback was not uncertain—the main uncertainty was in the mag-

*Actually in this instance payback plus 10 percent was used to compensate for the high levels of inflation at the time. Other adjustments to the basic payback measure might have included the cost of capital, depending on the circumstances.

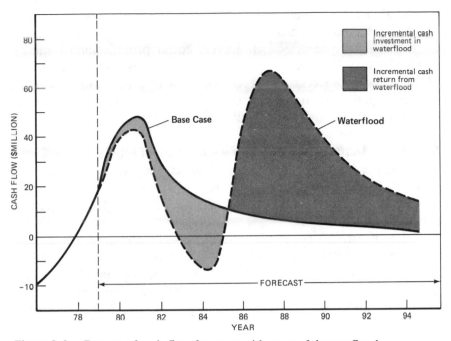

Figure 8-9. Pattern of cash flow forecasts with successful waterflood

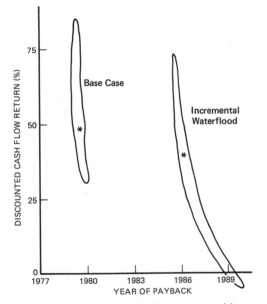

Figure 8-10. Clouds of uncertainty for the base case, and incremental waterflood
∗ = Company forecast.

nitude of the percentage of the discounted cash flow return, which varied from 30 to 85 percent.

Incremental waterflood, however, could provide handsome returns of nearly 75 percent on the incremental investment, but because of the uncertain success of the technique, the returns could be very low or even negative. Also, the year of payback of the incremental investment could be as early as 1985 or as late as 1990.

Sensitivity Analysis.   Two major events were of interest in sensitivity analysis, the impact on the cloud of uncertainty if waterflood were successful, and the effect of passing the windfall profits tax on oil drilling ventures. The cloud of uncertainty for the former event is shown in Figure 8-10.

If the uncertainty concerning the success of waterflood is removed as in Figure 8-11, the returns become more certain, eliminating the low and negative returns. In addition, the risk associated with long payback is reduced, being paid back by 1987. But the major issue is whether or not waterflood will be succesful. SCENSIM can only rep-

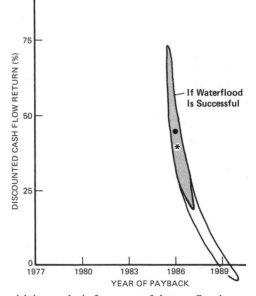

Figure 8-11.   Sensitivity analysis for successful waterflood

• = Mean for cloud of uncertainty, given the success of waterflood.

resent these changes; management must decide if they wish to take the risk.

Further analysis assuming the passage of the windfall profits tax (not shown) provided information that management felt was decisive. The cloud dropped significantly to maximum returns of less than 35 percent, with half the cloud in the negative returns region. Also, the payback extended far into the future, increasing the risks considerably. Of course, the windfall profits tax bill did pass, and waterflood was never undertaken. The SCENSIM approach provided information in a form that was of considerable assistance to the strategic scenario selection process. Management had a number of alternate uses for the capital, including drilling and primary field development, that were also presented within the SCENSIM format.

A CAPACITY EXPANSION EXAMPLE

This example deals with an issue of capacity expansion in an SBU of a large manufacturer that produced an "industrial" product; that is, it was sold to other manufacturers to cover or package their products, and was a relatively minor portion of the final product cost. It was sold to a variety of end-use industries with vastly different growth rates, from the computer to the furniture industries, so market penetration rates of the various end-users affected future sales levels of the product.

The product itself was somewhat unique in that it faced no direct competition from other identical products, although there was extensive functional competition from many other products that accomplished the same tasks based on very different technology. The product was relatively new compared to its functional competitors, and had technical advantages, but was more expensive. A major competitive issue was, "will customers pay more for improved performance?" The production process was continuous (as opposed to batch), was unique and difficult, and quality was a constant issue.

Strategic Events.   An extensive list of strategic events was elicited from the managers involved, the most important of which were as follows:

- State of the economy
- GNP growth

- Continuation of economic trends
- Cost inflation relative to functional competition
- Growth rates in end-use markets
- Penetration rates in end-use markets
- Product substitutability in specific end-use markets
- Technical feasibility in specific end-use markets
- Price-volume relationships in each market
- Distributor relationships (small volume compared to functional competitors)
- Foreign sales (exchange rate and shipping considerations)

After working with executives of this company to determine the events that they felt would impact their sales and earnings, it was possible to profile potential sales and earnings levels for 1985 as shown in Figure 8–12. Sales could range from a low of $150 million to a high of $250 million, with earnings ranging from about $35 million to almost $100 million. The sales forecast was $180 million, the mean sales for the cloud of uncertainty was about $195 million. However, existing manufacturing capacity limited sales to about $200 million, depending on the exact sales mix and price level. Therefore the issue

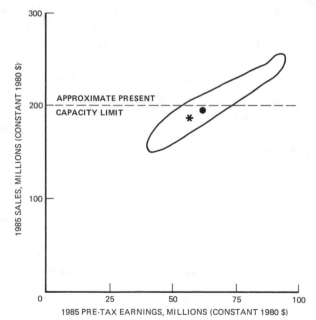

Figure 8–12.   Sales/earnings cloud of uncertainty for 1985 in relation to capacity

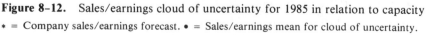

* = Company sales/earnings forecast. • = Sales/earnings mean for cloud of uncertainty.

quickly focused on strategies for adding capacity versus the chances for obtaining the additional sales.

Capacity Alternatives.   The company process engineers developed alternative ways of obtaining added capacity involving the elimination of bottlenecks in the process, which were termed "reamouts," and adding additional lines. There could be both an initial reamout and a second one, and these capacity increments could be used in combination with the additional lines, as shown in Figure 8–13 in a decision tree, resulting in six alternate strategic scenarios, numbered in parentheses at the right of the diagram. Alternative (6), the base case, involved no capacity additions. The resulting capacities (in thousands of pounds) are also shown at the right of the diagram. Actually, there were other alternatives involving minor process changes that have been omitted from this discussion, since they tend to complicate Figure 8–13 and the illustration that follows. The needed capacity could be obtained without a greenfield expansion, which had a somewhat higher investment/capacity ratio than any of the incremental means of obtaining capacity.

SCENSIM Results.   Since the alternate strategic scenarios involved differing investments, discounted cash flow return versus payout was used to profile the results. The clouds of uncertainty for alternatives

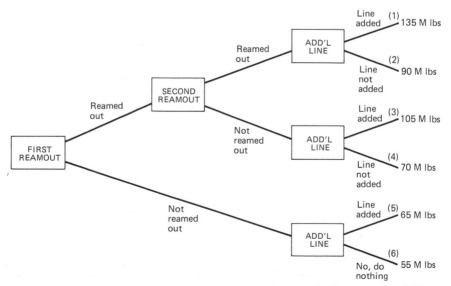

Figure 8-13.   Decision tree for some of the strategic scenarios for capacity additions

(2), (3), and (4) are shown in Figure 8-14. Alternative (4), the first reamout with no additional line, performs poorly, with returns in the range of 5 to 15 percent and payouts achieved in the late 1980s to the early 1990s. Adding an additional line through alternative (3) performs somewhat better, but not as well as alternative (2), both reamouts without added lines.

When both reamouts are performed, the second benefits from the first by absorbing investment costs in the first reamout that interact with resulting capacities for the second. The cloud of uncertainty for alternative (2) provides returns in the range of 18 to 37 percent, and achieves payout as early as 1986, but no later than 1990. Alternative (6), do nothing, involved probable opportunity costs of lost sales because of the lack of capacity, and was not seriously considered.

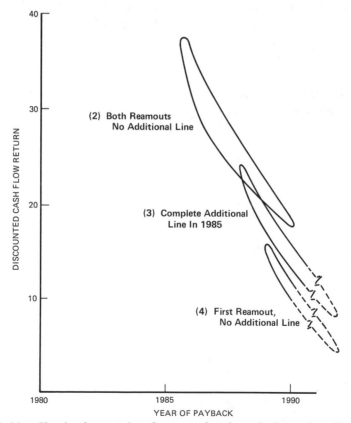

Figure 8-14. Clouds of uncertainty for expansion through alternatives (2), (3), and (4)

Nevertheless, these large opportunity costs provided additional financial justification for proceeding with capacity additions. The SCENSIM representation of the strategic scenarios helps to characterize alternative (2) as a dominant strategy, and it was adopted.

A CORPORATE PORTFOLIO ANALYSIS EXAMPLE

Given the SCENSIM methodology, the same concepts can be applied at the more aggregate corporate level. We simply move up one echelon, and SBUs become the components we examine, along with events that impact their sales and operating income, creating SBU clouds of uncertainty. The SBU clouds aggregate then to produce a corporate cloud of uncertainty. We then perform sensitivity analysis to examine the effects on SBUs and on the corporate clouds of uncertainty of whatever hypotheses for eliminating or controlling uncertainty that seem appropriate to the managers concerned.

The corporation in this example is the one used in the earlier example of product-line analysis. That example concerned one of the SBUs in this corporate analysis example, though over a larger planning horizon. The firm is a large high-technology company that develops most of its own products, and may invest hundreds of millions of dollars in development, plant and equipment, and market development to realize the potential of new products that may become SBUs in their portfolio if successful.

At the time of the analysis, corporate management had invested huge sums to implement a strategic plan for one of the SBUs, but there was great internal uncertainty about the decision, to the extent that consideration was being given to scrapping the plans midstream. Why? Because there was real concern about where to put scarce resources, not only within the SBU, as indicated in the previous example, but among all SBUs making up the corporation as a whole.

Some issues were political in nature, having military connotations. Whether some military procurement programs were implemented or not had great impact on what the company would do. Yet, short of lobbying and other attempts to influence, most of this uncertainty was outside corporate control. Even if the procurement programs went forward, there were alternate military plans that in one scenario required literally tons of the corporation's materials, but in another required very little. But in addition, because of the developmental nature of the product in question, there were still questions concerning its functional performance. It had worked in tests, but no one knew the full extent of its field performance.

It was in this extremely uncertain environment that the corporation was attempting to make crucial decisions concerning the use of its resources.

Strategic Events.   While the foregoing gives some flavor of the general corporate environment, there were 29 specific strategic events on which the SCENSIM analysis was based. These events can be categorized into six groups:

4   economic events (future state of the economy, rate of inflation, level of exchange rates and tariff business, and cost of energy)

7   political events (level of U.S. defense spending, funding levels for five specific military programs such as the B1 bomber and MX missile, level of foreign military spending, particularly NATO)

6   competitive events (five events dealing with potential actions of in-kind competitors to the various product lines, particularly expansion activities, and one event involving the potential entrance of a new functional competitor in two of the major product lines)

2   managerial events (outcome of labor negotiations affecting one SBU, and the success or failure of a proposed major cost reduction program)

8   technological events (applicability of various product lines to new end-use areas)

2   raw material supply events (the relative costs and availability of critical raw materials)

29

When effects of the events at the SBU level were calculated, the clouds of uncertainty for the five units appear as in Figure 8–15*a,* and the corporate cloud aggregates as in Figure 8–15*b.* Although the mean values of the SBU clouds (represented by the individual stars) add up to the mean value of the corporate cloud (the scales between the two graphs are not the same), the size and shape of the corporate cloud is not the simple sum of the SBU clouds. This occurs because events interact in a complex way in their effects on SBUs, and may cancel in

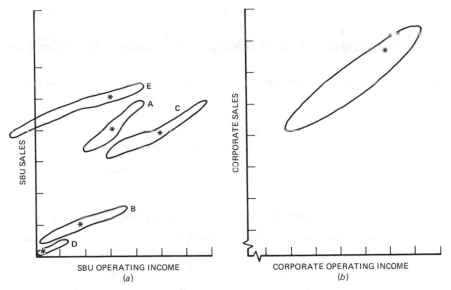

Figure 8-15. Forecast of 1986 sales-operating earnings clouds of uncertainty for (*a*) business units, and (*b*) the corporation as a whole

* = Mean sales-operating income for cloud of uncertainty.

some instances and be additive in others in forming the corporate cloud.

Figure 8–15*a* provides an uncertainty-characterization of the five SBUs. For example, although E has high levels of sales, it has high risk of profitability—under certain event impacts it can easily have operating losses in 1986. In fact, its profitability in terms of its percentage of operating income to sales is low, even for its mean or maximum performance.

On the other hand, C is very important to the portfolio, contributing a large operating income. C is quite profitable, but does not have a percentage of operating income to sales that is as high as the small mixed businesses of B and D. Both B and C have considerable uncertainty in their profitability, but unlike E, the risk is more balanced instead of being largely a downside risk.

Sensitivity Analyses. Some of the most interesting results come from the differential effects that event impacts have on SBUs, and the aggregate corporate effects. We will deal with only two of the many SCENSIM scenarios. For example, the occurrence of Event V, an un-

controllable event depending on the price of energy, seems to have upside impact on SBUs A and C, but downside impact on SBU E, as
shown in Figure 8–16, which indicates the effect on the clouds when
the uncertainty of Event V is removed. SBUs B and D are not affected
by the event. The aggregated effects on the corporate cloud are to
reduce sales-income uncertainty. While this event is very important to
SBUs A, C, and E, it is not so important to the corporation as a whole.
Though it depresses the market for E's products, this negative impact
is counterbalanced by its positive impact on A and C.

If an event is countercyclical to the other events, or if one or more
of the SBUs are counter in response, the individual managers of these
units may feel the effect rather strongly—as when Event V occurs—but the CEO of the corporation will not have a problem at the
corporate level because of the cancellation of effects, which actually
reduces his uncertainty.

Now, how much corporate risk is the result of a particular SBUs
performance? Or stated differently, how much corporate risk is removed if a particular SBU achieves its forecast? Since E exhibits so
much uncertainty, and can actually contribute losses for 1986, it is an

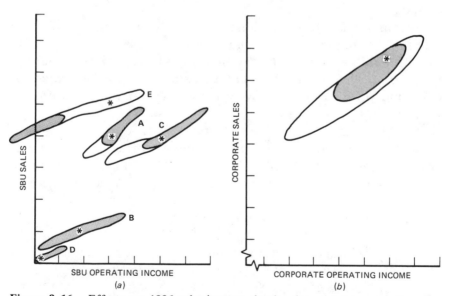

Figure 8-16. Effects on 1986 sales-income clouds of uncertainty assuming that
Event V occurs (*a*) for five SBUs, and (*b*) at the corporate level

obvious candidate for closer scrutiny. Figure 8–17 shows the effects on corporate risk if E's performance is as forecast. The effect is to reduce corporate risk somewhat, as might be expected.

The SCENSIM analysis is useful in two general ways at the corporate portfolio level. First, it performs a function in helping to sort out who should worry about what. What events have corporate impact, and which impact individual SBUs? If something like Event V occurs, the problem is really in the provinces rather than in Rome. The CEO probably should not become directly involved, unless he has lost faith that the managers of the SBUs directly affected can handle the situation, in which case he has a staffing problem.

Secondly, SCENSIM is useful in helping to distinguish controllable and uncontrollable impacts. Hand wringing does not lead to an understanding of which SBUs are contributing risk to the portfolio, or of the complex interactions between the risk contributions of SBUs. Which risks should be the responsibility of corporate and which the province of SBU managers? SCENSIM does not help solve these kinds of problems, but it does provide information in a way that gives managers insight into risk-problem solutions.

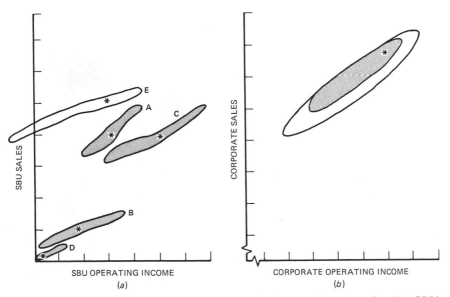

Figure 8–17. Effects on 1986 sales-income clouds of uncertainty assuming that SBU E's performance is as forecast (*a*) for five SBUs, and (*b*) at the corporate level

Concluding Remarks

SCENSIM assumes that the strategic scenarios are based on careful competitor analysis of the industry and its markets, and on an analysis of the business unit itself, revealing structural strengths and weaknesses. It is not a substitute for them. The strategic scenarios are management's own, and the events that create uncertainties are also management's. SCENSIM takes as raw material the scenarios and management's expression of the events that unsettle them or excite their imagination. These inputs are quantified and the impacts that result in the clouds of uncertainty calculated.

Appendix

Our objective in this appendix is to provide a computational example as well as additional information concerning the conceptual framework for simulating strategic scenarios by SCENSIM.

The SCENSIM technique relies on five elements

- A mathematical model of the business situation that relates inputs to outputs
- Forecasted values of the inputs
- Descriptions of the strategic events together with their impacts on the inputs
- Representation of results as a cloud of uncertainty
- Sensitivity analysis

We will discuss these five elements in the context of an example. Suppose a company has a single-product strategic business unit (SBU) with sales in two market segments, A and B. The desired outputs to be computed in the analysis are sales and earnings—the measure of the impacts of the events that we will specify.

MATHEMATICAL MODEL

Since we are concerned with strategic issues, the model of the business need not be complex. In fact, a detailed model is likely to be disadvantageous—it would require longer development time, and computation of the impacts of the myriad event-combinations would also be time and resource consuming. In the example situation, three simple logical relationships will suffice:

Sales = price × volume
Contribution = (price per unit − variable cost per unit) × volume
Earnings = contribution − fixed costs

These are simple accounting relationships. For both sales and contribution, it is necessary to sum over the two market segments. In order to condense these simple relationships, and to account for the two market segments, we adopt the following notation:

S = sales
p_i = price in the ith segment, either A or B

V_i = volume in the ith segment, either A or B
C = contribution
VC = variable cost in the ith segment, either A or B
FC = fixed costs
E = earnings

In mathematical form, the three relationships are:

$$S = \sum_{i=1}^{2} (p_i V_i) \tag{1}$$

$$C = \sum_{i=1}^{2} ((p_i - VC) V_i) \tag{2}$$

$$E = C - FC \tag{3}$$

Equations (1) and (3) provide the key outputs of interest, S and E. The reason for stating the relationships in precise mathematical form is that they can be computerized. Computerization is important for real applications, because of the large number of computations required.

VALUES OF INPUTS

We need input data in order to compute. These data would come from company records, and the price-volume data represents a forecast of volume at a given price. For this simple model, the data are:

VC = \$3.50
FC = \$200
V_A = 70 units at p_A = \$6.50/unit
V_B = 210 units at p_B = \$4.50/unit

For the *base case,* then, with no impacts of events to be defined below,

S = \$6.50 × 70 + \$4.50 × 210 = \$1400
C = (\$6.50 − \$3.50) × 70 + (\$4.50 − \$3.50) × 210 = \$420
E = \$420 − \$200 = \$220

The base case point of S = \$1400 and E = \$220 is plotted as an asterisk (*) in Figure 8–18.

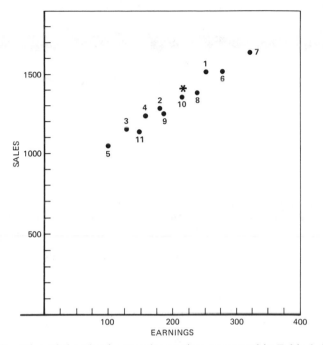

Figure 8-18. Plot of the 12 sales/earnings points computed in Table 8-2

STRATEGIC EVENTS AND THEIR IMPACTS

For this simple example we consider three strategic events:

- The state of the economy
- A competitor plant built
- Increased demand in Market A

The managers involved estimate the following impacts on the input variables for the two conditions, "economy up" and "economy down":

Economy Up

	PRICE	VOLUME	VARIABLE COST PER UNIT	FIXED COST
Market A	+ 3%	+ 4%	+ 2%	No impact
Market B	+ 2%	+ 6%		

The impacts on the outputs of the "economy up" event may be computed by the same three equations as $S = \$1509$ and $E = \$255$, and are plotted as the point 1 in Figure 8–18.

Economy Down

	PRICE	VOLUME	VARIABLE COST PER UNIT	FIXED COST
Market A	−1%	−6%	No impact	No impact
Market B	—	−10%		

The impacts on the outputs of the "economy down" event are $S = \$1274$ and $E = \$182$, and are plotted as point 2 in Figure 8–18.

The second event involves the rumor that a competitor plans to build a new plant that could impact prices and volumes. The estimated impact of this event on the input values is summarized here.

Competitor Builds New Plant

	PRICE	VOLUME	VARIABLE COST PER UNIT	FIXED COST
Market A	−5%	−5%	No impact	No impact
Market B	−2%	−20%		

The impact on sales and earnings is computed as $S = \$1152$ and $E = \$131$, plotted as point 3 in Figure 8–18.

Combination of Events.   Point 3 represents the estimate of sales/earnings impact of a new competitor plant in relation to the base case, independently. But this event could occur in combination with either an up or down economy. Therefore, we must compute for these two conditions, and they are represented as points 4 and 5 in Figure 8–18.

Finally, we consider the impact of the third event, increased usage in Market A.

Increased Usage in Market A

	PRICE	VOLUME	VARIABLE COST PER UNIT	FIXED COST
Market A	+4%	+20%	No impact	No impact
Market B	No impact	+6%		

Point 6 in Figure 8-18 represents this event, with points 7, 8, 9, 10, and 11 representing the combinations of this event with the state of the economy, and the impact of a possible new competitor plant. There are twelve possible outcomes summarized in Table 8-2: the base case, the basic event occurrences, and the event combinations, each of the points being labeled in Figure 8-18.

REPRESENTATION AS A CLOUD OF UNCERTAINTY

In Figure 8-19, we have drawn an envelope around the calculated points. We interpret this envelope of the points as the region of possible sales/earnings outcomes. By strict definition, only the points can occur, but when more events (with combinations) are included in the analysis, the density of points increases. But more important, real events have many more alternatives than our simple example, hence the interpretation of the envelope as defining a region of outcomes, or a cloud of uncertainty, seems justified.

These computations for the simple example complete a full round for a SCENSIM analysis. Other measures of the outcomes could have been used; for example, we could have substituted after-tax earnings by adding one more simple equation to the mathematical model,

$$\text{After-tax earnings} = \text{Earnings} \times \text{Effective tax rate.}$$

TABLE 8-2. **Sales/Earnings Impacts of Events and Combinations of Events**

	EVENTS				
POINT PLOTTED IN FIGURE 8-18	Economy	Competitor Plant	Increased Demand in Market A	SALES	EARNINGS
*	------------------------Base Case------------------------			$1400	$220
1	Up			1509	255
2	Down			1274	182
3		Yes		1152	131
4	Up	Yes		1241	158
5	Down	Yes		1049	101
6			Yes	1513	284
7	Up		Yes	1630	323
8	Down		Yes	1379	241
9		Yes	Yes	1253	186
10	Up	Yes	Yes	1350	218
11	Down	Yes	Yes	1144	152

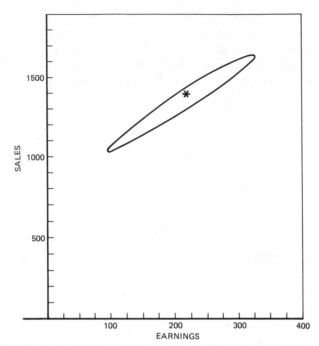

Figure 8-19. Cloud of uncertainty enclosing the 12 sales/earnings points

If return on assets (ROA) is a logical outcome measure, then the associated capital investment or assets for the product will be a required input. The ROA measure is computed by dividing earnings by the assets or the invested capital. The output measures that best illuminate the strategic situation should be used.

SENSITIVITY ANALYSIS

To investigate the sensitivity of the outcomes to the occurrence or nonoccurrence of an event, such as the building of a competitor plant in our simple example, we can examine the sales-earnings outcomes for both alternatives.

For example, what happens to the cloud of uncertainty defined by Figure 8-19 if the competitor plant is not built? We have already generated the data necessary to plot the sales/earnings points, and to draw the envelope defining the new cloud of uncertainty. The region is defined by points 1, 2, 6, 7, and 8 in Table 8-2 and Figure 8-18—all the points not containing a "yes" under the column headed "Competitor Plant." When a separate envelope is drawn to enclose these points, we have Figure 8-20, showing clearly how the uncertainty is reduced by eliminating this event. The company forecast, or base case, remains the same, assuming that it was really done with no consideration given to the possibility of the competitor expansion. The concept of sensitivity analysis can be expanded to include the effects of strategic alternatives.

THE COMBINATORIAL PROBLEM, AND THE SCALE OF COMPUTING REQUIREMENTS

For the simple example it was possible to compute the impacts for all twelve combinations of the event occurrences. For real problems, the number of combinations can become very large. Most of the real applications with which we have been involved had 20 to 30 events, with

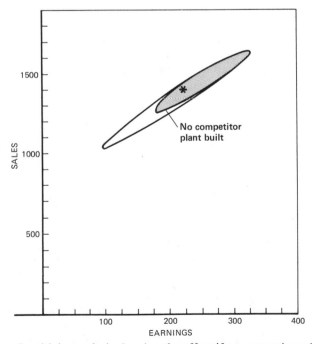

Figure 8-20.   Sensitivity analysis showing the effect if no competitor plant is built

up to five or six alternatives for each event. Events are included as long as they are judged to have meaningful impact on outputs and some chance of occurring, erring if necessary on more rather than fewer events. Our experience has been that beyond the 30 or so most important events, the impacts on output measures have been negligible.* But for 20 events, each with two alternatives to the base case, the number of combinations to compute approaches 3.5 billion. Clearly, it is not possible to evaluate them all.

One solution to the issue of large-scale computing requirements is to use Monte Carlo simulation. But this technique requires that probabilities be assigned to the occurrence of event alternatives. With Monte Carlo simulation, the more likely combinations are evaluated more often than the less likely, with unlikely combinations probably not evaluated at all.

As an alternative to Monte Carlo simulation, we assign probabilities of occurrence to each alternative, but evaluate only the likely combinations—those that have greater than a preset minimum probability of occurrence. The likely combinations become those used in SCENSIM analysis. The threshold probability is adjusted to yield a manageable number of combinations. The most likely few thousand combinations are usually sufficient to characterize the cloud of uncertainty. The advantage of the technique is that we examine only the likely combinations,† reducing computing requirements. Our experience indicates that the envelope of interest is relatively insensitive to the assigned probabilities when a reasonable number of events is used.

In the majority of our applications of SCENSIM a proprietary

---

*The importance of an event is related to its impact on a cloud of uncertainty—its size and shape. In applications where a large number of events have been developed, we have often deleted those having little discernible impact. But the process of determining that an event has little impact can be important. If an event was formulated, someone was concerned about it. On the other hand, if it has no impact, then clearly it is not strategic in nature. The process of filtering out small-impact events can often lead to a refocusing of attention on the important issues.

†A list of concerns and opportunities (events) rarely contains highly unlikely events. Unless you are in the dynamite manufacturing business, it is probably not worth while to include the event that the plant may blow up. Such events are very unlikely, and may be excluded. Instead of developing contingency plans for such occurrences, a business should protect themselves by purchasing insurance. And since strategic plans do not address such unlikely events occurring, we can exclude them from SCENSIM analysis. With a similar rationale, unlikely event combinations can be excluded as well.

computer program has been used. In some instances, unique application characteristics have required the development of custom-designed computer programs. But with the development and wide acceptance of spreadsheet software for microcomputers, the SCENSIM computing requirements are reasonable without the proprietary program.

Chapter 9

From Analysis to Plans and Action

We have already observed that if a thorough strategic analysis of industries, markets, and the SBU is performed, the competitors in the business will be understood and most of the strategic alternatives will be eliminated—the structural strengths and weaknesses of all players will be laid bare, revealing only a few viable courses of action.

Analysts and consultants can be very useful in performing this analysis, and in providing further analysis of risks in strategy formulation. But they cannot formulate a strategy for a company, nor can they implement the strategy developed. Strategy formulation involves value tradeoffs and an assumption of risks and responsibilities by the involved managers. Implementation cannot be delegated to outsiders.

This final chapter assumes the kinds of analysis that are the core of this book, places them in a broader context of the strategic planning process, and discusses the process of implementing these plans—moving from planning to strategic management. We will discuss the analytical methods developed in the book in relation to the decision to plan, the development of business unit strategic plans, the coordination of SBU plans within corporate strategic plans, and finally, the transition to strategic management.

The Decision to Plan

Some event usually triggers the decision to engage in strategic analysis and to develop strategic plans. Planning for its own sake is seldom useful, since sufficient time and effort must be diverted from current activities to the planning process. Resources must be committed and staff allocated and supported. There must be organizational commitment or the plans will be incomplete or not worth implementing. The day-to-day pressures of business tend to crowd out strategic planning—short-term issues somehow always seem more important or at least more immediate, a syndrome that must be resisted.

Triggering Events

The triggering source may be internal or external. Internal sources may be related to comparative performance—such as a loss of market share that may be traced perhaps to degenerating costs or quality relative to competitors. Poor performance can lead to a commitment to plan. A new chief executive can provide internal impetus to engage in strategic planning, but this kind of trigger is often interpreted as a mandate to plan, and may produce tacit agreement by managers rather than organizational commitment.

External triggers commonly produce an imperative for action. Changes in the business environment require a change, or at least an adjustment in strategy. Good examples are dramatic new product or process technologies, deregulation of an industry, or a dramatic price rise of a raw material or ingredient. The introduction of word processing required typewriter manufacturers to engage in strategic planning. The success of personal computers, and their outstanding word processing software has or should have sent the dedicated word processing manufacturers, such as Wang, back to the drawing boards. The continuous casting process decreased steel-making costs and required new strategic plans. Deregulation in the airline industry provided strategic opportunities for some companies, and deregulation in banking has triggered a dramatic realignment in the product lines of investment banks, brokerage houses, commercial banks, and savings and loan banks.

ORGANIZATIONAL COMMITMENT

External triggers are most likely to rally true support for the planning process. Nothing unifies an organization like an outside threat, or an innovative opportunity. Without both commitment and involvement of the organization, a successful planning process is less likely, and may not even be completed. But even if the planning process is completed, successful implementation without commitment is virtually impossible. Consultants—inside or outside—can be helpful in building commitment, but care must be taken to ensure that they are only a part of the planning team. Externally developed strategic plans are seldom implemented, because they lack the commitment generated by involvement.

Sufficient resources must have been allocated to the planning process, and they must remain sufficient. Planning takes time for absorption of new and innovative ideas. It is in part a process of changing opinions and biases, and working through the politics of organizational and personal impacts. Even if a plan could be developed quickly, time must be allocated for its absorption. While simple and perhaps obvious, these principles of commitment and involvement are routinely violated.

MANAGEMENT'S COMMITMENT

The commitment and involvement of top managers is vital. One of the signs of management commitment is the allocation of resources to the strategic planning effort. One of the benefits of hiring outside consultants is the signal it carries of managerial commitment—resources have been committed to the project that must be paid for. The involvement of top managers in the process is as important as the involvement of the rest of the organization.

Strategic Plans

All plans are not strategic in nature, though strategic plans may incorporate functional organizational units as important components. Basically, strategic plans are appropriate for SBUs (and new SBU ventures) and at the corporate level, and these two levels of strategic plans are merged for single-product companies. Issues appropriate for SBU strategies are not for corporate strategies and vice versa, but how the dual-level plans fit together is very important. A "top down" approach to planning tends to dictate elements of SBU plans; a "bottom up" approach involves the molding of corporate plans around those of SBUs. Both modes have their advantages and drawbacks, and a preference for one or the other may depend on the individual situation.

BUSINESS UNIT VERSUS CORPORATE PLANS

The plans for SBUs encompass all aspects of the business—marketing, production, distribution, finance, and new product development, with emphasis depending on the individual situation. What should the SBU do, and how should these goals be accomplished?

Corporate plans deal with more comprehensive issues. How does the portfolio of SBUs fit together? What units should be added or deleted to achieve corporate goals? Certain variables are dictated at the SBU level, for example, financial structure, but can be altered at the corporate level. The corporate plans deal with broader goals and how the individual SBU plans are interwoven to achieve the goals. Achieving these corporate goals results in specific missions for individual SBUs, and how the SBUs accomplish their missions is an issue in their plans.

TOP DOWN VERSUS BOTTOM UP

Achieving the correct interrelationships between SBU and corporate plans is not simple or easy. Experience shows that bottom up plans never seem to aggregate to a balanced portfolio—something important will be out of balance. For example, resources requested usually exceed corporate capability to provide them. Mature units want to keep the cash they are generating, and growth businesses often want more than they really need.

Top down planning provides constraints to SBUs in terms of missions to be accomplished, resources available, and so on, and should produce a balance in overall corporate planning. On the other hand, the top down approach overlooks the advantage of securing commitment through SBU involvement in the process, and sometimes forces an SBU into a strategy that may not be desirable. Some combination of the necessary balance achieved in the top down approach and the commitment achieved through the bottom up approach is often obtained in an iterative process representing a mixture of the two pure forms. Clearly, an SBU that is out of control needs direction to get it back on track. On the other hand, too much direction and control may stifle creativity and entrepreneurship.

Developing a Business Unit Strategic Plan

There are four basic phases to the process of developing an SBU strategic plan:

- analyzing the situation
- developing strategic alternatives
- selecting a strategy
- formulating detailed plans and budgets

This four-stage process is more like peeling an onion than the straightforward linear step-by-step process implied by the above list. Each layer of the process may reveal a need to cycle back to a reexamination of previous layers. First, we analyze the situation, and then start developing alternatives. But questions may arise that are not covered in the situation analysis, requiring a cycling back. Just when a strategy selection seems appropriate, new concerns arise requiring new information, and another recycling is required. Strategies change because competitors may change their strategies, or we may need to take account of shifts in the environment. The process is dynamic, and never completely done.

ANALYZING THE SITUATION—THE STRATEGY AUDIT

The strategy audit seeks to provide answers to the following questions:

- Who is doing what to whom?
- How are they doing it?

• What are the structural differences among competitors?
• What are the trends? Where are we going?

This audit is the basic analysis that precedes strategy formulation and implementation—it draws on the bulk of the analysis methodology that is the focus of this book. For an SBU, it analyzes the products and markets served—the product/market portfolio.

Competitor Positions and Momentums. Or, who is doing what to whom? First, who are the competitors? Answering this question is relatively simple for undifferentiated or commodity products, but when there is substantial product differentiation or in-kind competition the answer is not so straightforward. Managers often say that their product is unique and has no competitors, but there are usually substitutes, and every product must at least compete for its share of the purchasing dollar. Taking a broad view of competition is preferable to a narrow one—candidates can always be eliminated if it is concluded that they are not competitors.

Given a definition of product markets and competitors, the growth/share matrices and share/momentum charts discussed in Chapter 2 and the sector charts discussed in Chapter 3 are useful and meaningful ways to display the information to managers.

When used as a mechanism for display, without inferred strategic implications, the growth/share matrix is quite valuable. It shows the products in the SBU portfolio that are strong (high share) and weak (low share), and which are important (large sales volume) and those which are not (small sales volume). The growth/share matrix shows in a graphic manner those products that have potential for the future (high growth), and those that have little potential (low growth).

The share/momentum chart provides a graphic view of the trends. It provides a display indicating which products of competitors are gaining or losing market share, and how these gains and losses appear across the entire product portfolio. But the sector chart provides what may be the most important view of competitors, showing what is happening in terms of growth and relative market share for all competitors in each product market. These standard strategy charts, though overworked, are still the best ones, as long as it is understood that they are for display purposes, have no strategy implications in and of themselves, and carry with them no standard prescriptions.

Beyond understanding the positions and momentums of competitors by product markets, we need to understand the positions of the products in their value-added streams, particularly for intermediate goods. Is the component product a large or small part of the value added for the final product? If a small part, then component price has little effect on the end-product price. Supply relationships are also important—are all competitors equally affected by supply of critical raw materials or components, or does one or more have an advantage? And we need to characterize customers—do all competitors sell to the same set of customers, or is the market segmented? The competitive dynamics both up- and downstream can have impact.

Which particular part of the analysis that forms the strategy audit is most important? That depends on the situation—selecting the appropriate tools is part of the art, and experience certainly helps.

Competitive Forces—How Are the Competitors Doing It?   Once we know who is gaining market share, for example, we must try to understand how it is being achieved. A useful approach is to lay out the product market attributes, for example, price, quality, service, distribution, image. One might rank the competitors under each attribute, relating market share gains and losses to the attributes. If for example, the competitor with the lowest price is gaining the most market share, then it can be inferred that price is important.

Gaining insight into the meaning of the attribute rankings may require more sophisticated market research techniques. This use of market research is somewhat atypical. It relies on market research as an input rather than as an end in itself, focusing on hard facts rather than opinions. It does not ask customers what they want, but relates competitor rankings to behavior.*

Structural Differences.   In order to develop strategies that take advantage of structural differences, or result in structural change, we need to understand current structural differences among competitors. This objective is best accomplished by reviewing the value added stream for each product, taking into account each competitor's position. What is the importance of each stage in the stream, in terms of the proportion of the value added, and in which activities do each of the competitors participate? An example of such a value-added chart

---

*The problem is that when asked what they want, customers say they want everything—high quality, instant delivery, a great deal of service, extended credit, and all for a low price. Customers' tradeoffs for the various attributes are what is important and often missed by market research.

was shown in Figure 3-1 for the competitors in the titanium industry, showing the proportion of value added for mining the rutile, reducing the rutile to sponge, melting to ingot, forming, and, finally, fabrication of final products.

In a product where the participation in the different steps of the value-added stream leads to advantages in certain product attributes (cost, quality, etc.), then the competitors have structural differences, leading to hills and valleys in the playing field. Issues such as using a direct sales force versus distributors, or backward integration into raw materials versus the use of suppliers, are classic examples of participation in different stages of the value-added stream that may lead to structural advantages and disadvantages.

In some situations, it is sufficient to gain insight into where in the value-added chain each competitor is positioned. But when competitors differ in their process technologies, further analysis is needed. What are the advantages and disadvantages of the competing technologies? Which market segments are best served by the differing technologies?

In many industries, if not most, SBUs are not independent, they are interrelated. Production processes or technologies are shared among units. Sales and marketing staffs may not be dedicated to a single product or product line, but shared with others. When the value added in the interrelated activities is large, the interrelationships should be analyzed through activity analysis as was done for Deere & Company in Chapter 5. Activity-based analysis using activity-based growth/share and share/momentum charts is needed to give insight into cost positions and the strengths and weaknesses or competitors due to their particular value-added configurations. These analyses help focus on the economics of scope (due to the volume benefits of interrelated activities).

Impacts of Momentum and Trends.   What will happen if we make no change in strategy? The answer to this question provides a base case. Given an understanding of competitor positions and momentums, how competitors are accomplishing their aims, and structural differences, we analyze the current trends and projected positions. An expanding market can mask what is happening to relative position—sales and earnings can be increasing while the game is being lost. This was true during the personal computer market expansion when market expansion provided increasing sales but declining market share for several firms. Sector charts that project future positions, given current trends, help visualize what will happen without strategic changes or environmental shifts. Projected cost positions based on future volume may provide insights.

But analysis should go beyond simple extrapolation—it should take account of changes in the economy, the market, demographic shifts, and so on. Then the effects of future demand forecasts must be considered. If there is reason to believe that some products or product lines will grow in volume while others shrink, then an examination of how the activity structures of competitors will favor (or penalize) these mix changes is needed. Particularly in interrelated products, an assessment of how these forces will affect the competitive balance is useful.

Investigating product substitution and market saturation effects may upset the usual extrapolation forecasts. For example, word processing software used on personal computers has substituted for dedicated word processors—it is not clear, for example, that Wang took probable substitution into account in its strategy. A major shift in demand has resulted from the substitution.

Market saturation effects can also be dramatic, as manufacturers and retailers of personal computers have noted. A truly new product, such as personal computers, can have an explosive demand initially since no one owns them. But when those who wanted a PC own one, demand drops to a replacement level. And if the product is durable, as is the PC, the replacement level can be quite low. As simple as these concepts are, they are often forgotten.

DEVELOPING STRATEGIC ALTERNATIVES

Given the strategy audit (the analysis), the next step in developing an SBU strategic plan is to develop alternatives. The goals that provide the target need to be determined. Given the goals, SBU managers must develop strategies to achieve them, and that is the truly creative step. Once proposed, alternate strategies must be characterized in ways that allow informed choices to be made, and the SCENSIM technique presented in Chapter 8 has proven to be quite useful.

Goals.   What are we trying to achieve? Our discussion of top down versus bottom up processes is pertinent—if the process is top down, the goals are specified by the mission provided by corporate management; if bottom up, the goals are the SBU agenda; if some combination, the final result is an SBU mission that becomes SBU goals. The goals need to be stated explicitly—general statements are not sufficient, but they are good starting points. The mission represents a point of departure for stating specific goals; for example, if the mission is to generate cash, this must be made specific, if it is growth, then how much, if it is to extend market share, the target must be specified. But whatever the stated goals, they should be attainable. The strategy audit discussed earlier provides much of the hard data necessary to refine realistic goals.

Possible Strategies. The analysis required by the strategy audit should generate insights that lead to possible strategies. The best alternatives are usually those that play to the trends identified and take advantage of the structural differences between competitors. If some markets are being saturated, how can we structurally position ourselves for a competitive advantage in other nonsaturated market segments? What differences in supplier or distributor configurations might be exploited for particular market segments? How can we reposition ourselves in order to implement a competitive advantage? The essence of a really good possible strategy is the answer to the basic question, "How can we play our strengths against our competitors' weaknesses?

Experience helps, but familiarity with the specific situation, augmented through the analysis of the strategy audit, is of greater significance. Usually only a few viable strategies will make sense, but once articulated, they need to be characterized in useful ways.

Characterizing Alternatives. What might be the outcomes of each of the alternatives? Characterizing the alternatives and their possible outcomes often leads to improvements, variations, or combinations of alternatives that may be even better than the original ones.

The SCENSIM technique for characterizing alternatives is the method of choice in our experience. It provides a powerful visual representation of the opportunities, risks, and threats associated with the alternate strategies, and usually raises questions requiring further analysis. The crucial issue of how much risk to bear is a subtle one, and the answer to it can only be provided by the managers concerned, modified by the political, organizational, and personal relationships among them. The best that an analyst can do is to provide useful characterizations of the alternatives for managerial choice.

SELECTING AN SBU STRATEGY

There are two major issues in strategy selection: Will the strategy lead to the stated goals? and Does it fit the organization?

Strategic Fit.   Does the strategy achieve the goals? The more specific the stated goal, the better this question can be answered. But the degree of risk enters the forecast of goal achievement. A given alternative may be forecasted to achieve the goals, but there may be considerable risk associated with that forecast. Another alternative may not quite achieve the goals, but may have upside potential that could surpass the goals. Choosing between these kinds of alternatives is not a simple task.

One useful technique is to group the risks—events that have unfavorable outcomes in the SCENSIM analysis—into those that can be influenced and those that cannot. This partition often provides additional insight, for a large but potentially influenceable risk may be one that managers are willing to take, while one over which they have little control should perhaps be avoided.

Organizational Fit.   This issue has received a great deal of attention, certainly because strategies that do not fit the organization are not likely to work, whether or not they are brilliant. In the final analysis, the quality of a strategy is measured by whether it is successful in achieving goals. The best strategy, poorly executed, can be a complete failure, while a well-executed simple strategy can achieve a great deal.

If a strategy does not fit the organization, there is always the possibility of changing the organization and its people, but this is not easily done—and the extent of change may be more than originally envisioned. It is usually far better to develop a strategy that fits the organization than to attempt to mold the organization to the strategy.

A major, often overlooked, factor is the method of compensation of those involved in implementing the strategy. Managers and key staff clearly respond to the incentives under which they perform. A strategy focusing on long-term goals that is implemented by managers whose incomes are tied to short-term performance is doomed to failure.

FORMULATING DETAILED PLANS AND BUDGETS

The final step in developing an SBU strategic plan requires the communication of what the strategy is and how it is to be accomplished. Policies and procedures, role assignments, and the detailed allocation of resources, are usually expressed in the form of budgets reflecting the requirements of the chosen strategy. Reducing a strategic plan simply to budgets can strangle it—the intent of the plan is what is important, not the exact numbers.

Plans. Developing the plans themselves is the easy part, especially following the kind of process we have detailed. More important is the communication of the plan to everyone involved in its implementation. The intent and characterization of the strategic thrust are most important, yet planning documents are commonly full of numbers, table after table of dry representation of an exciting strategy. Graphic representation is more effective—it may not be as precise, but it will communicate intent. The plan needs to be effective in building commitment on the part of those who must make it work.

Roles. Each individual assigned an important implementation role must understand what he or she is to do, and why it is important to the success of the strategy. The "why" is crucial—without understanding the reasons for policies and procedures it is more difficult to adjust intelligently when circumstances change.

Policies and Procedures. People need to know how to react when unplanned events occur, and policies and procedures provide guidelines. These policies and procedures may change when new strategies are adopted. Communicating these changes helps communicate how the strategy is a point of departure, and is intended to help change behavior to that consistent with the new strategy.

Where we have a single product, the SBU plan is the corporate plan. But the common situation is that a number of SBUs exist, and we now consider the development of corporate strategy in this multiple SBU environment.

Developing a Corporate Strategic Plan

A corporate plan for a multiple SBU situation should be distinctly different from an SBU plan. The interrelationships among the SBU plans are of great significance in the corporate plan, while the competitors in each business, and how they compete, individual strengths and weaknesses, and so on are all parts of the individual SBU plans.

The corporate plan must focus on the way the individual SBUs fit together—the resource balance and the overall corporate direction. Issues that are "givens" at the SBU level are variable at the corporate level. For example, will the corporation be balanced in cash flow, or will it borrow to support new opportunities? What will be the dividend policy? What lines of business are appropriate for the corporation? The basic steps in a corporate plan are:

- Gaining portfolio perspective
- Achieving synergy, resource balance, and SBU value
- Detailing and communicating the corporate strategic plan

GAINING PORTFOLIO PERSPECTIVE—THE PORTFOLIO AUDIT

The elements and considerations of the portfolio audit are somewhat different from the strategy audit at the SBU level. The focus is on portfolio perspective. Detailed competitive issues for SBUs have already been addressed in the SBU strategy audit—we now want to know what the portfolio is, and how the units fit together.

Composition and Characteristics. What are we, and what are our SBUs? That is the first question. What are they? How large are they? What is their competitive position in the markets they serve? How profitable are they? Where do they seem to be going? These are the questions that the portfolio audit should answer.

A good place to start is to display the traditional growth/share matrix and share/momentum charts for the corporation. The growth/share matrix shows what the business units are, and their relative market share and projected growth. The share/momentum charts show trends. We stress again that these displays are not to be used for analysis or prescription, but to provide perspective on the existing portfolio. They can be augmented with other tools that provide display information on market attractiveness and cost for the SBUs making up the portfolio. For each SBU it is useful to develop a short synopsis book containing a summary sector chart supplemented with information concerning structural strengths and weaknesses, a statement of goals and missions, summary financial information with projections, and statements of strategies, opportunities, and threats. These booklets on each SBU can then be assembled with portfolio displays to form the basis for a corporate book, all designed for the function of helping to characterize the existing portfolio. Other unique materials can also be included, such as information showing focus on core technologies and macro flow charts.

SYNERGY, RESOURCE BALANCE, AND SBU VALUE

The next issue is concerned with how the units fit together. Fit has a number of dimensions: Does resource balance exist? Is the portfolio generating enough cash to fund future opportunities? Is it gaining competitive position or is it in broad retreat? Are there enough opportunities for the future, both from an economic perspective and to satisfy organizational needs for advancement and growth? What are the key activities in which the corporation is engaged, and are any of these activities themselves the basis for further growth and synergy? Displays similar to Figure 5-1, showing the Kodak growth/share matrix with all the thin film businesses highlighted help show the importance of core activities and the economics of scope, and perhaps also show which activities may be peripheral.

What contribution is each SBU making to the value of the corporation—which are adding and which subtracting from value? Displays such as Figure 1-4 for NL Industries or Figure 6-4 for Pacific Power and Light, showing which SBUs are earning in excess of their costs of capital, raise fundamental questions concerning the viability of some SBUs when the units are independent. But when there are core activities, such as with Kodak's thin film businesses, it is not so simple. Removing a business that feeds key activities can change the cost structure of other businesses in the portfolio; adding businesses that will feed the core activities can have the reverse effect.

Assessing the Future. If the current trends and momentum continue, what will the status be within a given time frame? This same issue was raised in SBU strategy development. While the portfolio could be out of balance at some point in time in terms of cash or perhaps growth, it cannot remain out of balance indefinitely without dire consequences.

Cash flow balance within the portfolio is particularly important, raising the issue of self-funded or sustainable growth. If the corporate growth is to be sustained by internal funds within some reasonable time period, it must generate enough profit to purchase assets to support its operations. In the simplest case, it will be a corporation with no debt, and the only new funding will come from profits. Since asset turnover cannot increase without limit, in the intermediate term the company can grow internally no faster than its return on equity. If it pays dividends, the maximum growth rate is reduced to the return on equity times the retention ratio, the proportion of the earnings retained. (In the short term it can grow faster if it can increase its asset turnover, but this increase is limited.) The corporation can borrow to obtain additional funds, but that source is also limited. If the debt-to-equity ratio is to remain constant, then the profits available to support new operations must come from retained earnings and a proportional amount of debt. This determines the maximum sustainable growth rate.[1] Growth faster than this rate requires increasing asset turnover or debt-to-equity ratio, and is not sustainable.

But it is not sufficient to consider only balance from a financial or cash flow viewpoint. Will there be enough high-growth businesses? How will the businesses relate to the core activities, and will there be enough core activity to maintain the low cost viability of those activities?

DETAILING AND COMMUNICATING THE CORPORATE
STRATEGIC PLAN

Given the analysis of the portfolio audit, the next step is to set corporate goals. Then SBU missions must be developed. If planning is top down, they will be set by corporate; if bottom up, the missions from SBUs must be distilled and combined, and checked for consistency with corporate goals. Finally, consideration must be given to portfolio additions or deletions.

Corporate Goals.   With or without advice, corporate goal setting is the province of the chief executive officer. The CEO must decide and be able to articulate what the corporation should be—a very difficult, but important task. A corporation without specific goals is like a ship adrift on unfriendly seas. But analysis is called for to check the goals for consistency and the probability of attainment. Inconsistent goals and certainly ones that cannot be achieved lead to frustration in the organization. A clear understanding of what is central in the portfolio needs to be articulated, in terms of market focus and activity bases.

SBU Missions. What should each SBU be doing? Whether the process is top down, bottom up, or some combination, there needs to be a final agreement on the mission of each unit. Missions tend to be expressed in terms of cash generation and use, growth and profitability, reflecting the need to maintain balance within the portfolio, including the possibility of increased or decreased debt. Therefore, one SBU's mission might be cash generation, while another is a net user of cash (presumably to expand market share, penetrate new markets, expand capacity, install new process technology, etc.).

There have been attempts to model the cash balance problem for optimum allocation. If all SBUs submitted multiple potential strategies—perhaps for growth, holding pattern, and cash generation—then the combinations could be analyzed and optimized for maximum corporate earnings, growth, or some other objective. Unfortunately, these schemes have met with limited success—it is difficult to obtain one well thought out strategic plan from each SBU, let alone three or four.

Acquisitions and Divestitures. When the portfolio lacks key elements, they must either be developed internally or acquired. In adding to the portfolio, account should be taken of core activities, as well as markets. The particular thrust may be market driven (IBM), or activity driven (Kodak), depending on the situation. For example, it is not surprising that Kodak has entered the floppy disk manufacturing business, since it plays to their core activity strength in thin film coating. Most successful acquisitions have played to corporate strengths.

Divestitures are common currently, probably because the previous acquisitions were not carefully considered. When SBUs do not fit the portfolio, divestment is the logical action. This does not mean that totally new ventures, divorced from the portfolio, should never be undertaken. If the core activities are old, perhaps based on old technology, and markets are mature and declining, a total shift in emphasis might be needed to breath new life into the organization. But the direction must be carefully thought out, and resource limits carefully considered.

THE CORPORATE STRATEGIC PLAN

The corporate strategic plan provides a vehicle for the dissemination of the goals, SBU missions, and portfolio balance. The planning documents generated in the process provide the raw material, but now that the strategy itself has been isolated, the objective shifts to communication and motivation.

Disseminating the Strategy.   The plan must be communicated to everyone involved in its implementation, so that it is well understood, and to gain commitment to its achievement. The communications may take several forms, depending on the target audience. We do not mean that this step should be the only one in communicating and gaining commitment, rather it is the last of a series of such steps. The involvement of line and staff officers in the planning process was designed to obtain their expertise as well as their commitment to the end result.

Dovetailing Business Unit Plans.   A part of the process of disseminating the plan must be focused on the fit of the SBUs in the plan. Each SBU must understand not only its mission, but how it fits into the grand plan. Just because a unit is placed on "hold," or is given a cash generation mission, does not mean that it is less important to the portfolio than one that has a growth mission.

Elitist units can cause morale problems for other units. For example, the MacIntosh division of Apple Computer was encouraged to think of themselves as the elite of the company. Meanwhile, the Apple IIs were furnishing the profits for the company. GM faces a similar potential problem with its Saturn unit. The corporate goals and each unit's role in achieving these goals must be clearly communicated, with emphasis on the unique contributions of each unit.

Moving from Strategic Planning to Strategic Management

When the planning cycle is complete, then what? Will everyone heave a sigh of relief and forget it all, since they can now return to normal activities? The real goal of strategic planning is to change the thinking of managers about their roles, markets, competitors, their fit in the organization, the fit of their SBUs, and so on. The planning cycle will have been a failure if the result is not implemented effectively.

We cannot plan for everything in great detail, so managers must fill that gap with strategic thinking on a day-to-day basis and manage strategically—strategy must be a part of every decision. Strategic issues should not arise only during the strategic planning cycle.

A reason for involving line managers and staff in the planning process is to facilitate their strategic thinking. Strategy is too important to be left to staff analysts. Analysts have an important contribution to make in providing the information necessary for strategy formulation, displaying it in useful ways, and acting as a sounding board. But once a strategy has been developed, only the managers can implement it and make it work. Their involvement leads to understanding, and to commitment.

Concluding Remarks

Implementation of strategy is important enough that books have been written on the subject.[2] If everyone understands what we intend to accomplish, why we are in a position to do it, and how the strategy is to be carried out, the rest of the process will be better understood and supported.

Given the strategy, it must be backed up with an appropriate organization structure that puts strength in the way of impediments to progress, and it must be staffed with managers who have the expertise and experience to implement it. These people need to be motivated by incentives placed squarely on the strategic objectives. They are the ones who will program and plan the actions that translate strategy to practice, motivate their subordinates, and focus their behavior on the new directions.

The "power of the purse" in allocating resources to ensure the success of the strategy is important, particularly when used in a positive sense. Not that funding should take the stance that throwing dollars at the strategy will make it work, but a resource-starved strategy is probably doomed. Risk analysis should precede the decision to follow a given course, but not be allowed to pick it to death after launch. Finally, controls are necessary and terribly important as a means of monitoring progress and knowing when to make mid-course corrections, but the emphasis of such controls should be forward looking rather than the traditional control loop based on historical information.

All mankind is divided into three classes: those that are immovable,
those that are movable, and those that move.

Benjamin Franklin

This book is written for those who move. The people who want to achieve something special—the movers and the shakers. These people have the inner motivation, and the vision to see what can be. But they need tools to analyze industries, markets, the intricacies of international competition, risks, themselves, and their competitors. Strategic analysis takes nothing away from the flamboyance of the movers in corporate life. Indeed, it adds a dimension of shrewdness that when combined with vision is a powerful competitive weapon.

We have said that if one performs a careful analysis of industries and markets, and of competitors' strengths and weaknesses, there are usually only a few viable strategies available, and they become fairly obvious. The power of strategic analysis is its ability to sweep away the nonproductive alternatives, and light up those that can add economic value to the firm.

Notes

Chapter 1: Objectives—Why Formulate Strategy?

1. See "Uniroyal: Back from the Brink and Ready to Put a Bigger Bet on Chemicals," *Business Week,* October 10, 1983.
2. See "Jonathan Scott's Surprising Failure at A&P," *Fortune,* November 6, 1978, pp. 34–44.
3. Peter Z. Grossman, "A&P: Should You Invest Along with the Germans?" *Financial World,* February 15, 1979.
4. Bowmar sued Texas Instruments, claiming that when they developed their hand-held calculator, they chose TI as the developer and supplier of MOS chips with assurances from TI that it would not exploit Bowmar's plans of construction and development, and that TI would be a supplier without conflict of interests. See "Bowmar Seeking $240M From TI in Antitrust Suit," *Electronic News,* December 9, 1974.
5. "Texas Instruments: Pushing Hard into the Consumer Markets," *Business Week,* August 24, 1974.
6. See Elwood S. Buffa, *Meeting the Competitive Challenge: Manufacturing Strategy for U.S. Companies* (Homewood, Ill.: Dow Jones-Irwin, 1984).
7. George A. Steiner, *Strategic Planning: What Every Manager Must Know* (New York: The Free Press, 1979), p. 3.
8. For a detailed discussion of the cost of capital, and the details of its estimation, see any modern corporate finance text, such as *Financial Theory and Corporate Policy,* by T. E. Copeland and J. F. Weston

(Boston: Addision-Wesley, 1983), or J. F. Weston and E. Brigham, *Managerial Finance* (Hinsdale, Ill.: Dryden Press, 1981).

Chapter 2: Strategic Analysis

1. See Bruce D. Henderson, "The Product Portfolio," The Boston Consulting Group, Perspective No. 66, Boston, 1970; Bruce D. Henderson, *Henderson on Corporate Strategy* (Cambridge, Mass.: Abt Books, 1979.

2. For additional discussion of these product portfolio methods, see Derek F. Abell and John S. Hammond, *Strategic Market Planning: Problems and Analytical Approaches* (Englewood Cliffs, N.J.: Prentice-Hall, 1979), or the three-part series by Arnoldo C. Hax and Nicolas S. Majluf, "Competitive Cost Dynamics: The Experience Curve," *Interfaces,* October 1982, pp. 50–61, "The Use of the Growth-Share Matrix in Strategic Planning," *Interfaces,* February 1983, pp. 46–60, and "The Use of the Industry Attractiveness–Business Strength Matrix in Strategic Planning," *Interfaces,* April 1983, pp. 54–71.

3. Arnoldo C. Hax and Nicholas S. Majluf, "The Use of the Growth-Share Matrix in Strategic Planning" *Interfaces,* February 1983, pp. 46–60.

4. Since it is attractiveness of the market that we seek to display, it is projected *market* growth rate that is used, not the projected growth rate of the particular company in the market.

5. Donald C. Hambrick and Ian C. MacMillan, "The Product Portfolio and Man's Best Friend," *California Management Review,* Fall 1982, pp. 84–95.

6. See Nariman K. Dhalla and Sonia Yuspeh, "Forget the Product Life Cycle," *Harvard Business Review,* January–February, 1976, pp. 78–92; and Rolando Polli and Victor J. Cook, "Validity of the Product Life Cycle," *The Journal of Business,* 1969, pp. 325–332.

7. One of the disadvantages of the joint venture form is the inability to move quickly in capacity expansion situations. The partners in the joint venture may find themselves with differing objectives and financial status, and all parties must approve.

8. See Michael E. Porter, *Competitive Strategy* (New York: The Free Press, 1980).

Chapter 3: Industry and Market Structures

1. The short record for RMI is due to the fact that RMI data is not separated in NL's 10-K report before 1979 or after 1980.

2. "The Shakeout in Software: It's Already Here," *Business Week*, August 20, 1984, pp. 102–104.

3. "A Shrinking Market Has Beermakers Brawling," *Business Week*, August 20, 1984, pp. 59–63.

4. *Ibid.*

5. *Ibid.*

Chapter 4: Productivity/Exchange-Rate Effects in Global Competition

1. Thomas J. Peters and Robert H. Waterman, Jr., *In Search of Excellence* (New York: Harper & Row, 1983).

2. Ira C. Magaziner and Robert B. Reich, *Minding America's Business: The Decline and Rise of the American Economy* (New York: Vintage Books, 1983), p. 32; see pp. 69–72 for a discussion of sheltered and traded businesses. See also Theodore Levitt, "The Globalization of Markets," *Harvard Business Review*, May–June 1983, pp. 92–102.

3. See Theodore Levitt, "The Globalization of Markets," *Harvard Business Review*, May–June 1983, pp. 92–102.

4. For a discussion of exchange rate determination, see Alan C. Shapiro, *Multinational Financial Management* (Boston: Allyn and Bacon, 1982), pp. 39–46; Peter H. Lindert and Charles P. Kindleberger, *International Ecomomics,* 7th ed. (Homewood, Ill.: Richard D. Irwin, 1982), pp. 321–325; and Herbert G. Grubel, *International Economics* (Homewood, Ill.: Richard D. Irwin, 1977), pp. 236–242.

5. Henry J. Gailliot, "Purchasing Power Parity as an Explanation of Long-Term Changes in Exchange Rates," *Journal of Money, Credit and Banking,* August 1970, pp. 348–357.

6. Rolf M. Treuherz, "Forecasting Foreign Exchange Rates in Inflationary Economics," *Financial Executive,* February 1969, pp. 57–60.

7. Jacob A. Frenkel, "The Forward Exchange Rate, Expectations and the Demand for Money: The German Hyperinflation," *American Economic Review,* September 1977, pp. 653–670.

8. Robert Z. Aliber and Clyde P. Stickney, "Accounting Measures of Foreign Exchange Exposure: The Long and Short of It," *Accounting Review,* January 1975, pp. 44–57.

9. See for example, *U.S. Industrial Competitiveness: A Comparison of Steel, Electronics, and Automobiles,* Office of Technology Assessment (OTA-ISC-135), July 1981, Appendix A, p. 170.

10. For a discussion of how Japan and the United States provide this support, see William G. Ouchi, *The M-Form Society* (Reading, Mass.:

Addison-Wesley, 1984), and Ira C. Magaziner and Robert B. Reich, *Minding America's Business: The Decline and Rise of the American Economy* (New York: Vintage Books, 1983), Chapters 22 and 23.

11. For a thorough analysis supporting this statement, see Ira C. Magaziner, and Robert B. Reich, *Minding America's Business: The Decline and Rise of the American Economy* (New York: Vintage Books, 1983).

12. For an analysis of policies in both the United States and its strongest national competitors, and the nature of national industrial policies, see Ira C. Magaziner and Robert B. Reich, *Minding America's Business: The Decline and Rise of the American Economy* (New York: Vintage Books, 1983).

13. Figure 4–5 does not include the Soviet Union and the People's Republic of China because they do not participate to any significant degree in world steel markets. The Soviet Union has the largest steel production in the world, having 1.4 times the 1982 production of Japan.

14. "Justice Department Drops Its Opposition to Merger of LTV, Republic Steel," *Los Angeles Times,* Business Section, March 22, 1984. Under the compromise agreement with the Justice Department, the merged company must sell two steel operations within six months or the government will appoint a receiver to sell them.

15. For an analysis of factor costs in the Japanese and U.S. steel industries, see Chapter 13 of Ira C. Magaziner and Robert B. Reich, *Minding America's Business: The Decline and Rise of the American Economy* (New York: Vintage Books, 1983).

16. These estimates for early 1985 are based on the data provided by industry members at the Iron and Steel Conference, UCLA, February 24–26, 1985.

17. "Big Steel's Winter of Woes," *Time,* January 24, 1983, p. 58.

18. See Ira C. Magaziner and Robert B. Reich, *Minding America's Business: The Decline and Rise of the American Economy* (New York: Vintage Books, 1983), p. 159.

19. "Time Runs Out for Steel," *Business Week,* June 13, 1983.

20. Because the auto industry is only a part of the larger transport equipment sector, its performance could have been better than the sector as a whole, though automobiles dominate the sector.

21. See for example, William J. Abernathy, Kim B. Clark, and Alan M. Kantrow, *Industrial Renaissance: Producing a Competitive Future for America* (New York: Basic Books, 1983), and "Small Car War: U.S. Volkswagen Has Problems With Price, Quality, and Japanese," *Wall Street Journal,* February 7, 1983.

22. See "Small Car War: U.S. Volkswagen Has Problems with Price, Quality, and Japanese," *Wall Street Journal,* February 7, 1983.

23. See James C. Abegglen, "How to Defend Your Business Against Japan," *Business Week,* August 15, 1983, p. 14.

24. Robert Wright, "Norway: Paradise Retained," *The Wilson Quarterly,* Spring 1984, p. 119.

25. "Coping with Oil," *The Wilson Quarterly,* Spring 1984, p. 132.

26. One of the commonly touted prescriptions for the exchange rate dilemma is to establish a foreign export base. This solution can be effective if most of the costs can be accumulated in the foreign country. Too often, however, foreign countries, and particularly underdeveloped or developing countries, do not have the supporting industrial infrastructure. Therefore, if a large fraction of the value added must be shipped in from the United States, then these costs are simply inflated by extra transportation costs. We do not say that the foreign location is necessarily a poor one, only that the issues are complex, and need careful study.

Chapter 5: Product and Activity Structures

1. "Battered Steiger Tractor Appears Prepared to Take Advantage of Economic Recovery," *Wall Street Journal,* July 8, 1983.

2. Donald C. Hambrick and Ian C. MacMillan, "The Product Portfolio and Man's Best Friend," *California Management Review,* Fall 1982, pp. 84–95.

Chapter 6: Diversification and Acquisitions

1. While overall third-quarter 1983 merger announcements increased 14 percent from the second quarter, the number involving closely held sellers increased 24 percent. See "Business Bulletin," *The Wall Street Journal,* December 22, 1983, p. 1.

2. "Do Mergers Really Work?" *Business Week,* June 3, 1985, pp. 88–100.

3. *New York Times,* October 28, 1983.

4. *The Wall Street Journal,* October 10, 1983.

5. *The Wall Street Journal,* December 22, 1983.

6. *The Wall Street Journal,* December 21, 1983.

7. T. J. Peters and R. H. Waterman, *In Search of Excellence* (New York: Harper & Row, 1982), Chapter 10.

8. Richard Rumelt, *Strategy, Structure, and Economic Performance* (Boston: Division of Research, Harvard Business School, 1974).

9. National Machine Tool Builders Assn., and "L.A. Machine-Tool Show

Reflects Gain by Japanese," *The Los Angeles Times,* Business Section, March 23, 1984.

10. "Do Mergers Really Work?" *Business Week,* June 3, 1985, pp. 88–100.

Chapter 7: Financial Implications of Strategic Positions

1. See, for example, T. E. Copeland and J. F. Weston, *Financial Theory and Corporate Policy,* 2d ed. (Boston: Addison Wesley, 1983), or J. F. Weston and E. Brigham, *Managerial Finance,* 7th ed. (Hinsdale, Ill.: Dryden Press, 1981).

2. See "How to Snoop on Your Competitors," *Fortune,* May 14, 1984, for some techniques that some companies use regularly to gather competitive intelligence. Though extreme, the study of aerial photographs is one of the techniques mentioned.

3. It is not surprising that the experience curve slopes were similar because both used the same basic process technology. With the same experience/cost relationship, Company B made better strategic use of growth, however.

4. See for example: B. G. Malkiel, "The Capital Formation Problem in the United States," *Journal of Finance,* May 1979, or Eugene F. Brigham and Dilip K. Shome, "The Risk Premium Approach to Estimating the Cost of Capital," *Proceedings of the Nineteenth Annual Iowa State University Regulatory Conference on Public Utility Valuation and Rate Making Process,* Iowa State University, 1980.

5. See Elwood S. Buffa, *Meeting the Competitive Challenge: Manufacturing Strategy for U.S. Companies* (Homewood, Ill.: Dow Jones-Irwin, 1984), Chapter 4 dealing with capacity strategy.

6. There were additional expansion alternatives in the actual situation.

7. Michael E. Porter, *Competitive Strategy* (New York: The Free Press, 1980).

8. *Ibid.*

9. Some industries may not exhibit the V-curve phenomenon, as when the industry comprises only a few large companies, or when barriers to entry preclude niche players. Agricultural chemicals is an example of the latter, with a regulatory barrier to entry.

Chapter 9: From Analysis to Plans and Action

1. For a detailed discussion of the concept of sustainable growth and derivation of formulas, see Alan J. Zakon, "Capital Structure Optimization,"

in *The Treasurer's Handbook,* edited by J. F. Weston and M. Goud-zwaard (Homewood, Ill.: Dow Jones-Irwin, 1976), Chapter 30.

2. See for example, Peter Lorange, *Implementation of Strategic Planning* (Englewood Cliffs, N.J.: Prentice-Hall, 1982), and Boris Yavitz and William H. Newman, *Strategy in Action: The Execution, Politics, and Payoff of Business Planning* (New York: The Free Press, 1982).

Index

A&P Food Stores, 4
Acquisitions: *see* Diversification and acquisitions
Activity interdependence, 25, 26
Activity structures: *see* Product and activity structures
Acton, Lord, 122
AFIA, 123
Agriculture, 75; *see also* Farm equipment industry
Airline industry, deregulation in, 53, 215
Allegheny International, 44
Allegheny Ludlum Steel Corporation, 43
Allied Chemical Corporation, 8
Allis-Chalmers Corporation, 116
All-Steel Corporation, 138
ALS, 43
American Can Company, 123, 125
American Cyanamid Company, 139, 140
American Home Products Corporation, 139, 140
American Hospital Supply, 139, 140
American Motors Corporation, 169
American Telephone & Telegraph Company (AT&T), 33, 123
Anheuser Busch, 31, 56–63
Apparel industry, 135–137

Apple Computer, 230
ARMCO, 44
Ashton Supply Company, 11
ASK Computer Systems, 55
Asset turnover, 228
    margins versus, 151–152, 157–158
Automation, 168
Automobile industry, 31, 86, 91–93, 169

Banking, deregulation in, 215
Basin Surveys, 11
Beer industry, 31, 56–63
Bell Laboratories, 33
Bethlehem Steel Corporation, 81
Boeing Aircraft, 120
Bogue, Marcus C., 65n
Boston Consulting Group (BCG), 13, 14
Bottom up planning, 217–218, 222–223
Bowmar Company, 4, 40, 120, 146
Brand image, 167
Brand usage share, 4–5
Bristol-Myers Company, 139, 140
Buffa, Elwood S., 65n

CAD/CAM (Computer Aided Design/Computer Aided Manufacturing), 168
Canada, steel industry in, 89–90

Capacity/demand patterns of titanium
    industry, 44–45
Capacity expansion, 160–165
    SCENSIM and, 195–199
Capacity growth rate, 47–48
Case, J. I., Company, 168–169
Cash cows, 16–18, 21
Cash flow balance, 227–228
Cash traps, 17
Caterpillar Tractor, 119, 120
Central location, 120
Chemical industry, 101, 134, 169–170
    market valuation in, 7–8
Chrysler Corporation, 169
Cigna Corporation, 123–125
Cincinnati Milicron, 63
Clorox, 143–145, 169–170
Cloud of sales/earnings uncertainty,
    179–183, 188–205, 209–210, 212n
Coca-Cola, 146
Colgate Palmolive, 143–145
Commitment, 216, 230–231
Comparative advantage, 74–75, 94–95
Competitive dynamics
    advantageous, 136–142
    in titanium industry, 46–49
Competitive position, 14, 16
Competitor ratings, 220
Complementary activity structure,
    142–143
Computer Associates International,
    Inc., 55
Computer software industry, 31, 53–55
Conoco, 123
Consolidated markets, 52–56, 64, 137,
    138, 143
Consultants, 214, 216
Consumer electronics industry, 63,
    101–106, 120
Controllable uncertainty, 182–183, 191
Coors beer, 56, 59, 62
Corporate goals, 228–229
Corporte portfolio analysis, SCENSIM
    and, 199–203
Corporate strategic plans, 216, 217,
    226–230
Cost leadership strategy, 165, 166
Cost/price experience curves, 26–28,
    33, 147–152
Cross and Trecker, 64
Crucible Specialty Company, 41, 43

Deere & Company, 113–120, 168–169
    growth/share matrix, 113, 119
Demographic trends, 135–136

Deregulation, 53, 142, 215
D-H Titanium, 59
Differentiation strategy, 165–167
Digital Research, 53, 54
Diversification and acquisitions, 32–33,
    123–146, 229
    hallmarks of effective, 131–146
    objectives of, 125–131
    related, 126–131
    by sector, 124–125
    unrelated, 126
Divestment, 18, 22
Dogs, 16–18, 32
    profitability and cash flow charac-
    teristics of, 20–22
Dow Chemical Corporation, 8, 49,
    139, 140
Dry battery industry, 64
Dupont de Nemours, E. I., & Com-
    pany, 101, 123, 169–170
Dutch Boy Paints, 11

Eastman Kodak Company, 171
    experience curves for amateur pho-
    tographic products, 26–29, 92
    growth/share matrix, 100–101, 143,
    227
Economic value of the firm, 7–12; see
    also Value-added streams
Economies of scale, 39
Economies of scope, 39, 100
Elitist units, 230
Emerson consumer electronics, 63
Energy costs in steel industry, 88
Equity returns, 7–8, 10–11; see also
    Return on equity (ROE)
Exchange rates, 68–74, 133, 134, 171
Experience curve, 14, 22–28, 32

Factor costs between international
    competitors, 86–92
Fairchild Company, 146
Farm equipment industry, 101, 111,
    113–120, 168–169
Fiat, 169
Financial implications of strategic posi-
    tions, 33–34, 147–171
    capacity expansion example, 160–165
    components of required return,
    157–160
    cost-price experience relationships
    among competitors, 147–152
    effects of corporate financial struc-
    ture, 152–156

generic strategies, 165–168
  V-curve, 168–170
Flexibility, 167
Fluor Company, 146
Focus, 165
Ford Motor Company, 116, 119, 121, 169
Fragmented markets, 52–55, 64, 137, 139–140
France, industrial portfolio (1970–1976), 76, 78–79
Franklin, Benjamin, 232
Futura Titanium, 41, 43
Future values, 7, 11–12

Gamble-Skogmo Company, 146
General Electric Company, 14
General Foods Corporation
  growth/share matrix, 14–15, 20
  share/momentum chart, 19–20
General Motors Corporation, 120, 230
Generic strategies, 165–168
Getty Oil Company, 123
Giddings & Lewis, 64
Global competition: *see* International strategic issues
Growth, 9–11, 125
Growth/share matrix, 13–18, 21, 29, 219, 221, 226
  Deere & Company, 113, 119
  Eastman Kodak, 100–101, 143, 227
  General Foods Corporation, 14–15, 20
  product based, 107–108
  titanium industry, 46–47

Hambrick, Donald C., 20, 22, 29
Harvesting, 18, 22
Heileman beer, 59, 62
Herman Miller office furniture company, 64, 138, 139
Hesston Company, 168–169
Hoffman La Roche, 140
Hon Company, 138, 139
Horizontal integration, 126, 127
Household products industry, 143–145, 169–170
Howmet Turbine Components Corporation, 41, 43, 49
Hurdle rates, 153–154

IBM Corporation, 101, 121, 138
Implementation of strategy, 34–35, 214–232
  business unit strategic plans, 216–225

corporate strategic plans, 216, 217, 226–230
  decision to plan, 215–216
In Search of Excellence (Peters and Waterman), 65, 127
Industry and market structures, 6–7, 30–31, 39–64, 137
  beer industry, 56–63
  capacity/demand patterns, 44–45
  competitive dynamics, 46–49
  margins, 49–51
  prices, 45–46
  types of, 51–56
  value added and activities, 40–44
Industry type, major acquisitions by, 124–125
Inflation, 69–71, 157–159
Information sources, 28–29
Information Unlimited Software, 55
Innovation, 167
Integrated circuits, 32
Internal triggers, 215
International activity bases, 120–121
International Harvester, 117, 119, 120, 169
International strategic issues, 6, 31, 65–95, 134, 135
  automobile industry, 91–93
  comparative advantage, 74–75, 94–95
  exchange rates, 68–74, 133, 134, 171
  national industrial portfolios, 66–68, 75–80
  steel industry, 80–93
International Titanium, 48, 50
Ishizuka Research, 48
Ivory, 5

Japanese industry, 6, 30, 31
  automobiles, 91–93
  consumer electronics, 63
  farm equipment, 116
  industrial portfolio (1970–1976), 76, 78–79
  machine tools, 64, 140–141
  steel, 80, 81, 83–90, 157–160, 171
  titanium, 41, 42, 45, 47–50
Johnson, S. C., Company, 143, 144
Johnson & Johnson, 139–140
Jones & Laughlin, 33, 81

Kobe Steel, 42, 43
Kubota, 116

Labor costs

Labor costs (*cont.*)
  automobile industry, 91
  steel industry, 87, 88–89
Lawrence Aviation Industries, 43
Learning curve: *see* Experience curve
Level-playing-field view, 6
Lever Brothers, 143–145
Lilly pharmaceutical company, 139,
  140
Lionel Corporation, 56
Lotus, 53, 54
LTV, 33, 81
LTV Steel Company, 33, 123, 158, 159
Lux, 5

Machine tool industry, 63–64, 140–141
MacMillan, Ian C., 20, 22, 29
Mallory Company, 64
Management commitment, 216,
  230–231
Management Science America, 55
Manifold business forms industry, 31,
  32, 39, 55–56, 138
Marcor Company, 146
Margin paradox, 33, 147, 149–151,
  156, 160, 171
Margins versus asset turnover,
  151–152, 157–158
Market attractiveness, 14, 15
Market niches, 56, 143
Market research, 220
Market saturation effects, 222
Market segmentation: *see* Segmenta-
  tion
Market share, 15, 18–21, 24–25
  relative, 14–15, 21, 106, 107, 114
Market structure: *see* Industry and
  market structures
Market-to-book ratios, 7–9, 130–131
Martin Marietta Aluminum, 41, 43
Massey Ferguson, 116, 120, 168–169
McKinsey & Company, 13
Mercedes Benz, 169
Merck & Company, Inc., 139, 140
MicroPro International Corporation,
  53–55
Mircosoft, 53, 54
Miller beer, 31, 56–62
Mini-mills, 82–83
Missions of SBUs, 229, 230
Mobil Oil Corporation, 146
Monte Carlo simulation, 212
Moore Business Forms, Inc., 31, 32,
  39, 55–56, 132, 138

Multidomestic production facilities,
  120

National Distillers and Chemical Cor-
  poration, 44
National industrial portfolios, 66–68,
  75–80
National Steel Company, 157–159
Net advantage, 75
Nippon Mining Company, 42, 43
Nippon Steel Company, 81, 83
NL Industries, 10–11, 29, 44, 126, 129,
  131, 146, 227
Norway, petroleum industry in, 93

Objectives of strategic analysis,
  3–12
Office furniture industry, 32, 39, 64,
  138–139
Oil field development strategy, 192–195
Olivetti, 123
On-Line Software International, 55
Operating margins, 144–145
  titanium industry, 49–50
Oregon Metallurgical Corporation
  (ORMET), 41, 43, 44, 48–50
Organizational commitment, 216
Organizational fit, 224–225
Organizational learning, 22
Osaka Titanium Company, 41, 42, 44,
  48–51, 53, 63
Output growth, 133–135
  versus productivity growth,
  66–68
Overall cost leadership, 165, 166

Pabst beer, 56, 59, 62
Pacific Power and Light Company,
  127–131, 146, 227
Panasonic, 63
Past growth, 19
Past market growth, 19
Peters, Thomas J., 65, 127
Petroleum industry, 67, 93, 126
Petrolog, 11
Pharmaceutical industry, 139–140
Philip Morris, 56–57
PIMS (Profit-Impact-of-Marketing-
  Strategies) program, 20–22
Porsche, 169
Porter, Michael, 165, 168
Portfolio audit, 226–227
Price-cost experience curve, 26–28, 33,
  147–152

Price/return structure, 154–156, 163
Prices in titanium industry, 45–46
Procter & Gamble Company, 101, 143–145
Product and activity structures, 32, 99–122, 221
  analysis of farm equipment industry, 113–120
  complementary, 142–143
  international, 120–121
  segmentation by product line and geography, 107–112, 121
  shared, 25, 26, 101–106, 142
Product life cycle analysis, 29
Product-line example of SCENSIM use, 183–191
Product mix, 3
Product portfolio analysis, 13–20
Product substitution, 222
Production design, 25–26
Productivity; *see also* International strategic issues
  versus output growth, 66–68
Projected market growth rate, 14–16
Publisher Readers Digest Associates, 55
Purchasing power parity, 69–74
Purex, 143–145

Quality, 167
Question marks, 16–18, 21

Radio Shack, 63
Rationalized exchange, 121
Raw material costs in steel industry, 87–88
RCA Corporation, 127
Reinvestment economics, 156
Related diversification and acquisitions, 126–131
Relative capacity share, 47–48
Relative market share, 14–15, 21, 106, 107, 114
Republic Steel Corporation, 33, 81, 123
Required return, components of, 157–160
Return on assets (ROA), 128–129, 152–156, 210
Return on equity (ROE), 130–131, 152–162, 228
Return on investment (ROI), 21
Returns, 9–11, 125

Risk relationships, 34; *see also* SCENSIM
RMI, 41, 43, 44, 48–50, 53, 60
Robotics, 168
Rohm & Haas, 8
Rucker Company, 11
Rumelt, Richard, 127

Sales/earnings forecast, 177–183, 188–213
Sanyo, 63
Scale, 9, 125
SCENSIM (SCENario SIMulation), 34, 175–213, 222–224
  capacity expansion example, 195–199
  computational procedure, 178, 205–213
  corporate portfolio analysis example, 199–203
  oil field development strategy, 192–195
  product-line example, 183–191
  sensitivity analysis with, 179–183, 189–191, 194–195, 201–203, 210–211
Schering-Plough Corporation, 140
Schlitz beer, 56, 59
Schlumberger Company, 146
Sector charts, 219, 222, 227
  beer industry, 57, 62
  computer software industry, 53–54
  fragmented, unconsolidated-stable, unconsolidated-unstable, and consolidated markets, 51–53
  machine tool industry, 141
  manifold business forms industry, 55–56
  office furniture industry, 139
  pharmaceutical industry, 140
  titanium industry, 46–49
Securities and Exchange Commission (SEC), 29
Segmentation, 52, 107–112, 121, 165–168
  farm equipment industry, 114–117
  by product line and geography, 107–112, 121
Sensitivity analysis with SCENSIM technique, 179–183, 189–191, 194–195, 201–203, 210–211
Share/momentum chart, 14, 18–20, 29, 219, 221, 226
  product-based, 108–112
  titanium industry, 46–47

Shared activity structures, 25, 26, 101–106, 142
Shooting stars, 17
Sirius Software, 55
Smithkline, 139, 140
Softsmith Corporation, 55
Sony, 63
Soricum Corporation, 55
Southern Pacific, Ticor Insurance unit, 123
Soviet titanium industry, 30, 41, 48–49, 50, 53
Specialization, 75, 94–95, 166
Sperry-New Holland, 168–169
St. Joe Company, 146
Standard deviations (SD), 21
Standard Register Company, 56
Stars, 16–18, 21
Stauffer chemical company, 8
Steel industry, 31, 80–93, 133, 157–160, 171
Steelcase Inc., 32, 39, 64, 138
Steiger Company, 117
Steiner, George, 6
Stewart & Stevenson Oil Tools, 11
Strategic alternatives, development of, 222–224
Strategic business unit (SBU), 13–14
missions of, 229, 230
Strategic fit, 224
Strategic management, 230–231
Strategic Planning Institute, 20
Strategic plans, 216–218
Strategic scenario analysis, SCENSIM for, 34, 175–213
Strategy, implementation of: see Implementation of strategy
Strategy audit, 218–222, 223
Stroh beer, 59, 62
Structural differences among competitors, 220–221
Structural issues: see Industry and market structures
Sumitomo Metal Industries, 42, 43
Sustainability, 9–11, 125

Teledyne Allvac Company, 41, 43
Tengelmann Company, 4
Texaco/Getty, 123
Texas Instruments, 4, 101, 145
3M Corporation, 139, 140
TIMET, 41, 44, 48–50, 53, 60, 126
Titanium Industries, 41, 43
Titanium industry, 30, 40–51, 53, 221

Titanium Metals Corporation of America (TIMET), 10
TOHO Titanium Company, 41, 42, 44, 48, 49, 51
Top down planning, 217–218, 222–223
Toyosha, 116
Toyota, 169
Toys-R-Us, 56
Triggering events, 215–216
Tsai, G., & Company, 123

Uncertainty, cloud of sales/earnings, 179–183, 188–205, 209–210, 212n
Unconsolidated-stable markets, 52, 53, 56, 57, 137
Unconsolidated-unstable markets, 52, 53, 137, 141–142
Uncontrollable uncertainty, 182–183, 191
Union Carbide Corporation, 64
Uniroyal, Inc., 3
United States Steel Corporation, 44, 81
Unrelated diversification and acquisitions, 126
Upjohn Company, The, 140

Value-added streams, 30, 220–221; see also Diversification and acquisitions
for farm equipment industry, 117–118
industry and market structures and, 40–44
V-curve, 34, 168–170
Vertical integration, 126–127
VisiCorp, 53–55

Wage rates, 87, 88–89
Wang laboratories, Inc., 215, 222
Warner-Lambert Company, 139, 140
Waterman, Robert H., Jr., 65, 127
West Germany
industrial portfolio (1970–1976), 76, 78–79
steel industry, 89–90, 171
"What if" analysis, 176, 178
Wickes Company, 146
Wine Spectrum, 146
Withdrawal, 18, 20, 142
Women, participation in labor force, 135–136
Word processing manufacturers, 215, 222
Wyman-Gordon Company, 41, 43